Arlington Heritage

VIGNETTES OF A VIRGINIA COUNTY

Cover Photograph — THE GLEBE HOUSE

IN ORDER TO PRESERVE AN AUTHENTIC RECORD OF THIS AREA, AS IT WAS AT A SPECIFIC DATE, THIS BOOK HAS PURPOSELY HAD NO MAJOR REVISIONS SINCE ITS ORIGINAL PUBLICATION IN 1959. SUBSEQUENTLY, MANY OF THE LANDMARKS HAVE BEEN DESTROYED.

THE AUTHOR

NATIONAL SOCIETY OF COLONIAL DAMES OF AMERICA IN THE DISTRICT OF COLUMBIA
"We consider ARLINGTON HERITAGE an inspiring educational contribution, and commend it as a book which will further the dissemination of history and patriotism. It symbolizes the aims for which our Society was founded. This book constitutes a tribute to the past, and an authentic source of knowledge for future generations."

THE BOARD

NATIONAL TRUST FOR HISTORIC PRESERVATION
"There is no substitute for the first-hand appreciative knowledge of the local historian; and in Eleanor Lee Templeman we have a dedicated expert who is recording the history of that county, Arlington, which has so many ties with the history of our nation."

RICHARD H. HOWLAND, *President*

VIRGINIA HISTORICAL SOCIETY
"Mrs. Templeman's ARLINGTON HERITAGE competently and graciously fulfills the need for a history of this small area which has loomed so large in the annals of the State."

JOHN MELVILLE JENNINGS. *Director*

Arlington Heritage

VIGNETTES OF A VIRGINIA COUNTY

ELEANOR LEE TEMPLEMAN

REVISED FROM MATERIAL

MUCH OF WHICH FIRST APPEARED

IN SERIAL FORM

IN

The Northern Virginia Sun

AVENEL BOOKS · NEW YORK

ARLINGTON HOUSE . . . The Robert E. Lee National Memorial

Copyright © MCMLIX by Eleanor Lee Templeman
Library of Congress Catalog Card Number: 59-10491
All rights reserved.
This edition is published by Avenel Books
a division of Crown Publishers, Inc.
by arrangement with the author
a b c d e f g h
Manufactured in the United States of America

This book is dedicated

in loving memory

to my mother,

ELLEN BEAUMONT CLARKSON READING,

and to my father,

ROBERT LEE READING.

Every life they touched

was spiritually enriched

by the contact.

PREFACE

Two years ago, I did not have the faintest intention of writing a book, and I am still surprised to find myself an author! The newspaper series from which it evolved grew out of an educational need; and the book is being published in response to public demand.

It was in 1957 that I became fully aware of the dearth of available information on Arlington County history. At that time, my son, then in the seventh grade, sought unsuccessfully for adequate reference material for the required report on local history. Also, to spur me on was the hope that public awareness of the importance and beauty of our landmarks might save some of them from needless destruction. Many have already gone, and others are threatened. Therefore, with a two-fold purpose, I started the series, ARLINGTON HERITAGE in the *Northern Virginia Sun* in March of 1957.

I am frequently asked whence I get my material. I did not personally know the stories of our landmarks and old homes, but each became a true-life mystery challenge to be solved. Each started with some one thing which aroused my curiosity: an ancient home or springhouse, a forgotten tombstone on a vacant lot, or an interesting notation on an old map. The first clue, however, was only the start of a long search. Much of the local history was in the recollections of early residents whose days were numbered, and whose family documents and records would eventually become scattered or destroyed. My work became a race against time.

When I see a home demolished, or a beautiful tree cut down, it hurts. I visualize the family who planned the house; I imagine their joy in moving into it and in planting the trees and shrubs to make it beautiful. Then I contemplate the unrolling of the scroll of life within its walls—new lives beginning, the peace of death as the cycle ends. . . . Yet life is continuous, each new generation is a link in an endless chain.

I am often reminded of a quotation from Longfellow's *The Builders* —

"All houses wherein men have lived and died
Are haunted houses. Through the open doors
The harmless phantoms on their errands glide
With feet that make no sound upon the floors."

I very strongly feel that houses symbolize the people who lived in them and that it is the human element which makes history a vital experience. Therefore, my book has concentrated upon the homes of Arlington County as the medium of unfolding the story of this very important fragment of America.

The intangible dividends of this research have been most rewarding. There has been the warm appreciation of the families whose ancestors pioneered in this area under extreme hardships, and prepared for us a good place to call "home". Sometimes I have had the pleasure of discovering for newcomers the history of some old home whose mellow beauty they have preserved. It has been heart-warming to have school children tell me how much they enjoyed my articles, which not only assisted them in their school assignments, but also taught them to observe more keenly the interesting things around them. They are learning to inquire into the unknown. Perhaps I have helped them to form the habit of associating tangible evidence with the spiritual values and fortitude required of those who fashioned our heritage. Always, the past is prelude to the future.

In a history of the county named for the mansion, which is the national memorial to Robert E. Lee, it seems fitting to include a resume of his life (aside from his activities in the Confederacy), and of his family background. Whereas these subjects are fully documented in voluminous books for the serious student and historian, there remained a need for a condensed version keyed to the interest of the general public.

Geographically and historically, Arlington County is closely tied to adjacent Alexandria, Fairfax County and the District of Columbia. Therefore, I have included brief sketches or references with pictures of these neighboring areas. Within the walls of Arlington House were interwoven the threads of life binding it together with many other great museum houses of Virginia. This accounts for inclusion of some Northern Virginia houses beyond our county borders: Woodlawn, Gunston Hall, and also Sully, which I hope will become a museum house in the near future.

* * * * *

A whole book could be devoted to the churches of Arlington and the spiritual growth of our community. With limitation of space, I have had to confine mention to those which were organized prior to the turn of the century, or later churches which evolved from these early congregations. I have added a few exceptions which seemed appropriate for special reasons. One such exception is on Catholicism, because of its outstanding educational achievements. I wish I could include all!

* * * * *

For two years, I have tried to write of the courageous women of Arlington who crusaded for all the fine things we enjoy today. Again, there were so many of them and I may have unknowingly omitted the name of some ardent worker who stayed in the background. I pay them homage for their lives of service, and hope that someone better qualified than I will record their individual achievements.

* * * * *

I recently read a list of more than twelve names for the conflict between the North and South. Whereas I personally prefer the term, "The War Between the States", I shall use the most generally accepted term, "The Civil War."

* * * * *

In writing of the area within the present boundaries of our county, for the sake of brevity, I shall designate the locality as "Arlington County" regardless of the county jurisdiction at the time to which I am referring.

* * * * *

Space limitations have prevented me from including all the data which have come to me within the past two years. Also, I have omitted material, no matter how interesting or amusing, which I thought might offend anyone. My intention is to bring knowledge and pleasure without injury.

* * * * *

I have endeavored to make each chapter a complete vignette, yet for the whole book to have some continuity. Because of the number of subjects and families involved, and the scope of time and territory covered, this has been exceedingly difficult. I hope that the final arrangement will be pleasing to the reader.

TABLE OF CONTENTS

Introduction

FROM its beginning in 1608, when Captain John Smith visited the Necostin Indian Village which stood near where the Marriott Motor Hotel now stands, the history of Arlington has been closely related to that of the State and the Nation. Following Smith's visit, the area was much frequented by men engaged in the Indian trade, but it did not become a settled community until about 1700. The first settlers were predominantly Virginians from the lower Potomac.

For another hundred years the area remained a remote corner of other larger Virginia counties. Its development was strongly influenced by the establishment of two neighboring towns; Alexandria (1749) and Georgetown (1751). The most significant factor in the history of Arlington, however, was the establishment of the Federal City across the river, in 1800.

Beginning in the early 1800's, Georgetown and Washington people were attracted to the sylvan beauty of nearby Virginia. Arlington County is embraced in a great curve of the Potomac at the "fall line" where the piedmont escarpment crosses the river, forming 200 foot palisades along our upper shoreline, terminating the tidal flow of the river at the county line. The orientation of these forested highlands, facing northeast above shadowed waters, has a definite effect upon the local climate. The air is fresher and many degrees cooler than the Federal City across the Potomac.

Some of the early Washingtonians sought permanent homes here and commuted, others came for the summer months. Many early statesmen and diplomats maintained hunting lodges. Local families catered to "paying guests".

Newcomers from all parts of the Union have continued to settle in our community in ever increasing numbers. Some of our most prominent families are descended from these newcomers of a hundred years ago, or later. Thus Arlington's heritage from the past is not strictly local, or even exclusively Virginian, but is truly national in character and interest.

Arlington became a separate political entity in 1801, when the area ceded by Virginia to the new Federal District was separated from Fairfax County and organized as Alexandria County. This area remained a part of this District of Columbia until 1846, when it was returned to Virginia, but not to Fairfax County. The town of Alexandria was separated from Alexandria County in 1852; the County was renamed Arlington in 1920.

Arlington's present name is, of course, derived from that of the mansion which George Washington Parke Custis built soon after 1800 on the heights overlooking the new city of Washington. Custis was Martha Washington's grandson, adopted by George Washington and brought up at Mount Vernon. His daughter married Robert Edward Lee, who came to regard Arlington House as his home, the tie which bound his allegiance to Virginia when the moment of decision came to him. Thus in this home and name are united the two finest traditions of Virginia.

The tragic events of 1861 were a time of trial for all the good people of Arlington County. The area was quickly overrun by the Federal forces and never relinquished. In time, twenty-two forts were erected within the county's present boundaries, as part of the defenses of Washington. The civil population was greatly outnumbered by the permanent garrison of these defenses, not to mention the occasional passages of the Army of the Potomac. A proper number of local sons slipped away to don Confederate gray. A notable number of the local daughters married boys in blue, who held a monopoly of the field for four long years. And a number of those who first came to this County with weapons in their hands returned after the war to make their homes here.

In 1900 this was still essentially a rural County, but thereafter it became increasingly suburban as homes and villages multiplied along the trolley lines that facilitated commuting to Washington. The influx of Government employees during World War I brought a great increase in population and a consolidation of the County into a single suburban community. The experience was repeated during the great expansion of Government employment in the era of the New Deal, and again during World War II, until now the County is almost solidly built up.

In all this new building and development, many of the County's ancient landmarks have been destroyed, while others have been hidden and forgotten. The composition of this book has been an adventure in the rediscovery of these lost landmarks and of the heritage they represent.

Indians, the First Families

PERIODICAL local finds have been made of Indian artifacts including pottery, projectile points, scrapers, mullers, tomahawks and other articles at widely scattered points, and belonging to different cultures. The last find, in 1958 in the 5300 block of 5th Street North, has been identified by experts at the Smithsonian Institution as belonging to the Middle or Late "Woodland" cultures which flourished from about 500 B.C. to 1400 A.D. Another important exploration in Arlington some years ago, at the mouth of Marcey Creek (now covered by the extension of the George Washington Parkway) established a new pottery type now classified as "Marcey Creek Ware" and tentatively dated as belonging to a culture which existed over 2,000 years ago.

The relationship of these early Indians to those found living here by Captain John Smith when he sailed up the Potomac in June, 1608, has never been traced. About these latter day Indians we know—from direct testimony—only that they existed, since Smith placed on his famous map the name of a village—Nameroughquena—the site of which as nearly as can be determined, was about where the Highway Bridge reaches the Virginia shore.

Since the river in those days was a link rather than a barrier—transportation by water was easier than by land—it is reasonable to assume that the Indians of Arlington were related to those on the other side of the Potomac in this area, who have been documented. They belonged to the Algonquian linguistic group and were called "Nacotchtanks" or "Necostins." This name has survived in slightly different forms as the Anacostia River and Analostan Island. On the latter, now Theodore Roosevelt Island, traces of an Indian village have been found.

At one time, the Necostins were members of the Powhatan Confederacy, but by 1608 they were asserting their independence of the Chief on the James River. They lived in family groups with perhaps thirty to sixty persons in a village. These villages were generally set on a rise of ground not far from a good spring, and near the river. Since the Indians had no horses, they preferred to travel by boat. They did not use birchbark canoes as in the north, but dugouts made from pine or tulip-poplar trees.

The houses were made of small poles fastened together at the top in a rounded form like an arbor. A replica of one of these houses has been on display at Jamestown. A demountable form of these houses (shown in the photograph) could be taken along on hunting trips.

The Indians of Arlington had none of what we think of as domesticated animals. They did have abundant wild fowl, fish, and animals which supplied not only food but a variety of other things. From the antlers of the deer, for instance, they got arrow tips and glue; from his bones, needles; from his entrails and sinews, thread and string; and from his hide, clothing, drumheads and thongs. The bear supplied meat, fat (used as an unguent as well as for cooking), clothing, bedding, and thongs. Other animals found in this area were the fox, beaver, otter, raccoon, squirrel, muskrat, possum, rabbit, wolf, elk, and even the buffalo.

In addition to the many wild plants which were eaten by the Indians, corn, beans, squash, and pumpkins were cultivated. Tobacco was used for ceremonial and medical purposes, not for enjoyment. Some of the Indian dishes are eaten today: succotash, hominy and corn pone which they called "ponap" or "appones." They had no salt unless they got it in trade, but they did have maple sugar and syrup. The Sugarland Run in nearby Fairfax County is testimony to the existence of sugar maples in this area. We know from the accounts of the early colonial rangers that their sap was used by the Indians for sugar.

Conditions of Indian life changed with the coming of the white man. Skins and corn were exchanged for metal pots, axes, knives, and hoes. Hogs and chickens were acquired. But also the encroachment of civilization meant less hunting ground, and the land-hunger of the European colonists led to incidents, one of the most famous of which precipitated Bacon's Rebellion. By 1679, the Indians moving westward had left Arlington.

NECOSTIN INDIANS . . . Exhibit of local Indian family group, using figures from the Smithsonian Institute.

The "Kingdom of Virginia"

ARLINGTON COUNTY'S written history goes back to Captain John Smith's voyage up the Potomac in 1608, although the circumstances leading to the colonization of Virginia began in England April 10, 1606, when King James I signed charters to the Plymouth and London Companies. The latter made the first permanent settlement at "James Cittie." Their second charter of 1609 as the "Virginia Company" granted jurisdiction over "all those lands . . . in that part of America called Virginia, from . . . Point Comfort . . . northward 200 miles . . . southward 200 miles . . . and all that space and circuit of land, lying from the sea coast of the precinct aforesaid, up into the land, throughout from sea to sea, west and northwest . . .".

This reflects the view of the best geographers of the day that the Pacific Ocean lapped the western side of the as yet unexplored and unnamed Appalachian Mountains. The third charter of 1612 included Bermuda which had been discovered in the meantime. The charter of the Virginia Company was annulled in 1624 by King James I, and its lands became a Crown Colony. By this time, the settlements were firmly established on and nearby the James River, and the Potomac River to the Falls was well known to traders with Indians.

The first limitations upon the extent of the "Kingdom of Virginia," as it was referred to by King Charles I, who succeeded his father in 1625, came with the grant to Lord Baltimore of a proprietorship over what became Maryland, patented in 1632 and with settlers arriving at St. Mary's in 1634. The most significant words of this grant, from the viewpoint of Arlington, are "the farther banks of the said river". They explain why the boundary between Arlington and the District of Columbia runs along the Virginia shore of the river and not in midstream, and why Roosevelt and Columbia Islands which lie along the Virginia shore are not part of Arlington and Virginia.

The land which is now Arlington County was originally a part of Northumberland County, which was created in 1648 and then included all the land between the Potomac and Rappahannock Rivers. Only the lower part of this area (the present Northumberland County) was settled at that time. As settlement extended up the Potomac, new counties were formed for the convenience of the frontier settlers. The first of these was Westmoreland, created in 1653 to include all the Virginia shore of the Potomac "from Machoactoke (Machodoc) River . . . to the falls above Necostins Towne". In 1664 Stafford County was created from the upper portion of Westmoreland; in 1731 the upper portion of Stafford, in turn, became Prince William County. In 1742 that part of Prince William north of Occoquan Creek and Bull Run became Fairfax County.

Maryland and Virginia authorities had agreed to meet in 1785 to discuss the controversy over the navigation of the Potomac and their joint boundary. The Commissioners who took part in this meeting did more than draw up a compact subsequently ratified by their respective States. From this meeting eventually came the call for the convention which resulted in the Constitution of the United States and the decision to set aside a tract of land ten miles square for the seat of the Federal Government.

The first decisive step toward a permanent Capital was taken in September 1787, when Congress was given authority to acquire the necessary site. Virginia in 1787 and Maryland in 1788, each realizing the advantage of having the location within its boundaries, offered ten square miles of land for that purpose. Other states made similar offers, with stormy debates in Congress. North and South each wanted the capital within its limits; neither side would approve two capitals, nor relinquish its hope of choice.

The deadlock was finally broken at a dinner party given by Thomas Jefferson. The solution involved an idea of Alexander Hamilton, the first Secretary of the Treasury, to promote a great national fiscal plan, of which an important part was the assumption of the Revolutionary War debts by the Federal Government.

Virginia, which had already amortized her war debts, led a block of Southern opposition. Jefferson was able to persuade Richard Bland Lee, first Representative of this area of Virginia, and a colleague, that the state would eventually benefit more than enough to offset the Assumption Tax by the choice of a Federal City site adjacent to it. Therefore, an exchange of votes was arranged over the after-dinner madeira. The Assumption measure was approved, and in July 1790, Congress enacted the Residence Act. This authorized the President to choose a site on the Potomac River between the mouth of Eastern Branch and the mouth of the Conococheague; a distance of about 105 miles.

Although familiar with the area, George Washington rode over it again, and in March 1791, he was authorized to lay out the "Territory of Columbia" so as to include land on both sides of the Potomac. The portion on the Virginia side of the river eventually became Alexandria County, then Arlington.

There is good reason to suspect that George Washington would have chosen the Virginia side of the Potomac for the Federal City, had he not feared criticism due to the fact that such a choice would have tremendously enhanced the value of vast acreage owned by himself, members of his family, and his most intimate friends, who had recognized the superior location in their choice of plantation sites.

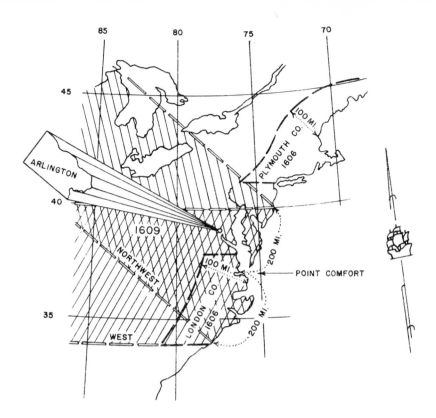

VIRGINIA COLONIES . . . Area included in the early charters of the Virginia
Company.

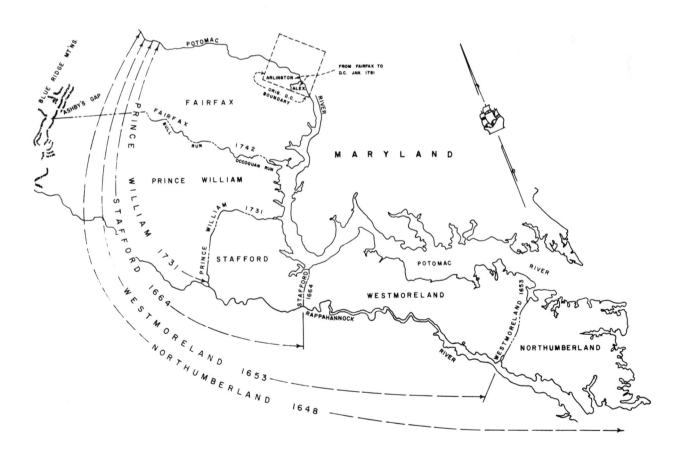

VIRGINIA COUNTIES . . . Sequence of jurisdiction of the area which eventually became Arlington County.

Fairfax, Arlington's Neighbor

UPON the creation of the new county of Fairfax in 1742, named after Thomas, the Sixth Lord Fairfax, the first court house was built at Spring Field, later known as Freedom Hill. Today, there is no settlement, nor even a ruin remaining, but the site was marked some years ago by a bronze plaque erected by the Fairfax Chapter of the Daughters of the American Revolution. It is on State Route Number 123 between Vienna and Tyson's Corner, about a half-mile south of the Leesburg Pike. The marker reads, "From this spot N. 20° W. 220′ stood the first Court House of Fairfax County, built in 1742, abandoned because of Indian Hostilities about 1752."

Documentation is lacking to verify the Indian menace, and it is more likely that it was abandoned because of inaccessibility. In 1752, Alexandria offered to construct a court house and jail without expense to the citizens of the county if they would move the county seat to that location. In 1791, Virginia contributed that part of Fairfax County which included Alexandria, to the Federal Government as her portion of the District of Columbia. This necessitated a change in the location of the Fairfax county seat, which was moved in 1799 to Providence which later became known as the town of Fairfax. The "Little River Turnpike" led from Alexandria through the site of the new county seat enroute to the river whose name it bore, at Aldie, on the way to the Shenandoah Valley.

Fairfax County's history is linked with the lives of three close friends who worked together in laying the foundation for America's Revolution. They were sometimes called "The Three Georges": George Washington, George Mason (see page 68), and George Johnston whose portrait hangs in the Court Room.

About 1750, when Johnston was practicing law in Winchester, he befriended the young surveyor, George Washington, and allowed him to use part of his law office. Young Washington's association with the middle-aged lawyer of strong character, high ideals, culture, and experience is credited with having influenced the formation of his character. In 1752, Johnston deeded his office to his young friend and moved to Alexandria. There he served as Presiding Justice of the Fairfax Court, Trustee of Alexandria, and then represented Fairfax County as a member of the House of Burgesses in Williamsburg. Thomas Jefferson credited him with the constitutional argument embodied in the famous resolution on the Stamp Act which Patrick Henry offered in Williamsburg May 30, 1765. Jefferson later wrote, ". . . the eloquence from Henry backed by the solid reasoning of Johnston prevailed . . ." George Johnston died in 1766, but left two sons to take their part in the Revolution which resulted from this stand against British tyranny.

At spectacular Great Falls in Fairfax County may be seen the locks of the "Potowmack Canal Company".

George Washington in 1784 studied the practicability of passing boats around the falls by a series of locks. This was one unit of a master plan to link navigation of the Potomac with the Ohio River. The company was formed the following year. George Washington spent a great deal of time making detailed surveys of the site, and then personally supervised the construction of the canal and the locks. He stayed with his friend, Bryan Fairfax, Eighth Lord Fairfax, at his estate "Towlston Grange" about three miles below the falls. Two locks which remain today in fair condition are each one hundred feet long by about fourteen feet deep, walled with huge blocks of hand-cut sandstone. Lower down, three locks were blasted through forty feet of solid rock cliff.

Nearby was established the town of Matildaville in 1790, named after the first wife of General "Light-Horse Harry" Lee. There was expectation that this would become an industrial center with the surplus water of the falls being used. However, the project was not successful, and after 1830, it was abandoned.

When the British occupied Washington for a time during the War of 1812, President James Madison and his cabinet moved temporarily to "Salona", a beautiful brick residence near McLean. Colonel John Mosby's capture of Union General Stoughton in Fairfax is related on page 122.

Fairfax County is notable for its famous museum houses: Mount Vernon, Woodlawn (see page 14), Gunston Hall (see page 68), and Sully (see page 42). Much important early religious activity took place within the county boundaries, and some of the finest pre-Revolutionary churches at the time of their construction were in Fairfax County: Falls Church, Pohick Church, and Christ Church (in Alexandria which is no longer part of Fairfax County).

In recent years, much of the farm land of Fairfax County has been developed into residential areas. Its population growth now ranks highest in the Nation. The segment of the George Washington Memorial Parkway to the new Central Intelligence Agency Headquarters beyond Langley is nearing completion. The University of Virginia will soon construct its Northern Virginia Branch at the south edge of the town of Fairfax. The largest Army Engineering Post of the Nation is located at Fort Belvoir, on the site of the original Fairfax family manor house. County clubs are replacing farms, and deluxe motels offer sylvan retreats to those who come to the Washington area.

The people of the Nation are fortunate in having the magnificent beauty of Great Falls preserved for posterity by the Fairfax County Park Authority which acquired sixteen acres in 1952.

Fairfax County, with these varied blessings, is a good place to visit, live, work, learn, worship, and play!

FAIRFAX COURT HOUSE . . . This building was constructed in 1799, and first used in 1800. Court has been held here continuously except a period during the Civil War, when Federal troops occupied the town of Fairfax and used the court house as a stable. Original wills of George and Martha Washington are displayed in the Records Room.

EARP'S ORDINARY . . . This house, believed to be over two centuries old, was formerly a tavern on the Little River Turnpike, one of Virginia's early roads. George Washington is said to have stopped here.

"Jurisdiction" Boundary Stones

THE land ceded by Maryland to the new "Territory of Columbia" was organized as Washington County; it included both old Georgetown and the new Federal City named for George Washington. The land ceded by Virginia was organized as Alexandria County, including the old town of Alexandria.

The boundaries of the prospective Territory of Columbia within Virginia were surveyed by Andrew Ellicott in 1791 and were marked by boundary stones at one-mile intervals. Of freestone, quarried at Aquia Creek down the Potomac, each was one foot square, four feet long, and cut at the top to form a four-sided pyramid. The stones were set two feet into the ground. Each bore the date "1791" and "Virginia" on the side facing the State, and "Jurisdiction of the United States" on the opposite side. They were often called "Jurisdiction Stones." If a marsh or stream prevented the stone from being placed at an accurate mile, the deviation was noted on the stone. A forty-foot lane spanning the survey line was cleared of trees.

George Washington, with Dr. Elisha Dick, officiated at the placing of the first stone on April 15, 1791, at Jones Point, Alexandria, where Great Hunting Creek enters the Potomac River. This was the south cornerstone. A lighthouse was later erected there, with a cross on the steps to mark the location of the stone beneath. The stones were numbered clockwise, beginning with No. 1 at each compass corner, running through No. 9 on all sides of the square.

Until 1801, each county remained under the jurisdiction of its respective State, with the privileges of citizenship including the right to vote in presidential elections.

As the years passed, the local residents came to believe the District government was favoring the commercial interests of Georgetown and Washington over those of Alexandria, and that their separation from Virginia was cutting them out of consideration in relation to the vigorous Virginia public works program of the 1840's. Also, a desire to regain a voice in state and national elections was brought up as a talking point. The Alexandrians therefore agitated for retrocession which was not approved until 1846, with Virginia jurisdiction restored in 1847.

In 1886, the United States Coast and Geodetic Survey determined the latitude and longitude of the four cornerstones by a re-survey which revealed that the supposed square was inaccurate, with the northwest line exceeding the ten miles by 63 feet, the southeast line by 270.5 feet, the northeast line by 263.1 feet, and the southwest line by 230.6 feet.

Marcus Baker wrote an article on the condition of these monuments in 1897 after traversing the entire boundary line and noting what he found. Of the ten along the present Arlington County line, only six were still standing in reasonably good condition; two had been broken off and the tops lost; one whole stone was lost; and another was broken off and lying several feet from its base. Legend has it that this last was broken off by an army wagon during the Civil War.

Between 1915 and 1920, chapters of the District of Columbia and Virginia Daughters of the American Revolution did a splendid work of locating the lost stone and pieces, having them restored to their bases, and protecting each by an iron fence. During the next quarter-century, these monuments suffered through a period of rapid growth of the County and abuse by those who had no interest in our historic heritage. In 1951 and 1952, the County undertook a program of boundary-stone reclamation and preservation. Fences were mended and painted, and one stone which had been buried beneath a shoulder of Leesburg Pike was unearthed.

With a renewed interest in such things, many people are enjoying hikes along the boundary to view the stones, or at least to see those in their vicinity. To help carry on this interest, here is a list of their locations:

SOUTHWEST STONES

No. 4 is the first along the Arlington County line, as the City of Alexandria cuts off the southern tip of the original area. It is in Fairlington on the shoulder of the Leesburg Pike about 200 feet north of the entrance to South Wakefield Street.

No. 5 is on South Walter Reed Drive, a few feet from the Leesburg Pike.

No. 6 is in the median strip of South Jefferson Street one block south of Columbia Pike.

No. 7 is at the back property line of Kenmore Junior High School grounds, north of 5th Road South.

No. 8 is in the Willston Apartment development, a few feet south of Wilson Boulevard and about 100 feet east of the water tower.

No. 9 is in East Falls Church on the east side of Van Buren Street and the south side of 18th Street North.

Just below 29th Street North, between Meridian Street of Falls Church and Arizona Street of Arlington is the only cornerstone. A small tract surrounding this stone has been purchased as a public park, jointly owned by the City of Falls Church and the Counties of Arlington and Fairfax.

NORTHWEST STONES

No. 1 is across North Powhatan Street from the reservoir on Minor Hill, west of Rockingham Street, adjacent to 3611 Powhatan Street, in the center of the block.

No. 2 is just west of Old Dominion Drive, via Edison Street, in the yard of the house at 5298 Old Dominion Drive. This stone has no fence.

No. 3 is the last one on the Virginia side of the river and is in the back yard of the house at 4013 North Tazewell Street.

BOUNDARY STONE . . . This stone marks the western corner of the original District of Columbia.

LYCEUM HALL ... Erected 1837 by the Lyceum Society as a lecture hall and to house the Alexandria Library which had been in operation for fifty years. Federal authorities used the building as a hospital during the Civil War. *201 S. Washington Street.*

RAMSAY HOUSE ... The oldest standing house of Alexandria, reputed to have been built about 1724 at Jones Point, thence moved in 1749 to its present site by William Ramsay, a founder and first mayor of Alexandria. *Corner of King and Fairfax Streets.*

CARLYLE HOUSE KEYSTONE . . . House erected 1752 by John Carlyle who married Sarah Fairfax; their initials appear on the keystone. John Carlyle was a founder of Alexandria and an early property owner of Arlington County. George Washington, five governors and leaders met here in 1755 with General Braddock to formulate plans for the French and Indian War. *121 N. Fairfax Street.*

ALEXANDRIA,

NO history of Arlington would be complete without including a bit about Alexandria, so many years a part of the county which bore its name until 1920.

In 1732, a group of Scottish merchants built a warehouse at West's Point at the mouth of Hunting Creek on the Potomac. The village of Belhaven grew up around the Hunting Creek Warehouse which had been chosen as a suitable port for the shipment of tobacco. By 1748, the town of Alexandria was incorporated and laid out across the creek from Belhaven, on land which had been owned by the Alexander family. The new site was probably chosen because silting of the creek would not affect the wharves on the main river.

The jurisdictional evolution of Alexandria was related in the Introduction on page 1, and in "Jurisdiction" Boundary Stones on page 8. Alexandria's 20th Century annexation of some of the adjacent county villages is detailed in "Subdivisions and Streets" on page 166.

In a churchyard in Alexandria is the grave of the "Unknown Soldier of the Revolutionary War." It is described on page 44.

Alexandria has a tragic romantic mystery which will probably never be solved. It is the identity of the "Female Stranger," buried in St. Paul's Cemetery in 1816. This lovely young woman was ill with typhoid fever

GADSBY'S TAVERN . . . Here George Washington recruited his first command in 1754, and in 1775 he presided at a public meeting which resulted in the adoption of the famous Fairfax County Resolves which had been drawn up by George Mason in protest against British oppression. *128-130 N. Royal Street.*

ROBERT E. LEE HOUSE . . . William Fitzhugh of Chatham Plantation purchased this house 1796. On July 7, 1804, his daughter Mary Lee, at the age of 16, married George Washington Parke Curtis and became the mistress of Arlington House. Robert E. Lee, when still a lad, moved to this Alexandria house with his widowed mother, brothers and sisters. *607 Oronoco Street.*

COLONIAL SEAPORT

CAPTAIN'S ROW . . . Many sea captains had their homes here adjacent to the waterfront; these houses are characteristic of seaport towns of Scotland and England. *100 block of Prince Street.*

when brought from a foreign ship to Gadsby's Tavern by her young husband. They concealed their identity but were obviously of gentle birth; speculation suggests nobility. The wife died within a few weeks, and after making arrangements for her burial and tombstone, the gentleman disappeared. Her tombstone reads, in part:

"To the memory of a FEMALE STRANGER whose mortal suffering terminated on the 14th day of October, 1816, aged 23 years and 8 months. This stone placed by her disconsolate husband in whose arms she sighed out her latest breath and who under God did his utmost to soothe the cold dead ear of death. How loved, how valued once avails thee not, to whom related, or by whom begot . . ."

Alexandria became a center of culture. Town-houses were maintained by many Virginia country gentlemen. George Washington considered it his home town. Here Lafayette was entertained in 1824 by Mayor John Roberts and other notable citizens. At the official dinner, Lafayette offered this toast, "To the City of Alexandria; may her prosperity and happiness more and more realize the fondest hopes of our venerated Washington!"

Many fine books have been written about this colonial city. Herewith are a few pictures which show many facets of its charm.

"Abingdon", Alexander-Custis Plantation

UNTIL it was destroyed by fire on March 5, 1930, "Abingdon", the plantation home of the Alexanders and later of the Custis family was possibly the oldest house in Arlington County. The foundations are still picturesque. In 1933, they were appropriately marked with a bronze plaque on a granite base, by the Association for the Preservation of Virginia Antiquities. The location is the hilltop above the National Airport, back of the "Nelly Custis Airmen's Lounge", near the base of the Radar Station.

John Alexander emigrated from Scotland in 1659, and patented 1,450 acres on the Potomac River twenty miles east of Fredericksburg in 1664. He bought 6,000 acres in this area from Robert Howson November 13, 1669, for 6,000 pounds of tobacco. Robert Howson was a shipmaster who had received his patent of October 21, 1669 for "headrights" for the settlers whom he had brought into the colony. About two miles wide, on the west bank of the Potomac, the grant extended from Hunting Creek (south of Alexandria) to the northern boundary of what later became "Arlington Plantation".

Abingdon was probably built by John Alexander's great-grandson Gerard, who inherited the site from his father in 1735. According to his father's will, Gerard was then living on "Holmes Island", but by 1741 he is recorded as residing on his inherited property. It is possible that the house had been built for one of the Alexanders' tenants prior to the time Gerard took residence and during the period that three generations of the family had resided on their King George County plantations.

A group of architects examined Abingdon a few months before it burned, with the hope that it could be restored. Examination disclosed it had originally been similar to "Wakefield"; a fine example of true colonial story-and-a-half architecture. Additions made during later periods included a high second story with sham pediment, two wing-rooms and a long porch.

When Martha Dandridge Custis Washington's son, "Jackie" (John Parke Custis), was twenty-one, he married Eleanor Calvert, granddaughter of the fifth and last Lord Baltimore. Within four years, their first two daughters were born at the "White House", the estate of the Custis family on the Pamunkey River. Anxious to reside closer to Mount Vernon, Jackie Custis in 1778 entered into negotiations with the sons of Gerard Alexander, Robert III and Gerard Jr., to buy their plantations on the upper Potomac.

The thousand acre Robert Alexander tract containing Abingdon was priced at twelve pounds per acre. The principal with compound interest was to be paid at the expiration of twenty-four years. The Gerard Alexander Jr. tract of 1,100 acres (separated from Robert's by the tract inherited by their brother Philip) was priced at eleven pounds per acre, to be paid in full by Christmas. George Washington futilely advised Jackie Custis against these contracts because of the high price, but most especially because of the compound interest clause.

Christmas Day, 1778 saw the contracts signed, and the young couple moved into Abingdon immediately. Here was born Nelly (Eleanor), March 21, 1779. The young mother was visiting the Calvert family home, Mount Airy, when she gave birth April 30, 1781 to a son, George Washington Parke Custis. Six months later, the young father died of "camp fever" contracted during the siege of Yorktown. General Washington was at his bedside. He and Martha adopted the two youngest Custis babies to bring up at Mount Vernon.

Jackie Custis' young widow and the two older children remained at Abingdon after her marriage in 1783 to Dr. David Stuart. They moved in 1792 to his home, "Hope Park" in Fairfax County; then about ten years later to "Ossian Hall" near Annandale.

Nelly Custis married General Washington's nephew, Lawrence Lewis of "Kenmore" at Mount Vernon, February 22, 1799. This was the last birthday of Washington's life. His wedding gift to the young couple was "Woodlawn Plantation". Nelly's brother, George inherited the Gerard Alexander Jr. tract which had been an outright purchase, upon coming of age in 1802. He took possession and thereon erected "Arlington House" where his daughter married Robert Edward Lee in 1831.

However, the Robert Alexander tract including Abingdon reverted to the Alexanders with a payment of seventy pounds per hundred acres annual rental for the twelve years use. Robert Alexander's heirs sold it to George Wise, from whom it was purchased in 1837 by Alexander Hunter who served for eighteen years as Marshal of the District of Columbia. As his name indicates, he was descended from the Alexander family. The Hunters had no children; therefore he willed Abingdon to his brother, Bushrod W. Hunter, in trust for his namesake nephew. When Bushrod and his son Alexander entered the Confederate Army, Abingdon was confiscated by the Federal Government. Young Alexander Hunter later won a suit for repossession through the assistance of James A. Garfield. It was soon sold, and was finally acquired by the Federal Government in 1940 as a site for the National Airport.

When the remains in the Alexander family burying ground were moved to Pohick Churchyard, along went those of "Long Tom", together with his tombstone. Family tradition rumors him to have been a treacherous Indian who was killed while ambushing a member of the family.

The threads of life have interwoven the families of Wakefield, Stratford Hall, Kenmore, Mount Vernon, Woodlawn, and Abingdon. Today, all except the latter which with Arlington House linked their destinies are historic shrines.

FOUNDATIONS OF ABINGDON . . . Built prior to 1741 probably by Gerard Alexander, destroyed by fire in 1930.

ABINGDON PLAQUE . . . Erected by the Association for Preservation of Virginia's Antiquities in 1933.

Woodlawn Plantation

THE LAFAYETTE BEDROOM . . . The principal guest chamber at Woodlawn is named for the Lewis' distinguished guest and lifelong friend, General Lafayette, who stayed here in 1824.

THE MUSIC ROOM . . . Music played an important part in the life of the Lewis family at Woodlawn, and this, the most elegant room of the mansion, is set for a musicale.

WOODLAWN . . . This late Georgian style mansion completed 1805, was designed by Wm. Thornton, first architect of the Capital, for Nelly Custis (Martha Washington's granddaughter raised at Mt. Vernon) and her husband, Major Lawrence Lewis (George Washington's nephew). The 2,000-acre plantation was a wedding gift from George Washington, who chose the mansion location as "a most beautiful site for a Gentleman's Seat." The garden and grounds were restored by the Garden Club of Virginia. House and grounds open daily 10 to 5 except Christmas. Administered by the National Trust for Historic Preservation. *On U. S. #1 south of Alexandria, 3 miles west of Mount Vernon.*

"Arlington House" and Its Builder

"ARLINGTON HOUSE", the national memorial to Robert Edward Lee, maintained by the National Park Service, belongs to the people of America. Recognition of the qualities of greatness which Lee possessed inspired Representative Cramton of Michigan to introduce a bill in 1925 which provided for the restoration of Arlington House in his honor.

Arlington House was not built by Robert E. Lee nor was it ever his legal property, but he considered it his home from 1831 to 1861. In 1854 he described it as "Arlington . . . where my affections and attachments are more firmly placed than at any place in the world."

George W. P. Custis was twenty-one when his grandmother, Martha Washington, died in 1802. He then went to his own land, across from Washington City, and began his house. Plans for its construction were probably drawn by the brilliant young English architect, George Hadfield. Finances had been strained in order to purchase belongings at the sale which settled Mrs. Washington's estate; therefore the less expensive parts of the Custis mansion were built first.

The Custis holdings, which included more than 15,000 acres throughout the state, provided the raw building materials. Pine for the flooring and woodwork came from the Pamunkey River estates in New Kent County. Bricks were baked of Virginia clay near the site.

The north wing of the house was constructed to shelter temporarily the Washington and Custis mementoes which had been stored in a cottage near the river. The new home was called "Mount Washington", which drew visitors interested in viewing the "Washington Treasury."

By 1804 Mr. Custis completed the south wing and brought home his bride, Mary Lee Fitzhugh from Alexandria. Shortly after her arrival Mount Washington was renamed Arlington House for the ancestral Custis home which had been built before 1680 on the Eastern Shore of Virginia.

While a scarcity of money originally delayed the completion of the mansion, this delay was prolonged by the War of 1812. Through 1815, the British blockade of the Chesapeake Bay prevented building supplies from being brought from the other Custis estates. When the danger of conflict came near Arlington in the form of invasion of the Capital City, Mr. Custis offered his active services to President Madison. This offer was declined because of his rheumatism. He then joined the ranks of the Peter Battery of Georgetown, and is said to have fired the last fieldpiece at the Battle of Bladensburg. While Mrs. Custis and their seven-year-old daughter watched the evacuation of the Capital City, Mr. Custis is reputed to have assisted Dolly Madison in rescuing the Gilbert Stuart portrait of General Washington from the White House.

"The Major," as Mr. Custis was called by his family, set a pattern of life at Arlington emulating what he had known at Mount Vernon. General Washington's ideas on agriculture and home industry prompted the experimental farm at Arlington. The annual "Arlington Sheep Shearings" with prizes for the best rams, began in 1805 and became popular events. They were an attempt to encourage the development of a native breed and assist in establishing an independent woolen industry. Mr. Custis was among the first to urge the creation of a Department of Agriculture, which eventually used his experimental farm, today known as the south area of Fort Myer.

On the shore of the originally clean and clear Potomac, Mr. Custis established "Arlington Spring", a favorite spot for picnickers and bathers. When an organization of merit (in the opinion of the master of Arlington) came to the spring, it was not unusual for a servant to appear with refreshments from the house on the hill. Frequently Mr. Custis' own celebrations at the spring included the entertainment of dignitaries beneath the shelter of the Washington War Tents decorated with flowers and paintings. The history of the smaller tent was sent to Mr. Custis in a letter from Colonel John Nicholas of Virginia, an officer of the Washington Life Guard. He said, "Although the Head Quarters were generally in a house, yet we always pitched the smaller tent in the yard or immediately adjacent to the Quarters, and to this tent the chief was in the constant habit of retiring to write his dispatches. His orders to the officer of the guard were: 'Let me not be disturbed; when I have completed my dispatches, I will come out myself . . .' From within these venerable canvas walls, emanated the momentous dispatches that guided the destinies of our country, in the most awful periods of the struggle for independence."

When people interested in the life of General George Washington came to the Federal City they were directed to Arlington House, whose white columns, gleaming in the sun, could easily be seen among the giant trees of what was almost virgin forest. Those who might come on foot would find resting stones placed along the carriage road which wound its way up from the river through the farm and the park to the house. Here Mr. Custis' hospitality was limited only by interest on the part of his guest.

Mr. Custis' Cultural Efforts

MR. CUSTIS did not always wait for the public to seek him out, but upon request or need would go forth to deliver addresses or show paintings and produce plays and manuscripts. The aim of all this endeavor was to publicize and keep alive the principles for which the Revolution had been fought and to see that General Washington's contributions were properly recognized. Mr. Custis' favorite patriotic occasions were Washington's Birthday, Saint Patrick's Day, and Independence Day. Some of his speeches would be as timely today as they were in the decades that followed the establishment of the Republic. His oratory was sincere and courageous even if at times a bit long. He usually celebrated Washington's Birthday at a ball held at Gadsby's Tavern in Alexandria.

His support of the patriotic principles of religious liberties culminated in his active celebration of Saint Patrick's Day. In a day when a strong anti-foreign feeling threatened the liberty of religion so carefully guaranteed in the First Amendment to the Constitution, Mr. Custis took a courageous position with other prominent citizens to protect the rights of his fellow Americans and to relieve the suffering of oppressed people abroad. He associated the cause for Irish liberty with the principles of the American Revolution. Mr. Custis went forth to meet the Irish of Washington City more than twenty-seven times between 1802 and 1857. He earned the title "Old Orator for Irish Liberty."

In one of his speeches he suggested that the American symbol of the rattlesnake with its motto, "Don't tread on me", be incorporated with the Irish harp as the symbol of free Ireland. The day on which this speech was delivered was much like the other Saint Patrick's Day celebrations. The celebrants gathered at the Masonic Hall and at Saint Patrick's Church in Washington. At high noon the United States Marine Band led the procession to the 14th Street wharf to welcome members of "The Hibernian Society of Alexandria." As the green flag became visible at the bow of their boat, the band struck up the air *Saint Patrick's Day*. Mr. Custis in his green coat was prominent among the leaders of the procession en route to the banquet hall on Pennsylvania Avenue, where there were speeches and toasts.

Recently on Saint Patrick's Day it has become the custom for Irish groups to gather at Arlington to plant shamrocks on Mr. Custis' grave in compliance with his wish expressed in 1844, ". . . years after my mortal body shall have been laid in the bosom of our common mother, some honest Irish heart may come, and dropping a shamrock on my grave, cry 'God bless him.'"

Mr. Custis, as the adopted son of Washington, always took a prominent part in the Fourth of July celebrations in Washington and Alexandria. Through him we can easily trace the Federal City's observance of Independence Day, started by a sunrise salute at the Navy Yard. Citizenry then gathered at the Capitol for the official ceremonies, thence to the White House for the President's reception, followed in the late afternoon by smaller informal gatherings.

Frequently the most sparkling of these celebrations took place at Mr. Custis' own Arlington Spring. Here he entertained the Marquis de Lafayette. In the traditional toasts and speeches, the past was memorialized and future plans for the Country were outlined. Patriotic tunes were included.

In 1848, Mr. Custis officiated at the laying of the cornerstone of the Washington Monument. In the years that followed he joined officials in placing state stones in the Monument as part of "the Glorious Fourth," while informal celebrations continued at Arlington Spring.

With Mr. Custis' death in 1857 and civil conflict in 1861-1865, the former glories of the "Fourth" at Arlington Spring disappeared. However, Mr. Custis' toast for the Fourth of July has not lost its timeliness: "The cause of civil and religious liberty—May the nations of the old world, when another half century shall elapse, be as independent and free . . . as we."

Mr. Custis was interested in writing plays and in the encouragement of native American drama. His best known play, *Pocahontas, or the Settlers of Virginia*, was produced in Philadelphia in 1830 and met with immediate success. His plays and literary endeavors, including his *Recollections of Washington* and *Conversations with Lafayette*, were composed in the "office" and "study" at Arlington.

Appreciation of the fine Custis and Washington family portraits inspired this versatile gentleman with an early interest in art. He became a self-taught, untrained artist whose paintings are interesting primitives. Examples may be seen at the rear of the center hall and over the doors of the south servant quarters.

Intellectual pursuits with a highly individual flavor and colorful execution endeared Mr. Custis to his family and friends but caused strangers to consider him a bit eccentric. The personal anecdotes concerning him are countless, and earned for him a distinct reputation. To Mary, his wife, he was a loving husband; to his daughter, he was the father from whom she had never received an unkind word; to General Lee, he was the man who had treated him as a son since childhood; and to the Lee children, he was their beloved "Grandpa." To us he is the personal link between Washington and Lee, a tie between the men of the Revolution and the Civil War.

SHAMROCKS FOR REMEMBRANCE . . . Historians of the National Capital Parks water shamrocks planted on the grave of G. W. P. Custis in a St. Patrick's Day ceremony inaugurated in 1956.

"First Lady" of Arlington House

MR. CUSTIS chose wisely when he invited sixteen-year-old Molly Fitzhugh to be his bride. Mary Lee Fitzhugh was born April 22, 1788 at "Chatham" on the Rappahannock River. While she was ten or eleven, her father, William Henry Fitzhugh moved the family to Alexandria, where they lived while awaiting completion of a handsome house on their "Ravensworth" estate near Annandale in Fairfax County. The original grant of approximately 20,000 acres was made in 1686 to William Fitzhugh, "Baron of Ravensworth", who was born in England in 1651 and died on his Potomac River estate near Wakefield in 1701. He never lived on his Ravensworth plantation but had French Huguenot tenant farmers raise tobacco there. Molly's father, the namesake and great-grandson of the emigrant, was the first of the family to reside at Ravensworth. Molly was frequently with her parents when they visited the Washingtons at Mount Vernon, where she became acquainted with George Washington Parke Custis, seven years her senior.

It was no surprise to family or friends when Molly became Mr. Custis' bride on July 7, 1804. From official records and family letters, her place in the life of Arlington is sketched. One love letter in the collection at the Custis-Lee Mansion shows her to have been a girl of sensitive and beautiful character, possessing a maturity far beyond her years.

The Custises set up housekeeping in the two wings. Molly is not known to have complained of the inconvenient location of the kitchen in one wing and the dining room in the other with no covered connection. However, as soon as the center section was completed, the dining room was immediately moved to a nearer and more convenient location. While her husband was busy with his cultural and agricultural pursuits, Molly undertook the organization of daily routine and the care of the servants. Deeply religious, she made Christian faith the motivating force of activity on the estate. She believed that her first duty toward the servants was to educate them to know God. Morning and evening prayers were held with the servants in reverent attendance.

In order to reach the goals of religious education, Molly taught Sunday school in the north wing. Later her influence was responsible for the construction of a chapel on the southwest section of the estate. The Virginia Theological Seminary provided student preachers for this work. Molly Custis became actively interested in the work of the Episcopal Church through her cousin, Bishop Meade.

Her feeling of responsibility for the servants went far beyond providing proper food and clothing. She cared for the sick and summoned a doctor for serious illness. Medicine was purchased wholesale in Alexandria and administered by her under a doctor's direction. She sought a just and practical solution to the problem of slavery which would bring freedom and status for "the People". One of her rare trips to Washington City was to witness the Supreme Court hearings on a re-colonization case. In order that the people of Arlington might be prepared to receive their freedom, for which Mr. Custis' will provided, she taught them to read and write and where possible provided for their training in a trade or skill which would enable them to earn a living.

From her portrait, the young mistress of Arlington appears to have had light brown hair and blond complexion. Her attractive face is heart-shaped and indicative of strong character. She was level-headed and somewhat retiring, a good temperamental balance for her husband. She managed the house in a well-organized manner and maintained an atmosphere of gracious hospitality. Miss Molly and her household lists were a source of amusement to her young relatives.

The Custises looked forward to a household of happy children. The early deaths of three of their four children were a great sorrow. Their love and attention was centered on their only surviving daughter, Mary Ann Randolph Custis, whom they reared in the traditions of Mount Vernon and Chatham. Mrs. Custis' sincere piety set an example of true Christian living for her daughter to follow.

The Arlington garden was especially dear to Molly Custis and her daughter. Molly helped plan and plant the area south and west of the south wing of the house soon after her arrival in 1804. Eventually her daughter and granddaughters shared her interest in this garden. Here bloomed their favorite flowers until the beginning of the Civil War. In 1825, Charles Carter Lee presented her with a moss rose for this garden with a poem. Her young friends and relatives always found her a sympathetic advisor in affairs concerning the heart of belles and beaux and the related language of flowers. The ladies of her acquaintance traded plantings, much as they exchanged favorite recipes. The beauty of Molly's garden and her talent with flowers was a family legend. Sick plants were frequently brought to Arlington for her revitalizing touch.

Today when one visits the Custis-Lee Mansion, Molly's garden is only lawn, shaded by a giant elm. The exact location and list of original plantings are recorded, and there is hope that the garden will some day be restored as a fitting tribute to all the ladies of Arlington.

MRS. G. W. P. CUSTIS . . . An original portrait by Cephas Thompson owned
by Mrs. George Bolling Lee.

Lee-Custis Wedding

MARY ANN RANDOLPH CUSTIS was only one month old when she was brought to Arlington from "Annefield" in Clark County, Virginia, where she was born on October 10, 1808. Attractive but never beautiful, it was her personality and spirit which endeared her from girlhood to her cousins and friends.

Her mother gave her religious training and taught her academic subjects and the art of homemaking. Her father was especially interested in her art and music training.

Robert Edward Lee was not more than four and she three when his mother, Ann Hill Carter Lee, took him to Arlington for his first social call on the Custis family. The Lees had just moved to Alexandria from "Stratford Hall" in Westmoreland County. Robert's father, "Light-Horse Harry" Lee, was a close friend of Mrs. Custis' brother. In the years that followed, the friendship of the Custis and Fitzhugh families sustained Mrs. Lee through a life of sadness, ill health, and financial difficulty. Arlington became the place of many happy childhood memories for all five of the Lee children, who were always most welcome. Years later, Mary Custis Lee recalled that as children she and Robert had planted trees in front of Arlington as a symbol of their affections.

Through the years the handsome faces of the Lee boys of Alexandria came and went. It was the face of Robert that remained most clearly in the mind and later the heart of Mary Custis. Mary was twenty-one when he was graduated in 1829 from West Point. He returned home to find that his mother was dying at Ravensworth. The care Robert was able to give her in this last illness gave her comfort and increased the respect and love of his friends and relatives. Comfort and sympathy were his at Arlington House. Before his return to Army duty, much had been done to restore his good spirits.

It was the summer of 1830 when Lieutenant Robert E. Lee, on leave, proposed to Mary Custis and was accepted. In a letter from Fortress Monroe to his brother, Charles Carter Lee, dated June 15th of the following year, he wrote, "The day has been fixed and it is to be the 30th of June . . . Can you come and see it done? I expect to leave here on the *Potomac* on the 29th and reach Alexandria Thursday morning. Go out to Arlington in the afternoon . . ."

While Lee made his plans, the Custises prepared Arlington for the wedding of their only child to a young man whom they had known and loved since childhood. As the day approached, the house was readied and the kitchens were active in anticipation of the wedding and the days of entertaining that would follow. Mary chose her attendants from among her cousins and childhood friends: Britannia Peter of Tudor Place (Georgetown), Julia Calvert of Maryland, Angelica Lewis of Woodlawn, Marietta Turner of Kinlock, Mary Goldsborough of Maryland, and Catherine Mason of Mason's Island as maid of honor. Robert had chosen his brother Sydney Smith Lee as his best man, and Tom Turner (his cousin) and four Army friends as groomsmen.

The bride and her attendants dressed for the occasion in the rooms of the second floor; the men, in the north wing of Arlington. That evening, as the appointed time of eight-thirty passed without the arrival of the minister from the Virginia Theological Seminary, apprehension grew. Anxious eyes strained through the slashing rain as lightning revealed the empty road from the Seminary. At last the pounding of a horse's hoofs announced his approach.

Marietta Turner later described his arrival: "Much fun arose from the appearance of the Reverend Reuel Keith, who arrived drenched to the skin. Although a tall man, he was compelled to conduct the nuptial service in the clothes of my cousin, George Washington Parke Custis, a very great gentleman but a very small man so far as inches were concerned."

When the wedding march began, the bride's attendants descended the stairs, followed by the bride on the arm of her father. The bridal party assembled in the family parlor and the Reverend Mr. Keith read the service from the Episcopal Book of Common Prayer.

The entertainment centered in the main hall, the family parlor, the family dining room, and the large dining room in the south wing. The silver and crystal used were Washington, Custis, and Fitzhugh family heirlooms. The gaiety of the party was not dampened by the rain outside.

As was the custom, the wedding party spent the first night at the home of the bride. Then each in turn would entertain the group at their homes if they were in the neighborhood or on the route of the bridal trip. Marietta's description of this event stimulates the imagination: "This evening was one to be long remembered. My cousin, always a modest and affectionate girl, was never lovelier, and Robert Lee, with his bright eyes and high color was the picture of a cavalier. The elegance and simplicity of the bride's parents, presiding over the feast, and the happiness of the grinning servants . . . remain in my memory as a piece of Virginia life pleasant to recall."

Mrs. Lee, who anticipated that as an army wife she would become "a wanderer on the face of the earth," did not foresee that they would consider Arlington as their home for thirty years.

ROBERT EDWARD LEE . . .

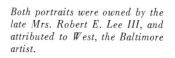

*Both portraits were owned by the
late Mrs. Robert E. Lee III, and
attributed to West, the Baltimore
artist.*

MRS. ROBERT EDWARD LEE . . .

The Lee Children

LIEUTENANT Robert E. Lee had been graduated from the United States Military Academy in 1829, standing second in his class. Because of his academic record, he was given an opportunity to serve in the corps of the engineers, which he did. He had reported to the corps at Cockspur Island, Georgia, for his first tour of duty. Here he had drawn plans and assisted in the construction of Fort Pulaski. In 1831 he was transferred to Fortress Monroe at Old Point Comfort, Virginia.

Practical experience in construction and maintenance continued. Mrs. Lee had come to Fortress Monroe as a bride, and in 1832 their first child had been born there. Lieutenant Lee came to Fortress Monroe an inexperienced officer; he left in 1834 qualified to direct major engineering projects. At this time, orders took him to Washington City as assistant to the Chief of Engineers.

When the Lees came home to Arlington from Fortress Monroe, they brought with them their first-born. This child was no stranger to Arlington and had the nickname of Boo, not a very sedate substitute for the rather formidable George Washington Custis Lee. In later years he was known as Custis Lee, but when he returned as a boy, his grandfather—for whom he was named—was delighted with Boo. Despite his father's efforts to establish a separate residence for the Lees in Washington, the Custises' wishes prevailed in the face of a Washington housing shortage. The Lees were given the second floor, and the Custises kept their quarters in the north wing, where they had lived in the early days of Mount Washington and Arlington.

Three years later, Lieutenant Lee was given an opportunity to demonstrate his ability. When silt deposits in the Mississippi River threatened to destroy the harbor at St. Louis, Missouri, he was placed in charge of the work.

Lieutenant and Mrs. Lee took Custis and a second son, William Henry Fitzhugh (Rooney), to St. Louis with them in 1837. Lieutenant Lee was to be stationed at Jefferson Barracks and he wished his family to be with him. They left Mary, their little girl, with the Custises, fearing that she was too frail to make the trip. There were unexpected difficulties and Lee was unable to bring the family back to Arlington until 1839. He did a brilliant job in St. Louis. Army funds failing, his plans were implemented by the city and the harbor was saved. In 1849 he left St. Louis holding the rank of captain and having established his reputation as an engineer.

In the ensuing years, there was seldom a time when some of the family were not at Arlington. Shortly after the return from St. Louis, Anne Carter Lee was born. Before she was two years old, the whole family went to Fort Hamilton, New York, where two of the children subsequently suffered serious injury. Rooney, despite warnings, played with sharp garden tools in imitation of his idol, the Irish gardener for whom he was nicknamed, and suffered the loss of several fingers. More serious was Annie's loss of sight in one eye as the result of a fall on a pair of scissors.

The family welcomed the birth of Eleanor Agnes in 1841 and Robert Edward, Junior (called Rob) in 1843. Both born at Arlington, they were soon introduced to their father's career by joining the family unit at Fort Hamilton. The family usually returned to Arlington for Christmas and summer vacations but spent the rest of the time at their father's post, where they attended school.

Fort Hamilton in New York on the Narrows across from Manhattan Island claimed Captain Lee's services for five years. Routine tasks absorbed his talent and time. In 1846 the war with Mexico ended this tour of duty. When Captain Lee went to the front, he left his family in the safe hands of the Custises. His youngest child, Mildred, was only a few months old; she would be almost three before he returned.

After fifteen years of Army life, Mary and her children came home to Arlington for an indefinite stay. Captain Lee had his first taste of war. He was assigned to General Wool's command. In January, 1847, his services were requested by General Winfield Scott.

Robert Lee's courage and performance of duty earned for him a Brevet Major's rank at Cerro Gordo, a Brevet Lieutenant Colonelcy at Contreras Churubusco, and a Brevet Colonelcy at Chapultepec. His services in the Mexican War won the lasting admiration of General Scott.

THE CHILDREN'S PLAYROOM . . .

Christmas at Arlington House

CHILDHOOD at Arlington was happy. Acres of wild flowers were scattered in the oak park of the ridge and the lush meadows toward the Potomac. Bathing and picnics took place at Arlington Spring in the summer. Ice skating on the Alexandria Canal and sleighing were their winter sports. The girls became fond of gardening in their own flower beds. The boys were invited to test physical skills and strength in frolics with their father. There were startled guests who came upon a familiar family scene in the parlor, where Robert E. Lee, Senior, was wont to stretch out on the floor and, for the price of tickled feet, tell stories to the children kept busy in this pursuit. The whole family was fond of pets; cats, dogs, and horses were special favorites.

Typical of good times shared were their Christmases. This happy and holy season signaled a return of the Lee family to Arlington. "Home for the holidays" was a phrase full of real meaning for Robert E. Lee, his wife, and their seven children. The Custises treasured the annual reunion with their daughter's family as their most cherished Christmas gift, and prepared for it with happy anticipation.

About the seventeenth of December, the Arlington servants began to gather greens—holly, myrtle (laurel), ivy, running cedar, and pine—to decorate the portraits, mantels, doors, and windows. This was "bringing in Christmas"! A huge yule log was prepared, in the true English and Mount Vernon tradition. for Mr. Custis to ride on as it was brought to the parlor fireplace on Christmas Eve. Handmade decorations of religious symbols of Christmas were prepared; gold and silver angels and stars shone among the greens.

Regardless of distance or weather, the Lees usually arrived at Arlington the week before Christmas. In a long letter to Custis Lee, who had to remain at West Point during the holidays, Robert E. Lee wrote his absent son a full description of all the festivities which took place at Arlington in 1851. That was the winter that the Lee family was stationed in Baltimore, and their trip to Washington on "the cars" was delayed by snow and frost on the tracks. Colonel Lee described it as the coldest Christmas since 1835. Mr. Custis and "Old Daniel" were at the depot with the carriage for Mrs. Lee, Mary, Annie, Agnes, Mildred, and Rob: Rooney and his father walked to Arlington through the snow.

Grandma Custis had eagerly awaited the family arrival, with the smiling house-servants who had been busy preparing favorite Christmas delights. From five-year-old Mildred to seventeen-year-old Mary, the young people participated in the excitement of anticipation of the great day to come.

Before daybreak on Christmas morning the children were up to explore the depths of the stockings they had hung by their beds, sharing their fun with the two older generations. As soon as the members of the family were dressed and "Christmas gifted", presents were delivered to the servant quarters. The adults and older children then attended Christmas services at Christ Church in Alexandria, bringing back guests to spend a few days enjoying the gaiety of Arlington. Rooney and his friends skated the six miles home from church along the Alexandria Canal.

The feast of the afternoon featured turkey, cold ham, plum pudding, and mince pie. Games and music followed in the parlor before the yule log crackling on the hearth. Baby Mildred still clutched her doll, which had not left her embrace since dawn. This was a Christmas to be cherished for those who gathered at Arlington. As a red sunset reflected on the blanket of snow covering the oak park, Mrs. Custis led the family and guests in Evening Prayer.

Between 1831 and 1861, Robert E. Lee was able to get home twenty-four times. However, many times his presence was the result of arduous travel under strenuous conditions. The few times it was impossible for him to be there, the Custises sent a bit of Arlington to cheer his Christmas meal.

On December 20, 1856, Robert E. Lee sent the following Christmas greeting to his family from his post at Fort Benson, Texas: "I hope nothing will happen to mar or disturb the pleasure of the fireside at Arlington, but that you may all assemble around its comfortable hearth with grateful, cheerful and contented hearts. My prayers and thoughts will be with you and all will receive my fervent salutations. I hope nothing will be omitted that I could have done to make each one happy . . ."

The materials of decorating and means of travel have changed in the past century, but the spirit of Robert E. Lee's wish for his loved ones has not greatly altered since the first Christmas Day!

The Lee children enjoyed the pleasures of country life mingled with periods of living at the service posts as their father advanced slowly in his chosen career. Holidays were described in Colonel Lee's letters as filled with childlike delights. The richness of their family life was based on a strong spiritual foundation fostered in the atmosphere of the Custis home.

Home From The Mexican War

UPON his return from Mexico in 1848, Colonel Lee found seven pairs of children's eyes eagerly watching for their hero father and the treasures he was bringing them, among which were a pony, "Santa Anna", and the war horse, "Grace Darling". Along came the Colonel's Irish groom to keep the children spellbound with his war tales.

That fall Colonel Lee assumed duties in Baltimore, Maryland. He supervised the construction of Fort Carroll for additional protection of the harbor.

In the fall of 1852, he was appointed the ninth Superintendent of the United States Military Academy at West Point. It was at this post that the entire Lee family was together for the last time. The eldest son, Custis Lee, attended the Academy while the other six children were in school on the post.

The sudden death of Mrs. Custis on April 23, 1853 occurred the day following her sixty-fifth birthday. Her husband chose the burial site in the oak park southwest of the mansion. Robert E. Lee ordered the simple and dignified tombstone from Robert E. Mounitz, a famous sculptor of New York. Engraved upon it were lilies-of-the-valley and heartsease, with the quotation, "Blessed are the pure in heart, for they shall see God".

This death left a gap in the family which would never be filled. Her seven grandchildren, ranging in age from seven to twenty-one, deeply missed "Dear Grandma" who had helped rear them. The servants missed "Miss Molly's" sensitive interest and unceasing concern for their spiritual and physical welfare. The void she left in the hearts of her husband and daughter was a deep and lasting one. The example she had set remained alive and dear in the memory of all who had known her.

Two years after Mrs. Custis' death, West Point duty came to an end with Colonel Lee's transfer from the staff of the Engineering Corps to the Second Cavalry. Congress had authorized the organization of this unit to control the Indians and bandits in the West. As-signment to this regiment at Camp Cooper, Texas, took Colonel Lee away from his family for a longer time than at any previous period in his peacetime service. The children's schooling, family obligations, and emergencies kept Mrs. Lee at Arlington and prevented her from joining him.

Late in 1857, Mr. Custis died at the age of seventy-six. His was Arlington's first military funeral, complete with dirge, uniformed escort, and gun salute. His grave was marked by a small obelisk. News of Mr. Custis' death caused Colonel Lee immediately to request extended leave. Returning home, he took up the complicated task of straightening out the Custis estate. As executor of the estate, it became his responsibility to pay the bills and salvage what he could for his children, who were Mr. Custis's heirs. He used his own funds to put the three major estates on a self-supporting basis. Custis Lee, who inherited Arlington from his grandfather, sent the deed to his father, but Lee did not feel it right to accept it. He was still on leave struggling with Mr. Custis's estate when General Scott ordered him to Harpers Ferry with a detachment of marines from the Washington Marine Barracks to quell a slave rebellion led by John Brown. Tradition tells us that the messenger sent by General Scott was a young lieutenant in his office, James Ewell Brown Stuart. Little did they foresee their future as officers of the Confederacy.

In 1860, George Washington Custis Lee was stationed at Fort Washington, close enough to Arlington to keep an eye on the estate and the family. This relieved Colonel Lee of the burden of immediate supervision, and he returned to the Second Cavalry to resume his career. Tensions had been mounting between the North and the South, and the signs of danger were clear to this veteran soldier.

But returning to Texas in the spring of 1860, he was not fully aware of the country's proximity to the war which had been averted so often in the past. He was unaware, too, that this would be his last tour of duty with the United States Army.

COLONEL ROBERT E. LEE . . . United States Army.

The Decision

THE national tensions which Colonel Lee left in the Spring of 1860 at Arlington were whipped to frenzied bitterness and secession throughout the South before Christmas. Texas seceded in February 1861, and Colonel Robert E. Lee returned to his native Virginia on the first of March. He had reflected concern for his country in January, when he observed, "I am anxious that Virginia should keep right, and as she was chiefly instrumental in the formation of the Constitution, so I would wish that she might be able to maintain it and save the union." It was the end of March when he accepted with honor a full colonel's commission signed by President Lincoln. The Lee family continued to pray that a bloody fratricidal war might be averted. This was the position of many in Virginia when on April 12, Fort Sumter was fired on in Charleston, South Carolina.

With the fall of Fort Sumter on Sunday, April 14, a critical series of events began which would drastically change the life of Robert E. Lee and his country. On April 15 President Abraham Lincoln, determined to uphold his oath of office and preserve the Union, called for 75,000 volunteers. The following day the Virginia Legislature went into secret session which culminated on the 17th in passage of the ordinance of secession. This news was not confirmed in Northern Virginia or Washington City until the 19th.

While Virginia considered secession, Colonel Lee received notes from General Winfield Scott and Mr. Francis Blair requesting visits on the 18th in Washington City. Loyalty to Virginia was foremost in his mind as he awaited the decision of his native state. He had earlier stated: "If the Union is dissolved and the government disrupted I shall return to my native state and share the miseries of my people and save in defense will draw my sword on none."

It was in this frame of mind that Robert E. Lee listened as Francis Blair offered him the command of a large Federal Army. With true recognition of Lee's ability, men in high places had recommended him to the President, who in turn authorized Francis Blair to approach Lee with the offer of command.

Seven years later Lee described his reaction: "I declined the offer he made me to take command of the army that was to be brought into the field, stating as candidly and as courteously as I could, that though opposed to secession and deprecating war, I could take no part in an invasion of the Southern States."

Colonel Lee went from the Blair House across Pennsylvania Avenue to the office of his old commander, General Scott. He recounted the interview to General Scott, who is reputed to have said: "Lee, you have made the greatest mistake of your life; and I feared it would be so."

On his way back to Arlington, Lee stopped to discuss the state of the union and his own position with his brother, Sidney Smith Lee, who was on active duty with the U. S. Navy and faced the same general conditions. They planned to confer again before either took action. This was not to be the case.

The next day Robert E. Lee learned from the Alexandria paper that the Virginia Legislature had passed the ordinance of secession. He is quoted as saying, "I am one of those dull creatures who cannot see the good of secession."

Colonel Lee knew that initiation of hostilities would not wait for the Virginia referendum on the ordinance. Officers of his rank and experience would soon be under orders. If he meant to resign with honor he had to act. With a heavy heart he returned home to Arlington.

On the evening of April 19, Arlington was ablaze with light and filled with relatives and close friends who, hearing of the actions of the Legislature, sought knowledge of Lee's course of action. Colonel Lee paced and prayed until after midnight, when he descended the stairs from his bedroom to hand Mrs. Lee his letter of resignation. Its significance and the price it had cost were evident.

On Sunday morning he attended services at Christ Church in Alexandria, and on his return home received a letter conveying the governor's invitation to confer with him in Richmond. On the morning of April 22, 1861, Robert E. Lee left Arlington never to return.

As he turned his back on the Potomac to board the train for Richmond he could not have known that the next time he saw its waters he would be the Commander of the Army of Northern Virginia moving toward the battle of Antietam. The part his military genius would play in the following years of conflict was obscured from his view.

Three years after the end of the war, Lee said: "I did only what my duty demanded. I could have taken no other course without dishonor. And if it were to be done over again, I should act in precisely the same manner."

Although this action had cost him his home, and his professional career, it earned for him the rewards of honor, peace of conscience, and universal respect.

ARLINGTON HOUSE . . .

A Fond Farewell

APRIL, 1861, was cold; so unseasonably cold that Mrs. Robert E. Lee noted of all the spring flowers only the "yellows" were in bloom. If one believed in signs, indeed the earth seemed to reflect the cold grip of fear which grasped the hearts of reasonable men and women who saw their world about to crumble around them.

The Colonel's resignation and departure for the capital of the State was an accomplished fact before the family realized its full significance. Soldiers poured into Washington City in answer to Mr. Lincoln's call for volunteers. Arlington sat alone among the trees. Mrs. Lee refused to think of the future. She even attempted to convince Custis Lee, still busy completing his task of preparing the defenses at Fort Washington, Maryland, that if Virginia had to make a stand, the guns should be placed on Arlington Heights and the estate protected. Her son must have been a bit amused at this civilian thinking, in view of the large troop concentration across the Potomac, and Virginia's lack of readiness. He was awaiting his final salary payment before ending his career with the United States Army, and escorting his mother and sisters to a safer place.

Mrs. Lee's refusal to abandon her girlhood home was understandable. But even she was a bit frightened when Orton Williams rode over from the War Department to warn her that the whole Union Army now gathering in the city would cross the Long Bridge to take the ridge in a matter of hours. Later he returned to correct the hours to days, but the alarm had been effective. This army wife began to pack, to follow her soldier husband to one more post. Although now fifty-three and crippled by arthritis, this was the life she had chosen and she did not falter. She had traveled over half the continent; she may have thought now it would be only necessary to go a short distance for a few weeks until all this war talk blew over and things returned to normal. Even Mrs. Lee could not believe all of her desperate hopes. She took the treasures her father had carefully carried across the roads from Mount Vernon fifty-nine years before, to the basement. There she and the trusted servants packed them carefully away. The war tents, the Cincinnati china, and other mementoes were carefully protected from the elements. Mentally she chose from a collection of nearly sixty years of family living the precious and the needed to take with her. Frequently, Washington possessions remained and Lee possessions went.

The heavily laden Arlington carriage and wagons rolled between Arlington and the homes of friends and relatives in Alexandria, Georgetown, and Fairfax County. Custis was insistent that he see her and the girls safely to Aunt Maria Fitzhugh's Ravensworth before he went to join his father in Richmond. Lee's letters grew more persistent that she leave.

It was after the tenth of May that Custis finally persuaded his mother to join the girls, who had gone ahead. General Lee wrote from Richmond that the boxes sent for safekeeping were received and sent on to Lexington, where they would survive the War.

Arlington was in its glory as Mrs. Lee said a tearful goodbye to the servants, leaving directions for the care of the house and grounds, as well as letters for the officer whom she was certain would soon take quarters in her house. She turned over the keys to Selina Grey, as she had turned over the keys to many quarters in the past.

As the carriage turned around the garden and headed northwest to Ravensworth, she realized how different this departure was. In her mind's eye she may have seen the torches of the Union Army which would announce the pending troop movement. But when this became fact, Arlington stood alone and empty in the darkness of her park. The warm air of a May night carried the pungent and belyingly peaceful odors of her flowering shrubs, and frightened servants watched from the sheltering trees as the flaming torches crossed Long Bridge in the moonlight and troops began to ascend the hill.

RAVENSWORTH SPRING . . .
The plantation home was built during the 1700's by William Fitzhugh, and burned August 1, 1926. The springhouse and handsome brick stables are all that remain of the original structures. *About 2 miles southwest of Annandale, Fairfax County, on Braddock Road.*

ARLINGTON SPRING . . .
Nothing remains to mark the site.

Strangers at Arlington

THE movement of Union troops into Virginia in the spring of 1861 was described by General Samuel P. Heintzelman: "At 9 p.m. officers were sent to the colonels, directing them to march to the Washington end of the Long Bridge . . . to enter on the bridge at 2 a.m. on the 24th day of May." Before dawn, men of the regular army and volunteers moved south across the Potomac and took their positions on Arlington Heights and in Alexandria.

A little later that day General Charles W. Sandford, in command of troops on the Virginia side of the river, inspected Arlington estate. "Finding the mansion vacated by the family, I stated to some of the servants left there that had the family remained, I would have established a guard for their security from annoyance; but, in consequence of their absence, that I would, by occupying it myself, be responsible for the perfect care and security of the house and everything in and about it."

The day before the army moved into Virginia, Agnes Lee had written her sister, Mildred, from Ravensworth where she and her mother had taken refuge, "Arlington Heights are still unoccupied though there is a report they are to be possessed by a New York regiment in a day or two." On the 26th, the Eighth New York Militia encamped at Arlington. A short time later, General McDowell wrote to Mrs. R. E. Lee of his arrival at her estate: "Everything has been done as you desired with respect to your servants. . . . When you desire to return, every facility will be given you for so doing. I trust, Madam, you will not consider it an intrusion if I say I have the most sincere sympathy for your distress, and that, as far as is compatible with my duty, I shall always be ready to do whatever may alleviate it." General McDowell maintained his headquarters and sleeping tent outside the mansion in the garden. He had Colonel Lyons of the New York Militia occupying the first floor of the house to protect the property. Mrs. Lee, years after the war, remembered his conscientious care of her home, which became the headquarters for the Army of the Potomac. Thousands of men in blue slept upon Arlington's grounds. During the four long years which followed, they burned some of her oak forests for warmth, drank from her cool springs, and enjoyed food from her fields.

The men of the Eighth New York gently guarded this house on the hill, which had become a symbol of beauty, contrasted with the grim battles that were ahead. These were the men who had volunteered for three months service on April 20 but were held over to participate in the grim First Battle of Manassas and stain Bull Run with their blood.

While General Lee and his sons were on the battlefields, the ladies of the family stayed with family and friends until they could go to a house that General Lee had secured for them in Richmond, where they were settled by the close of 1862.

By January of 1864, a strong ring of forts for the defense of Washington City had been constructed and were sufficient protection for the Capital. No longer was Arlington House necessary for the transaction of Army business.

A law had been passed permitting commissioners to be appointed for the conquered territories of the South, with authority to assess the land for federal taxes. Arlington was among the estates thus affected. Money for the payment of these taxes ($92.07) was presented at the collection office in Alexandria by a cousin of Mrs. Lee, but the collectors refused to accept it from any other than the hands of the property owner in person, who was a semi-invalid in Richmond. Upon this technicality, the Federal Government confiscated Arlington and bid it in, at public auction, for $26,800 in 1864.

In June of 1864, at the suggestion of Quartermaster General Montgomery C. Meigs, the Secretary of War designated part of the estate as Arlington National Cemetery.

Because of what was recognized as illegal seizure, the government's title was considered in jeopardy for nearly two decades, during which time the Government continued to use Arlington Estate as a cemetery and the mansion as the office. The title case had been introduced into the courts in the fall of 1873 when Mrs. Lee's death made her eldest son the legal heir, in accordance with his Grandfather Custis' will. After ten years of litigation, Custis Lee's title to Arlington Estate was established; he accepted $150,000 compensation, and the Government's title was cleared.

Mrs. Lee, on her last visit to her Aunt Maria at Ravensworth in the spring of 1873 came to Arlington. The servants were still living and working at the house which was then the Cemetery Headquarters. They recognized their old Mistress with much affection. Without leaving her carriage, Mrs. Lee accepted a cool sip of water from the well west of the house and then drove away through the west gate without looking back.

War Department.
June 15, 1'64.

...iots that the ground...
...rounding the Arling...
...Mansion, nor ex=
...ing 200 acres, be en...
...ed be for a Military
...etry in which shall
...interred the bodies
...ll soldiers dying in
...Hospitals in the vicini...
...Washington or Alex=
...ria, after the ground...
...used at Alexandria
...illed.

...ten to Genl Rucker
...Bache & Genl Augur
...June 1'4
...letter to See of War
...23 66

The Arlington Mansion and the
grounds immediately surrounding it are
appropriated for a Military Cemetery.
The bodies of all soldiers dying
in the Hospitals of the vicinity of
Washington and Alexandria will be
interred in this Cemetery.
The Quartermaster General is
charged with the execution of this
order. He will cause the grounds,
not exceeding two hundred acres, to be
immediately surveyed, laid out, and
enclosed for this purpose,

June 15. 1864

Edwin M Stanton
Secretary of War

Lee's Post-War Years

"AFTER four years of arduous service marked by unsurpassed courage and fortitude the Army of Northern Virginia has been compelled to yield to overwhelming numbers and resources. . . ."

The spring of 1865 brought peace to the United States. A bitter Civil War ceased and some of the tired men who fought it returned to their families and homes. At the close of the War, Robert E. Lee and his family still occupied the house in Richmond, Virginia, at 707 Franklin Street, with little hope of ever returning to Arlington.

Robert E. Lee was one of the older men of this generation. Returning to peacetime status, he found himself without a profession. The life of a soldier was the only one he had known. His thirty-two years of exemplary service in the United States Army had reflected an ability which recommended him for high command. He had performed his duty as he saw it. His military ability enhanced by his strength of character and dignity of person inspired respect and love in the hearts of the people who followed him. The value of his service to Virginia and the Confederacy cannot be measured.

All soldiers who laid down their arms at Appomattox Court House were granted amnesty. In spite of this, there was much talk of treason trials for officers of high rank. It was the firm stand of General U. S. Grant which prevented this talk from becoming a reality. General Robert E. Lee without work or a home was not without a country in the uncertain days that closed the War. Although he was offered a mansion in a foreign country, he chose to remain in Virginia and share the fate of his people. He felt it was his duty to stay and do all in his power to bind up the Nation's wounds.

It was not until August that an offer of employment came which he felt he should accept. The Board of Trustees of Washington College elected him the president of their institution. Experience as Superintendent of the United States Military Academy at West Point had helped prepare him for such a position. This small, almost bankrupt, college at Lexington, Virginia, offered him an opportunity to serve. By Christmas 1865, he was able to take his family to Lexington. When the War began, his youngest child was fifteen years old. Now Rob and Rooney were beginning to farm the impoverished estates left to them by their Grandfather Custis. Custis Lee became a professor at Virginia Military Institute, which adjoined the campus of Washington College. The girls remained with General and Mrs. Lee—all the girls but Annie—whose sudden death in 1862 was a source of family grief.

For the last five years of his life Robert E. Lee was able to guide young men, many of whom had served with him in a sterner school. He marked the difference in function between a military school, such as West Point, and a civilian institution of higher learning such as Washington College. He saw the duty of education as preparing men to develop their talent as instruments with which to work in this world in order to merit their eternal reward.

In October 1870, Robert E. Lee died and was buried in the crypt beneath the chapel which he helped build at Washington College. North and South both mourned his loss. *The New York Sun* spoke of Lee as "an able soldier, a sincere Christian, and an honest man," while *The New York Herald* linked his name with that of Lincoln. . . . "Lee and Lincoln—both so whole in mind and heart and purpose that even war could not damage them."

Lee had lived in the spirit of the words from Lincoln's second inaugural address, "With malice toward none, with charity for all . . . let us strive on . . . to do all which may achieve a just and lasting peace among ourselves, and with all nations." In similar terms General Lee had written the Governor of Virginia . . . "All should unite in honest efforts to obliterate the effects of the War and to restore the blessings of peace." Here were fine and noble men worthy of emulation. It is fitting that the National Memorials maintained in their honor be joined by Arlington Memorial Bridge across the River which once divided the Nation.

APPROACH TO ARLINGTON MEMORIAL BRIDGE . . .

TOMB OF ROBERT E. LEE . . . in the chapel of Washington and Lee University at Lexington, Virginia.

Lee Family, Jamestown to Arlington

IT is through Arlington House, the mansion made famous as the home of the Confederate general Robert E. Lee and now his National Memorial, and Arlington National Cemetery which was established on Arlington Plantation, that the name of our county is known throughout the world. It therefore seems fitting that a history of Arlington County should include a brief resumé of the branches of the Lee family who were early landowners of this county and of "Leesylvania", the plantation of General Lee's branch of the family.

The first Lee to own land in Arlington County was Thomas Lee, the builder of Stratford Hall in Westmoreland County. Stratford is owned and maintained by the Robert E. Lee Memorial Foundation as a public shrine honoring the birthplace of the Confederate General, hence many people are surprised to learn that he is not descended from Thomas Lee, although a relative. Robert E. Lee's ancestral home was Leesylvania, described in the following chapter. Robert's father, General Henry ("Light-Horse Harry") Lee of Leesylvania had first married Matilda Lee, his second cousin, the granddaughter of Thomas Lee. The young couple lived at Stratford, and following Matilda's early death, Henry married her friend, Anne Hill Carter. She came to Stratford as a bride to care for her two stepchildren, and there she bore her own children, including Robert Edward Lee.

Thomas Lee has been so strongly identified with Stratford Hall that we tend to overlook his family's associations with Jamestown and Williamsburg, and his own activities in the northern part of Virginia. His emigrant grandparents, Richard Lee and Anne Constable, reached Jamestown on the same ship in 1639. Anne was a ward of the new governor, Sir Francis Wyatt, and it was to the governor's brick residence that Richard Lee came a-courting. They were married in the first brick church of Jamestown, on the site of the present picturesque ruins.

Their first home was on the north side of the York River, from which they fled with their infant son to escape the Indian Massacre of 1644. They built again on the safer south side of the river, where they lived for nine years before establishing their "Paradise Plantation" at Gloucester. Their final home was on Dividing Creek (near Kilmarnock) where they are buried.

Richard Lee was Clerk of the Quarter Court, Attorney General of Virginia, High Sheriff of York County, Burgess of York, Secretary of State, and member of the Council. His son, Richard Lee II, become a member of the Council when he was not yet thirty, and was appointed Naval Officer and Receiver of Customs of the Potomac. His son, Thomas Lee, was born in 1690. Another son, Henry I, was the progenitor of Robert E. Lee's branch of the family.

In 1711, when Thomas was but twenty-one years old, he was given power of attorney by Lady Fairfax as Resident Agent of the Northern Neck Proprietary, and administered her affairs for five years until the return from England of his brother-in-law, Edmund Jennings, who then took over the responsibility. Thomas Lee, who had become familiar with the entire area, then devoted his time to establishing his land grants. In 1718 he acquired 4,200 acres in Fauquier County, including the site of Warrenton. The following year he secured 3,700 acres at the Falls of the Potomac, extending down into present Arlington County to the mouth of Pimmit Run, where he built a tobacco warehouse. He eventually acquired 16,000 acres in Loudoun County. The town of Leesburg bears his name.

Thomas Lee succeeded his father as Naval Officer for the Potomac, served as Gentleman Justice of Westmoreland, and was elected Burgess in 1720. In 1722 he married Hannah Ludwell. They lived on the Machodoc Plantation of Richard Lee II near Hague in Westmoreland County, and three years later started construction of Stratford Hall, completed in 1729. February 4th of that year, the Machodoc House was burned by felons whom Thomas, as Justice of the Peace, had condemned. Queen Caroline of England sent over several hundred pounds to lessen the loss which arose from Lee's performance of public duty. This money helped complete Stratford so that they were soon able to move into their new home.

Thomas Lee rose in public affairs, negotiated the Treaty of Lancaster with the Iroquois Indians which opened up the Ohio basin for settlement, and became President of the Ohio Company organized in 1748 for colonization. He later became President of the Council and Acting Governor of the Colony until his death in 1750. Thomas Lee produced a fine crop of young rebels; five of his six sons were leaders in the rebellion against England.

Richard Henry Lee in 1756 drafted the Westmoreland Resolves, pledging life and fortune to the cause of liberty. In 1759 he introduced legislation which, if passed, would have abolished the slave trade. He introduced the resolution for independence. He and his brother, Francis Lightfoot Lee, were the only brothers to sign the resulting Declaration of Independence. Another brother, Thomas Ludwell Lee, took an active part in the Virginia Convention, served on the Committee of Safety, and became a Judge of the General Court of Virginia.

The two youngest brothers, William and Arthur Lee, both served in important diplomatic posts for America, which caused each to lose a personal fortune. Charles C. Tansill, Professor of History of Georgetown University, states that we would have lost the Revolution had it not been for Arthur Lee's diplomatic achievements in France. He obtained the first promise of French aid.

Stratford Hall therefore honors not only the beloved Confederate General who happened to be born there, but also his illustrious kinsmen who helped build our Nation and secure its liberty!

COBBS HALL BURIAL GROUND . . . Here in May 1958, the Society of
the Lees of Virginia dedicated a plaque at the grave of Richard Lee, who came
from England in 1639.

Leesylvania Plantation

FEW know the history of the ancestral plantation of Robert E. Lee's branch of the Lee family, "Leesylvania" in Prince William County between Woodbridge and Dumfries. More specifically, it lies between Neabsco and Powell Creeks, extending from the Potomac River on back inland to include lands west of U. S. Highway No. 1. The mansion house burned down in the 1790's, which accounts for this historic site being relatively unknown to the general public.

Now, all that remains marking the site of the home are traces of the foundations at the crest of the ridge overlooking the Potomac, and the graves of General Lee's grandparents on a moss-covered knoll at the end of the garden, overlooking Neabsco Bay. Later adjacent Fairfax family burials are marked by engraved stones protected by an iron fence, but the tombstones of the Lee graves disappeared over a century ago.

The vast acreage of the Leesylvania tract was patented in 1658 by Gervais Dodson, who shortly conveyed it to Councilor Henry Corbin of Pecatone Plantation in Westmoreland County. Corbin willed it to his daughter, Laetitia, in 1675, the year following her marriage to Richard Lee II, son of Richard Lee, the emigrant. Young Richard, a graduate of Oxford, was already a member of the Governor's Council at the time of their marriage. They continued to reside in Westmoreland County at their Machodoc plantation near The Hague. Laetitia Lee died in 1706. Her will left the distant plantation to their son, Henry Lee I, who was then fifteen. When about thirty-two, he married Mary Bland of Williamsburg and the James River plantations. They also lived in Westmoreland County at "Lee Hall", part of the Machodoc plantation.

It was not until their son Henry Lee II inherited Leesylvania, upon his father's death in 1747, that a member of the Lee family resided on the plantation which had belonged to the family for four generations, spanning nearly ninety years. Henry Lee II won the hand of Lucy Grymes, the auburn-haired "Lowland Beauty" who had been unsuccessfully wooed by George Washington. They were married on December 1. 1753, in Bruton Parish Church, Williamsburg, and soon departed for their new home on Leesylvania Plantation.

There Henry Lee II served as presiding Justice of Prince William, County Lieutenant (head of the County militia), and member of the House of Burgesses. He also represented Prince William County in the Virginia Revolutionary Conventions. He died in 1787, followed five years later by his wife. Both were buried in the family graveyard at the far end of their garden, where daffodils still bloom in the springtime.

Among their eight children born at Leesylvania were Henry III ("Light-Horse Harry," 1756-1818), cavalry colonel in the Revolution, Governor of Virginia 1791-1794, and the father of Robert E. Lee; Charles Lee (1758-1815), George Washington's personal attorney and Attorney General of the United States 1795-1801; Richard Bland Lee (1761-1827), the first Congressman representing Northern Virginia 1789-1795, and the person most responsible for choice of the site of the Federal City; Edmund Jennings Lee (1772-1843), Mayor of Alexandria 1814-1818, eminent lawyer and churchman. His legal efforts saved from confiscation the "Glebe Lands" of Fairfax Parish (within present Arlington County), as related on page 174.

Leesylvania was inherited by Charles Lee, whose son Alfred sold it in 1825 to Henry Fairfax. The Lee mansion had burned soon after the death of Lucy Grymes Lee, although there were other homes on the plantation mentioned in her husband's will.

The home in which the Fairfax family resided was half-way down the slope toward Freestone Point; it possibly predated the mansion. The Fairfax home burned down in 1910. The ruins of the walls and a chimney can be seen today, and the foundations of the bank-barn. At the extreme point of land, where Neabsco Creek enters the Potomac, there is a cliff upon which was a Confederate fort during the Civil War.

Surrounded on three sides by water, Leesylvania's rugged terrain, ancient forest, historic sites, and breathtaking views offer unlimited opportunity for a beautiful resort if properly developed with recognition of the desirability of preservation of these features.

The peninsula was purchased in 1957 by a group of men with such a project in mind. Nearly one million dollars has already been invested along the Potomac beach in swimming pools, board walks, picturesque picnic areas, and other facilities. It is hoped that future plans of the Freestone Holding Company will create a recreation area worthy of Leesylvania's historic heritage.

THE SPINNING-WHEEL . . . of Robert E. Lee's grandmother, Lucy Grymes Lee, of Leesylvania, and the spirit lamp from her son's home, Sully, lend inspiration to the author for her historical research. The desk (circa 1740) belonged to Colonial Governor John Reading of New Jersey. Fleet Surgeon Bailey Washington, III brought the chess set from the Mediterranean in 1836. He married Ann Matilda Lee of Sully, first cousin of the Confederate General.

FAIRFAX GRAVES . . . The Fairfax burials were made in the graveyard established by the Lee family whose tombstones have disappeared.

Sully Plantation House at Chantilly

"SULLY", the country home of Richard Bland Lee, lies in Fairfax County many miles beyond the Arlington County line. His influence had such a direct bearing on the establishment of what eventually became our county that it seems appropriate to include its history in this book.

Sully plantation was acquired in 1957 by the Federal Aviation Administration as it lay within the boundaries of the Dulles International Airport at Chantilly. However, realizing the historical importance of the house, Congress assigned the home and 36.3 acres to the Fairfax County Park Authority to be operated as a public museum.

The house was erected in 1794 by Richard Bland Lee upon land which had been granted in 1712 to his grandfather, Henry Lee I of Westmoreland County. The plantation was operated by tenants until Richard Bland Lee, third generation owner came there as a young bachelor. He lived in a comfortable two-story log house, no longer existing.

Richard Bland Lee served in the Virginia Assembly as early as 1784 when he was but twenty-three years old. He became the first Congressman from Northern Virginia in 1789. This man achieved national importance when he became the person most responsible for selecting the site of the Federal City, as related on page 4.

On June 19, 1794, he married Elizabeth Collings of Philadelphia, and brought her to his Virginia plantation. They spent their honeymoon in the log house while their new home was being built.

In December of that year, Richard Lee Tuberville of Fairfax County married his cousin Henrietta Lee, daughter of Richard Henry Lee of "Chantilly", Westmoreland County. They built a home near Sully and named it for the bride's birthplace. The name of Chantilly has remained for the neighborhood, although the house itself was destroyed in the mid-1800's.

The Richard Bland Lees probably engaged Colonel James Wren as the architect of their new home. He was a friend of the family, is known to have designed other homes in the Chantilly area, and the construction of Sully has many of his architectural characteristics. It is of beaded poplar clapboard over brick on a stone foundation.

A wide center hall, running the width of the house, contains a fine stairway and opens to spacious, well-proportioned rooms on both sides. Of special interest are the mantels which have often been sketched for reproduction. All the major rooms have fireplaces. Original random-width pine floors are still intact, as are the doors and their hardware.

The separate kitchen originally connected to the main house by a breezeway contains a huge fireplace, with quarters upstairs for the household servants. The breezeway was removed in the mid-1800's when an attached kitchen was added. The old smokehouse and toolhouse remain standing.

In the Library of Congress is a letter written by Thomas Lee Shippen to his father, Dr. William Shippen of Philadelphia, twice elected a member of the Continental Congress. The letter, dated October 24, 1797 contains a description of his visit to Sully . . . "We arrived here yesterday from Leesburg before dinner, and the great importunity of the delightful family has persuaded us to pass this day with them . . . I would fain give you some idea of the elegance in which this kinsman of ours has settled himself. . . .

"The house is new, built by himself about 3 years ago and lately furnished from Philadelphia with every article of silver, mahogany, Wilton carpeting, and glassware that can be conceived of that you will find in the very best furnished houses in Philadelphia . . . completely equipped with every luxury as well as convenience."

General and Mrs. Washington were devoted to the young couple at Sully. They attended the christening of Richard Bland Lee, II, and presented a set of fine crystal wine glasses to toast the health of the baby. It is interesting to recall that Richard Bland Lee was the son of Lucy Grymes, George Washington's youthful sweetheart.

The Lees' most intimate friends were James and Dolly Madison, the wives having met as girls in a Quaker school in Philadelphia. Elizabeth was Dolly's bridesmaid upon her marriage to John Todd, a Philadelphia lawyer. Biographies of Dolly Madison are based largely upon the letters in the Library of Congress containing the lifetime correspondence of these two friends.

Richard Bland Lee was appointed one of the three commissioners to superintend the re-erection of the public buildings in Washington destroyed by the British August 12th, 1814. In order to better serve his country, he gave up life at his beloved plantation and bought a house in the then newly developed fashionable section of southwest Washington called "Greenleaf Point". This townhouse at the northeast corner of 6th and N Streets, S.W. is marked with a bronze plaque placed on it in 1950 by the National Capital Sesquicentennial Commission.

In 1815, Richard Bland Lee was appointed Commissioner to Adjudicate Claims arising from loss or destruction of property during the War of 1812. In 1819, President Monroe appointed him Judge of the Orphans' Court of the District of Columbia, on which he served until his death March 12, 1827. He was buried in Congressional Cemetery.

Upon moving to Washington, Richard Bland Lee had sold his plantation to his cousin, Francis Lightfoot Lee, a graduate of Harvard. Among his children were Major John Fitzgerald Lee, the first Judge Advocate of the Army, and Rear-Admiral Samuel Phillips Lee of the Navy. It was the latter who married Elizabeth Blair. They resided in the Lee portion of the Blair-Lee House, now the President's Guest House.

SULLY . . . Erected 1794 by Richard Bland Lee.

THE STONE DEPENDENCY...
This picturesque building is documented as having been erected shortly after 1800 as a dairy house. This explains the absence of a fireplace on the first floor, although there is one upstairs in living-quarters.

In Sacred Memory

AS we look back through the years to the history of beautiful Arlington Estate as a final resting place of generations of Americans, we find that the first burial was of a Custis cousin, Mrs. Mary Randolph, who died in January, 1828 at the age of sixty-six. Her grave is enclosed by a brick wall, and is down the slope from the front of the house in a shaded dell. She was a frequent visitor at Arlington and expressed the wish to be buried there. Her own home, "Tuckahoe", was going out of family ownership. Her youngest son, Burwell Randolph, while a midshipman at the United States Naval Academy, fell from a mast and was crippled. Her devoted care of him is said to have hastened her death. Her tombstone reads, ". . . a victim of maternal love and duty. As a tribute of filial gratitude this monument is dedicated to her exalted virtues by her youngest son, 'Requiescat in pace.'"

The Custis family burying ground in the oak park south of the mansion was chosen in 1853 at the time of the death of Mrs. Custis, as related on page 28. This little private cemetery, enclosed by an iron fence, is excluded from the surrounding National Cemetery, and is still owned by the living descendents.

The most beautiful burial site at Arlington is the grave of Major Pierre Charles L'Enfant, directly before the mansion, overlooking the city which he designed in 1791. A bas relief of the Federal City is on his tombstone. He was born in France in 1754 and came to America in 1777 to fight in our Revolution.

In 1814 he was engaged to reconstruct Fort Washington across the Potomac from Mount Vernon, but he was relieved of his commission in 1815. He then made his home nearby with the Digges family at "Warburton Manor", and moved with them to "Chillum Castle Manor" in Prince Georges County, Maryland, where he died and was buried in their family cemetery in 1825. His remains were interred at Arlington in 1909. The Columbia Historical Society celebrated the two-hundredth anniversary of his birth on August 2, 1954, with Major General U. S. Grant, III, presiding.

The oldest remains at Arlington Cemetery are those of three Revolutionary soldiers whose bodies were re-interred there between 1907 and 1911. None were battle casualties. Paymaster Joseph Carlton died

in 1812 and John Folin in 1841. General James McCubbin Lingan died in 1812. He was killed by mob violence in his effort to uphold the freedom of the press. His friend "Light-Horse Harry" Lee sustained serious injury in his attempt to protect General Lingan. He was first buried in Georgetown and young George Washington Parke Custis delivered his eulogy. He was re-interred in Arlington in 1908.

For the grave of the "Unknown Soldier of the Revolution," we must go to the grounds of Alexandria's Presbyterian Meeting House at 321 South Fairfax Street, built between 1767 and 1772. The human remains, with buttons and fragments of a Revolutionary uniform, were found in the churchyard in 1826 when a foundation was being dug for adjacent St. Mary's Chapel (Catholic) which fronts on South Royal Street. They were re-interred near the meeting house wall, and a record of this made in the church archives in 1875 by William Gregory. In 1926, a temporary marker was erected by the American Legion, and in 1929 a marble plaque was placed on the grave by the Children of the American Revolution. The inscription thereon reads as follows:

"Here lies a soldier of the Revolution whose identity is known but to God. His was an idealism that recognized a Supreme Being. That planted religious liberty on our shores. That overthrew despotism. That established a people's government. That wrote a constitution setting metes and bounds of delegated authority. That fixed a standard of values upon men above gold and lifted high the force of civil liberty along the pathways of mankind. In ourselves his soul exists as part of ours, his memory's mansion."

At Arlington Cemetery are the graves of fourteen unknown soldiers and sailors of the War of 1812. Their remains were found in 1905 at the site of Washington Barracks near the Treasury and re-interred in the National Cemetery. Three known dead who served in the War of 1812 are buried at Arlington: Lieutenant John T. Ritchie died in 1831 and was first buried in the old Presbyterian Cemetery of Georgetown and moved in 1892. Captain John Givinn, U. S. N., died in Sicily in 1849. His remains were later brought back and interred at Arlington. Lieutenant Colonel Hugh Auld died in 1820 and was re-interred in 1935.

Footnote—4th printing:

In the spring of 1963, President John Fitzgerald Kennedy and Secretary McNamara, seeking a moment of relief from the cares of office in these troubled times, went privately to Arlington House. There, in the room in which Robert E. Lee, in agony of spirit, had written his resignation from the United States Army, they paid homage to his strength and nobility of character. Afterwards, on the lawn in front of the house, the President, enjoying the beauty of the spring day and the view of Washington, was moved to exclaim, "I could stay here forever!" . . . In November, he was laid to rest at the foot of Arlington House lawn (near the site pictured on the frontispiece of this book); his wish fulfilled!

AMPHITHEATRE DETAIL . . .

Arlington National Cemetery

IT was May 13, 1864, that the Custis Estate was officially opened as Arlington National Cemetery for burial of those who had died in service. That day William Christman, a nineteen-year-old private of Company G, 84th Pennsylvania, was laid to rest in the oak park. By June 30 of the following year, there had been 5,003 official burials. On August 6, 1866, the bones of 1,791 unknown Union soldiers were added from the Manassas Battlefields and by September this number had increased to 2,111. Eventually there were 11,911 known and 5,349 unknown Union Civil War burials, which included military and civilian, white and colored, men, women, and children. The Union Civil War Monument south of Arlington Mansion resembles a Greek sarcophagus. One of the finest equestrian statues honors the memory of General Phil Kearny of New Jersey who was killed at Chantilly in Fairfax County, Virginia.

The beautiful Confederate Monument, erected by the United Daughters of the Confederacy, was dedicated on June 4, 1914, by President Woodrow Wilson. The remains of 400 soldiers were buried there. The inscription reads, "Not for fame or reward, not for place or for rank, not lured by ambition or goaded by necessity, but in simple obedience to duty as they understood it, these men suffered all, sacrificed all, dared all and died."

The cemetery's most prominent entrance is the Memorial Gate at the end of the Arlington Memorial Bridge Drive, opened on February 27, 1937. Here the drive divides, with a gate on either side. The north gate is named in honor of Admiral Winfield Scott Schley, who in 1884 commanded the expedition which rescued the Arctic explorer Adolphus Greely. He also commanded the American fleet at the Battle of Santiago in 1898. The south gate honors Theodore Roosevelt, our twenty-sixth president. He commanded the "Roughriders" in the famous charge at San Juan Hill in Cuba during the Spanish-American War.

To the north of this main entrance is the "Sheridan Gate", whose entablature honors the Union General. The supporting columns were originally erected in 1818 in the portico of the War Office in Washington and were moved to Arlington in 1879. The four columns honor Scott, Lincoln, Stanton, and Grant. This gate arches over the original entrance used by the Custis-Lee family. At the extreme northeast end of the cemetery is the "Ord and Weitzel Gate".

South of the main entrance is the "McClellan Gate". Still further south is the "Treasury Gate", which was originally erected in Washington near the Treasury Building.

The "Fort Myer Gate" is on the west side and near it is the chapel from which military burials are conducted.

Soldiers of the Spanish-American War are honored by a slender shaft topped by a spread-eagle on a globe, erected by the National Society, Colonial Dames of America. Another monument is to the "Roughriders". The Navy and Marine Corps are honored by the "Maine Monument", which is actually the mast of the battleship *Maine,* blown up in Havana Harbor, February 15, 1898. The following year, 63 known and 102 unknown bodies of soldiers and sailors of this disaster were re-interred in Arlington Cemetery. In 1910, Congress approved raising the sunken ship and in 1912, 66 more bodies were recovered, (only one of which was identified) and brought back for burial beneath the original mast in Arlington, dedicated on February 15, 1915.

Among later monuments of great beauty is the Canadian Cross, "Erected by the Citizens of Canada in Honor of the Citizens of the United States who Served in the Canadian Army and Gave Their Lives 1914-1918." Another is the "Army and Navy Nurse Memorial," unveiled in 1938. The statue is the work of sculptress Frances Rich, daughter of actress Irene Rich. The "Peary Monument" was erected in 1922 by the National Geographic Society to honor Admiral Robert E. Peary, 1856-1920, who discovered the North Pole on April 6, 1909. It is a stone globe with a bronze star placed at the North Pole.

On Memorial Day, 1923, Mrs. Warren G. Harding started a beautiful custom by planting an elm tree at Arlington in honor of the Girl Scouts of America. Two years later, the North Carolina Daughters of the Confederacy followed by planting a long-needle pine in memory of Anne Carter Lee, (the daughter of Robert E. Lee) who died in 1862 at the age of twenty-three.

The latest memorial tree is a young California redwood, planted on October 15, 1956, by the postmistress of Sequoia National Park in memory of her son, Lt. Howard F. Liddell, whose fighter plane was shot down near Iwo Jima, June 1945. One could not find a more beautiful symbol of the continuity of life after death than a living tree memorial!

May 30, 1958, climaxed a week dedicated to the honor of all unidentified heroes of World War II and Korea, with the interment at Arlington National Cemetery of the two symbolic bodies. They rest beside the remains of the "Unknown Soldier" of World War I, before the Memorial Amphitheatre which was dedicated in May 1920.

Spanning the Potomac to the National Cemetery is Arlington Memorial Bridge. Built on the axis connecting the National Memorials to Abraham Lincoln and to Robert E. Lee, it symbolizes the present bond between the North and the South.

The handsome equestrian statues at one end were sculptured by James Earle Fraser, who had designed the "End of the Trail", the Indian-buffalo nickel, and many noted works. Each of the bridge groups, eighteen feet high, is of a horse flanked by two symbolic figures. At that time, 1951, they were the largest bronze castings ever made, and were cast in Italy at the expense of the Italian Government as a symbol of the renewed friendship of the two nations.

MAST OF THE MAINE . . .

GATEWAY . . .

Arlington's Other Memorials

IN addition to the National Cemetery and the memorials within it, our county has some other beautiful and interesting memorials. The Iwo Jima statue is the newest and most famous. Dedicated by President Eisenhower November 10, 1954, it honors the men of the United States Marine Corps who have given their lives to their country since November 10, 1775. On the base is inscribed, "Uncommon Valor was a Common Virtue."

The gigantic statue of five Marines and one Sailor raising the American flag on the crest of Mount Suribachi on Iwo Jima Island is the work of sculptor Felix W. deWeldon. He was on duty with the Navy when the photograph by Joe Rosenthal was teletyped to headquarters. Mr. deWeldon was so inspired that he worked uninterruptedly forty-eight hours to complete a small scale model, now at the Naval Academy Museum. From this, he made a life-sized model which is placed at the entrance of the Quantico Marine Base. His final achievement, an engineering marvel, is the seventy-eight foot high statue (including the base) now in a seven and a half acre park north of Arlington National Cemetery.

On Columbia Island between Arlington Memorial Bridge and Highway Bridge is another beautiful and unusual piece of sculpture. It depicts seven sea gulls in flight above the crest of a billowing wave. It is the work of Beni del Piatta. The inscription reads, "To Strong Souls and Ready Valor of Those Men of the United States Who in the Navy, the Merchant Marine, and Other Paths of Activity Upon the Waters of the World Have Given Life or Still Offer It in the Performance of Heroic Deeds, This Monument is Dedicated by a Grateful People."

In the Court House grounds is a handsome stone memorial to those who fell in the two World Wars, erected by Arlington Post No. 139 and its Auxiliary Unit of the American Legion, and the Citizens of Arlington. The names of those who fell in both conflicts are engraved upon the stone.

A plaque beneath a fine oak near the corner of 15th Street and Court House Road reads: "Mother's Tree, Dedicated May 11, 1924 by the Women's Civic Club of Clarendon, Virginia." Beneath another tree, which died during the 1957 drought, is a plaque reading, "Memorial Tree, World War, Dedicated to the Boys of Arlington County, Virginia, Who Gave Their Lives in the Cause of Humanity. By the Women's Civic Club of Clarendon, November 11, 1923." The names are listed beneath.

The three cannons and the bronze bell mounted on the stone monument are a memorial gift to Arlington County from the heirs of Frank Hume, early civic and educational leader of the county. He was born in Culpeper in 1843, and volunteered at sixteen in the Mississippi Zuaves. He was wounded at Gettysburg, and returned home to find that all his brothers had been killed and the home burned. He dedicated his life to philanthropic work, and purchased "Warwick Estate" in 1879 in what was then the southwest corner of Arlington County (now on the northwest corner of Alexandria). At the University of Virginia there is a memorial fountain erected in appreciation of his generosity in educational endeavors.

The gifts to Arlington County were from Mr. Hume's personal collection. The handsome bronze bell is a trophy of the gun vessel *Monitor Nantucket,* which was struck fifty-one times during the bombardment of Fort Sumter in Charleston Harbor, where the first shots of the Civil War were fired.

The three cannons are numbered for identification. Number 1 is a naval gun which was kept at the White House during the term of President Andrew Jackson for firing salutes at various celebrations during his presidency, including the dedication of the Jackson City cornerstone. It is probable that the gun had been used in the Battle of New Orleans, where "Old Hickory" whipped the British fifteen days after the end of the War of 1812, the news having been delayed. During the Civil War, the gun was hidden by Southern sympathizers in the marshes of the Potomac. Gun Number 2 was manufactured by Noble Brothers of Rome, Georgia, and was used by the Georgia Battery escorting Confederate President Jefferson Davis at the time of his capture. Being hard pressed by the Federal Cavalry near the Savannah River, they burned the carriage and spiked the gun to make it useless to their captors.

Gun Number 3 was originally on a steamboat belonging to the State of Virginia, in use from Washington to Baltimore. It was seized by the Federals from the Alexandria dock at the outbreak of the Civil War. A party of daring young Confederates conceived a plan to recapture the vessel. Disguised as women schoolteachers, they booked passage for a trip advertised as a teachers' excursion. As it steamed past Mount Vernon, they doffed their disguises, each displaying a brace of pistols. They seized command, ran the vessel ashore to discharge the passengers, and proceeded down the Potomac. Upon receiving report of the daring escapade, the Federal authorities in Washington dispatched a speedy revenue cutter with a long-range rifle. Overtaken near Quantico, the Confederates ran ashore, scuttled the boat, and escaped into the Virginia wilderness. The gun remained on the shore with the derelict vessel until after the war, when it was acquired by Mr. Hume.

HONOR TO MEN OF THE SEA . . .

MEMORIAL TO UNITED
STATES MARINES . . .

Old Mills Have Vanished

THROUGHOUT the years, songs have been sung, poems written and pictures painted of old mills. They represent man's first harnessing of natural power. Their sites have often determined the location of pioneer settlements. It is to be regretted that none of the old mills of Arlington County still exist.

The smaller mills, such as those of the Balls, were intended primarily for grinding home produce. The larger ones were of a commercial nature. The early merchant mills were licensed to issue script used as a medium of exchange before banks were established in the isolated communities.

One such mill was built on Pimmit Run below the Potomac palisades on land patented in 1719 by Thomas Lee. After various ownership changes, it was acquired in 1789 by Philip Richard Fendall, a distinguished attorney and banker of Alexandria, and Lewis Hipkins, who apparently was in charge of operations until his death in 1794 from hydrophobia, as related on page 178. When the mill property was mortgaged in 1803, it was described as "a good merchant mill, brewery, distillery, and sundry other improvements." Various mills were operated at this site through the 1890's, the last having been rebuilt on the stone ruins of the one burned down during the Civil War.

Much of the information we have on the early mills and various other aspects of the life here in early days is from the records of the series of lawsuits involving the Alexander family holdings. When the John Alexander lands were finally surveyed, there were nearer 8,000 acres than the previously assumed 6,000 for which he had paid six hogsheads of tobacco in 1669. This discrepancy together with the uncertainty over the exact boundaries led to frequent and prolonged litigation which was not finally settled until 1790.

From testimony given in 1767, we learn that a mill was built on Four Mile Run in the Shirlington area between Doctor's Branch and *lower* Long Branch. Doctor's Branch was named for Doctor Michael Dunghill (later spelled Dangill), who was reported to have lived there for a short time "and then absconded." Long Branch enters the run about a mile from the river. (This is referred to as *lower* Long Branch so as not to confuse it with another stream of the same name which enters the run in Glencarlyn, and which will be referred to as *upper* Long Branch.)

The above mentioned mill was referred to in a patent of 1719 as "Chubb's Mill". A witness stated, "Chubbs Mill was built by one Lilliard who died and Chubb married his widow and then the Mill was called 'Chubb's Mill'."

A transaction of the 1740's mentions Edward Masterson's Mill near the site of Chubb's Mill; its site is in the Jenny Dean Park. Another document spots a mill of the 1760's nearby, built by John Carlyle of Alexandria and patronized by George Washington.

The site of John Ball's mill is up Four Mile Run

and opposite the mouth of Lubber Run, spelled "Lover Run" on some old maps. He died in 1766. His will refers to his mill stock. The estate inventory mentions a broken pair of millstones and a pair of new millstones, frog and spindle. In the yard of his home on the hill is a millstone which may be one of those and should be safeguarded as the one tangible part of a colonial mill of Arlington County.

The Fairfax Order Book shows that in 1754, John Colville was granted permission to erect a water gristmill on Lubber Run near its confluence with Four Mile Run.

In 1803, Philip Alexander appears to have had a mill on "Mill Branch of Shallow Creek", now Roach's Run. James Roach who bought that tract and built Prospect Hill in 1841, also purchased 36 acres in 1852 on Four Mile Run adjacent to the Columbian Factory and Mill; which processed cotton. The 1864 map shows Roach's Mill near the crossing of Arlington Ridge Road.

These documents also spot the location of the first place where shoes were commercially made in the County. Evan Thomas patented land on Four Mile Run near these mills in 1719, "built a small house for the reception of his family and dyed [sic]." His widow married "one Rigbey", a shoemaker who used the Thomas cabin for his shop and built a better one for his family. A witness stated that "Rigbey run away" but that Mrs. Rigbey, her son William Thomas and two daughters stayed on. One daughter married Thomas Whitford and the other, Robert King.

George Washington's diary tells us of the mills further up Four Mile Run and along *upper* Long Branch. The entry of April 22, 1785 states, "Took an early breakfast at Abingdon. Accompanied by Mr. Stuart [who married the widow of Martha Washington's son] and Lund Washington, and having sent for Mr. Moses Ball, who attended, I went to a corner of the above land . . . below the ruins of an old mill." The site was on Moses Ball's property. On Long Branch are traces of what may have been the millrace and building site.

George Washington Parke Custis built a water gristmill in 1836 on Four Mile Run at Columbia Pike on land bequeathed to him by George Washington. It was in turn inherited by his grandson, Custis Lee. The mill was ravaged during the Civil War.

In the early 1800's, John Mason built a mill on Spout Run, between the river and Doubleday Bridge. The mill used the waters of Spout Run and of the next stream up the river, Windy Run. Traces of the Windy Run millrace are still visible above the palisades, rounding the promontory and joining the Spout Run millrace above the mill. These two millraces have been erroneously identified by some as earthworks of nearby Fort Smith. The stone walls of the mill were destroyed by construction of the Spout Run Parkway, and part of the Windy Run race by that of the George Washington Memorial Parkway.

ARLINGTON MILL . . .
Ruins after the Civil War.

ARLINGTON MILL . . .
Brigade passing the mill on
its way to occupy Munson's
Hill.

Early Roads and Rival Turnpikes

THE earliest road in Arlington County of which we have direct evidence followed a route much like that of present-day Shirley Highway from near Glebe Road to the Arlington Ridge cut-off. It was referred to in the early 1700's as a "wood's path". It ran from Cameron Mill on Hunting Creek to the ferry which crossed the Potomac from below what is now Rosslyn to the mouth of Rock Creek. A survey of 1743 shows this road running along (lower) Long Branch much as Army-Navy Drive does now. Travelers from Cameron Mill crossed Four Mile Run near its convergence with this stream at a ford known as the "Upper Horse Crossing".

The Alexandria-Georgetown Road as it came to be called, wound through Green Valley, a name later applied to the area further west. At the head of the valley, the road climbed over "Hoe Hill", crossed the plain at the foot of Arlington Heights and went on to the ferry. Although the path had become a stage road by the time George Washington traveled it to supervise the laying-out of the Federal City, this ferry remained the only river crossing in the vicinity for travelers to or from the south. Later Thomas Jefferson must have come this way as he traveled on horseback from Monticello to become President.

The valley road acquired a rival route, probably about 1840, when the "new graveled road" was built. This ran along the ridge from just south of the crossing of the ferry route with Columbia Pike, constructed in 1808, and descended along the line of Lang Street to Four Mile Run which it crossed on a picturesque double-arch stone bridge. These two roads were considered as alternate routes in 1887 by the Mount Vernon Avenue Association which proposed to construct a memorial highway linking the home of George Washington with the Capital City named in his honor. In the conviction that the bridge across the Potomac to the Arlington National Cemetery would be built shortly—"a work of supreme public necessity," the Association directed that routes for the Memorial Highway be surveyed. The bridge was not built until 1932, and these plans came to naught. However, for many years Arlington Ridge Road was known as Mount Vernon Avenue.

Another road of the mid-1700's was the "Road to the Falls", which left the Alexandria-Georgetown Road near the "Horse Crossing" and wound across the County toward the Little Falls. Within the last mile and a half from the river, it converged with another road from Falls Church. This cross-County road has come to have the name of Glebe Road since it linked Christ Church of Alexandria with the Glebe lands. In the early days, however, various stretches of it bore many different names, and another unrelated route was called Glebe Road. It led from Mason's Ferry to the Glebe House by way of Breckin's Branch (along present Kirkwood Road) and up its western tributary.

As the lands away from the river were settled, access to them by road became important. Some of the main traffic arteries of modern Arlington have a tale to tell of former times when Alexandria and Georgetown were in fierce competition for the trade of northern Virginia. They were originally turnpike roads built by private stock companies to draw traffic from the inadequately maintained public roads and lead it into one or another of the rival towns. Turnpikes were toll roads on which the travelers were stopped at turnstiles or turnpikes to pay their fare before proceeding.

Alexandria was first in this field. The principal roads leading from there to the northwest were the old route later identified as Braddock Road to Falls Church and beyond, and the route to the Sugarlands beyond Dranesville by way of the headwaters of Pimmit Run.

Georgetown bid for the inland Virginia trade by building the Falls Bridge, later called Chain Bridge, in 1797, but for the time being relied on the existing public road from the west, now Route 123, and the Little Falls Road from Falls Church to bring traffic to the Falls Bridge. Georgetown was also approached by a wagon road from Falls Church that ran to the ferry. Although the ferry was by now operated by the Masons, the road was known as Awbury's Road named for an earlier ferry-master. The present Wilson Boulevard follows portions of this route.

Alexandria opened the turnpike era by building Little River Turnpike to the Shenandoah Valley with a branch from Providence (Fairfax) to Warrenton. This road was begun in 1802 and completed to the Little River at Aldie in 1806, to Warrenton in 1810, and to the Valley in 1816. To tap the trade of the Federal City an Alexandrian built in 1808 the Long Bridge at the site of the present Railway Bridge, across the Potomac. Later that year, turnpikes were begun from the bridgehead: one to Alexandria was first called River Road or the Washington-Alexandria Turnpike, now Jefferson Davis Highway; the second, named Columbian Turnpike, connected with the Little River Turnpike in Annandale.

Georgetown responded to these developments, first by building a turnpike in 1809 from the Mason's ferry landing through Custis lands connecting with Columbian Turnpike and the earlier road to Alexandria along Green Valley, and second, by building a turnpike to Leesburg by way of Chain Bridge, utilizing the trace of the old Sugarland Trail. The road was begun in 1813 and completed within seven years.

Alexandria replied to Georgetown's Leesburg turnpike by developing the old road through present Seven Corners and Falls Church as a turnpike, now the Leesburg Pike. This project was begun in 1818, but was not completed until 1838. Meanwhile, an Alexandria group built Aqueduct Bridge to connect the Chesapeake and Ohio Canal at Georgetown with the Alexandria Canal, with a superstructure which accommodated vehicles and stock. In 1852, the Georgetown group built a new plank road from the Aqueduct Bridge through Falls Church to Providence (Fairfax).

TOLLHOUSE AT BROAD RUN . . . Erected
in 1761, this tollhouse still stands adjacent to
a double-arch stone bridge on the Alexandria-
Leesburg Pike.

ROLLING ROAD'S ROCK RAINBOW . . .
West of Dranesville, the banks of Sugarland
Run have eroded from the old stone bridge,
leaving the shell of masonry. Along this route
were rolled hogsheads of tobacco drawn by
oxen.

Chain Bridge near Little Falls

IN 1608 Captain John Smith went "as high as the falls." A cross on his map of 1612 marking "how far hath been discovered" is judged to be just above the site of Chain Bridge at Little Falls. In 1631, Henry Fleet made a detailed account of the long-established Indian river crossing. The local Necostin Indians were accustomed to meet trading parties of the Iroquois and to act as middlemen in the exchange of English trade goods for northern furs. There the Necostins also had a notable fishery. Great sturgeon were so plentiful that as many as thirty were caught in a single night. Though rarely seen now, they remained plentiful enough for Gilbert Vanderwerken in the 1850's to use their oil for lubrication of his omnibuses which he operated in Washington. However, these shores remain popular with fishermen, especially during the annual runs of shad and herring.

On the south side of the river near Little Falls, two well-defined trails led away from the crossing. One, now called Fairfax Road, runs up the river to the Sugarlands, an extensive tract of sugar maples famous in early times. The other followed Pimmit Run a short distance, then veered south connecting with the present Glebe Road at Walker Chapel and continuing west on Little Falls Road to the site of Falls Church.

In 1719 when the Iroquois were still the dominant power on the upper Potomac, Thomas Lee, not yet of Stratford, patented a large tract of land at Great Falls, extending down to include the mouth of Pimmit Run. He thought to exploit the ancient Sugarlands trail as a portage around the Falls to his landing on navigable water at the mouth of the Run. Fear of the Iroquois, however, retarded settlement above the Falls.

The first bridge over the Potomac was built in 1797 by the Georgetown Bridge Company at the ancient Indian crossing and was named The Falls Bridge. The chief traffic over it consisted of droves of cattle enroute to the Georgetown auction pens. To bring a better price by weight, the animals were well watered at Pimmit Run. These loads proved too much for the wooden structure and it was condemned and replaced in 1804. Six months later the new bridge was carried away by a flood.

Warned by these experiences, the company in 1808 constructed a bridge suspended by iron chains of four-and-a-half foot links anchored in low masonry towers. Although still officially designated The Falls Bridge, this structure was so unique and considered such a marvel of modern engineering that it became known as "Chain Bridge". The oak flooring was carried away by a flood in 1810 and replaced the following year.

An incidental consequence of the opening of The Falls Bridge was the development of a dueling ground on Pimmit Run near the Virginia end of the bridge.

Just back of the tumbling palisades, the stream meanders through a broad secluded meadow. Here in 1826, Henry Clay, Secretary of State, and John Randolph of Roanoke, Senator from Virginia, vented their malice in a bloodless duel. Clay's bullet pierced the ample folds of Randolph's dressing gown but missed flesh. Randolph fired into the air. The astonished antagonists embraced each other, rejoicing that neither was injured!

Chain Bridge lasted until 1852 when it collapsed. Caught beneath it, between the underbeams, was a man named Bull Fizzle. He had the reputation of being indestructable, and was extricated unhurt from the debris.

The bridge was replaced in 1852 by a heavy wooden crossbeam structure. However, the renown of Chain Bridge had been so great that its popular name has been used for all its chainless successors.

Chain Bridge was of great importance during the Civil War as the connection between Federal troops in Fairfax County and the reserve encampments at Tennellytown on the District side. The first Union Army sentinel to be court-martialled for sleeping at his post had fallen asleep on the District end of the bridge. Private William Scott of the 3rd Vermont Volunteers had taken a friend's place on the night of August 31, 1861, after keeping guard all day. He was sentenced to be shot, but his case was carried to President Lincoln who pardoned him. He made a fine record in the Army and was killed seven months later during the Campaign in Virginia.

By 1874, the bridge had to be rebuilt, this time of steel. The Reverend David Mutersbaugh of Fairfax was selected to make a test of its strength. He loaded a six-horse wagon with wood and drove across to Georgetown. Reloading with wet gas lime fertilizer, considered a heavy load, he drove back over the bridge and declared that it could bear "any load it would ever be called upon to carry." The bridge withstood complete inundation in 1889 at the time of the Johnstown flood.

In 1927 the bridge was closed for a year to permit repairs to the abutment on the Virginia side resulting from years of pounding of Potomac floods and ice jams. A concrete pier was constructed. However, the heavy flood of 1936 tore through the superstructure, and within two years the bridge was replaced by a higher steel cantilever girder structure. At the dedication June 1938, a link of the old chain, found by Bertram G. Foster and given to Mrs. Truett of "Falls Grove" (page 126-128) was presented to the "Oldest Inhabitants of the District of Columbia" who conducted the ceremony.

OLD CHAIN BRIDGE . . . From an early etching.

POTOMAC IN FLOOD . . . High water at Great Falls reveals the enormous power of the Potomac.

The Chapmans' "Summer Hill"

BETWEEN the Abingdon estate and the estuary of Four Mile Run lay a 150-acre tract which comprised a plantation named "Summer Hill". It was part of the 6,000-acre tract purchased by John Alexander in 1669. In 1687 he deeded this 150-acre plot to John Pimmitt whose son and heir, George Pimmitt, sold it in 1707 to William Harper. It was subsequently deeded in 1732 to Thomas Pearson, son of Captain Simon Pearson who had accumulated lands adjacent to the Alexander holdings since 1707.

In the meantime, John Alexander and then his son, Robert I (died 1704) and grandson, Major Robert II (died 1735) continued to reside at "Caledon", the plantation patented in 1664 down the Potomac in what is now King George County. Major Robert's sons, Gerard and John, were the first Alexanders to reside on the Four Mile Run property. Gerard took the north bank of the estuary, minus the aforementioned 150-acre plot, and built Abingdon. John took the south bank. In 1734 he married Susanna Pearson, daughter of Captain Simon Pearson, and they built "Preston" facing Four Mile Run estuary. Her sister, Constantia Pearson, who married Nathaniel Chapman, talked their brother, John Pearson, into letting them have his 150-acre tract so that she and her sister could be neighbors across the estuary. The Chapmans built their home, Summer Hill, shortly thereafter.

Nathaniel Chapman was an experienced ironmaster with business interests in both Maryland and Virginia. He was a charter member of the Ohio Company. Augustine and Lawrence Washington each named him an executor of his estate. After residing some years at Summer Hill, the Chapmans moved to Charles County, Maryland.

Summer Hill was inherited by Pearson Chapman (1745-1784) upon his father's death in 1760, but six years later he deeded it to his brother George, who wished to return to the old plantation with their widowed mother. In the meantime, Pearson resided at "Mount Aventine", a handsome Georgian house on his Charles County inheritance across the Potomac from Gunston Hall. Washington mentions visiting there.

In 1774 George Chapman, living with his mother at Summer Hill, married Amelia Macrae, daughter of a wealthy Scottish merchant of Dumfries who had married George's aunt, Elizabeth Pearson. George's mother died in 1791. Her will written in 1768, provided for the education of her grandchildren. She also directed that they receive silverware engraved with the Chapman-Pearson coats-of-arms. A "mourning ring" was bequeathed to her intimate friend Mrs. George Mason of Gunston Hall. By the time of her death twenty-nine years later, the estate had undergone changes which prevented the fulfillment of some of her requests, such as the construction of a vault. She had directed her executors ". . . to build a vault fronting on the creek in the square of the garden opposite the graves on the old plantation at Four Mile Creek . . . in which vault I desire my body to be deposited, and also the bodys of my children, and such other relatives as there are buried, and as to the remains of Mr. Chapman [Jonathan], my late husband's father who lies buried in the same place, I leave it to the discretion of my sons and daughters whether the same shall be interred in the vault or not. I direct my executors to erect a tombstone over my late husband who lies buried in Baltimore County. . . ."

George died in 1815, leaving the estate to his widow, who died four years later. Summer Hill was willed to the daughter, Louisa Chapman, who married Alexander Hunter, U. S. Marshal for the District of Columbia.

This couple eventually owned both the 150 acres of Summer Hill as well as Abingdon plantation, which Alexander Hunter purchased, as related on page 12.

Upon the death of Alexander Hunter, his widow in 1851 sold Summer Hill, terminating over a century of Chapman ownership. The family burying ground at Summer Hill was excluded from the sale and remained in possession of the family. In 1940 the site was required for the construction of the National Airport. Miss Helen Chapman Calvert of Alexandria supervised the transfer of the remains to a family lot at Pohick Church which had been purchased by her mother. Sixteen of the eighteen bodies were identified and are properly marked at their new resting place.

WASHINGTON NATIONAL AIRPORT . . . Summer Hill Plantation was
acquired for the airport, and dredged land added.

James Roach's "Prospect Hill"

THE handsome late-Federal mansion just north of The Little Tea House at 1230 South Arlington Ridge Road is now the home of Mrs. Philip Campbell, widow of the Honorable Philip Campbell who bought it in 1913. The house, named Prospect Hill, was built about 1841 by James Roach, on what was possibly the site of "Montpelier", the very early home of Benjamin Sebastian. Its commanding view from the crest of the ridge would make it the obvious choice of any builder. Early records refer to this ridge as "Hoe Hill".

This property which was part of the estate of John Alexander (see page 12) had been inherited by his great-grandson, Gerard Alexander. In 1733, Alexander leased what was probably this tract to Sebastian who two years before had been his overseer and collector of rents. Sebastian Springs and the stream they form at the base of the hill have perpetuated his name.

There is a legend that Sebastian and his father were Spanish pirates forced ashore in Virginia, later making their way up the Potomac and becoming respectable citizens. However, the facts we know about them are more dignified if less romantic; they come from the documentation of the Alexander lawsuits mentioned on page 50. Benjamin Sebastian was obviously a well-educated man, and the only witness styled "Gent", a title not given lightly in those days. In the testimony of 1768, he gave his age as sixty-two, and stated that he had lived in the neighborhood for thirty-eight years. It is clear that his opinion was highly respected. He had, at various times, served the Alexander family as an attorney.

He died in 1770, leaving a life interest in a substantial estate to his "beloved wife" Priscilla, making his two daughters, Elizabeth and Behethliam, his heirs. Although in his will he styles himself "Sr.", there is no mention of a son.

In 1811, the Hoe Hill tract passed from the Alexander family into the possession of William Henry Washington. It is doubtful that any of the Washingtons lived there although it changed hands within the family a number of times until taken over by the Bank of the United States on April 5, 1836. On March 30, 1838, it was purchased by Philip Roach, who died June 9th of that same spring, leaving it to his son James.

Philip Roach, his wife, son James and two daughters, Mary and Elizabeth, had come from Ireland to New York, and thence to Alexandria. His tombstone reads, "To the memory of Philip Roach, Esq., a native of Wicklow, Ireland, deceased June 9, 1838, aged 50 years. Cut off in the midst of usefulness. True to his God, Charitable to his neighbors, universal regret followed him to the grave. In him the town lost a friend."

On June 29th of the previous year, James Roach had married Elizabeth, daughter of Dr. James Carson of Alexandria. They lived at "Oakville" near Alexandria while James built the mansion for his bride. The bricks were made at the plant which Philip and James had established on their clay lowlands toward the river. The house is beautifully proportioned and detailed, with a two-story center section and one-story wings on each side. Brick-walled pathways lead to servant quarters which are also of brick. The original huge brass locks remain on the doors. One of the most interesting rooms is the kitchen with the oven built into the wall beside the massive fireplace.

The Roach brick plant and masonry business secured the contracts for the Alexandria, Loudoun and Hampshire Railroad and much of the stonework of the Alexandria Canal. Maps of 1864 show that the Roaches operated mills on Roach's Run and on Four Mile Run.

Edwardina S. Warren, a great granddaughter of the builder of the mansion, has loaned me a letter written about 1915 to her mother who was the only grandchild of the builder to be born at the mansion. The letter is from Elizabeth Roach (Sister Mary Aloysia), the first native of this area to enter the Order of the Holy Cross. She wrote:—

". . . The Union soldiers came to Prospect Hill 2 A.M. on May 24, 1861 and took possession of the house. James Roach [the builder] and his son James Carson Roach were made prisoners. Philip was at Georgetown College; left there for the Confederate Army; was taken prisoner, sent to the old Capital Prison, then to Fort Warren, Boston, and released August 1865. James Roach and his son were not allowed even to go to church, but the good Jesuits at the College often said Mass in his home. Mrs. Roach had to sign a pass for herself and family to go to Washington or Alexandria. Even the funerals had to have passes. The soldiers burned a two-story farmhouse and a large barn, killed ducks, turkeys and chickens, rooted up the vegetable garden, and turned the Government cattle in to graze in the front yard to destroy shrubs and everything. Many a night the family were awakened by the soldiers tramping through the house under pretext of finding fire arms. No wonder James Roach, his wife and daughter died during the war; their hearts were broken over their lovely home being destroyed. Forts Albany and Runyon were built on his farm and the trees cut down to build them. The soldiers went through with axes and fire to destroy the undergrowth. No wonder the mill cannot be found; the soldiers gathered the grain into the mill and burned it. After James Carson Roach married, the family moved to Alexandria and James lived there until he died. . . . Call it injustice or what you will; James Roach's children have lost their home!"

The difficulties experienced by the Roach family were typical of those encountered by many in this area as a consequence of the Civil War. Loss of their mills and farm equipment led to impoverishment, and the necessity for settling James Roach's estate resulted in the sale of the properties under court order on October 14, 1869.

PROSPECT HILL . . . Handsome Federal Mansion, built in 1841 by James
Roach.

The Frasers of Green Valley

ONE of the least expected things to encounter on a golf course is a private cemetery; yet that is what happens when playing at the Army-Navy Country Club. In a grove of trees near the 26th green are a number of tombstones enclosed by an iron fence. This plot was on the plantation of the Fraser family. William Fraser (1749-1824), his wife Mary, their son Anthony R. Fraser (1794-1881), his wife Presha Lee Fraser (1799-1859), and other members of the family are buried there.

The Frasers originated in Scotland. Simon Fraser (Lord Lovat) was the last man beheaded in the Tower of London, in 1747. According to family tradition, his nephew Daniel Fraser, arrived in Tidewater, Virginia as a stowaway aboard a ship at the age of sixteen. He was discovered and indentured to pay off the cost of his passage. When the indenture was cleared five years later, he married his master's daughter, Mary Beall of "Brandon".

Fraser family records indicate that their son, William, left Westmoreland County to settle in this area as a tenant of the Alexanders, with a lease dated 1758. It was probably his son William (Junior) who in 1804 leased some land from Walter Stoddard Alexander for the purpose of building his "houses" in Green Valley. The valley was possibly named for James Green, who is recorded as living in the vicinity of the present club house in the mid 1700's.

It was his son Anthony Fraser (born 1794) who eventually acquired about a thousand acres along both sides of *lower* Long Branch. About 1821 he built "Green Valley Manor" in an oak forest across the valley from the present Country Club. This handsome residence was destroyed by fire in 1924. A considerable acreage of the home site remains intact, extending from the Oak Ridge School grounds at the crest of the hill, down to Army-Navy Drive in the valley. The new Gunston Junior High School is on former Fraser property at 28th and South Lang Streets.

Fraser Road leads off 23rd Street South to the attractive home which was enlarged from the original slave quarters after the mansion burned. Adjacent is the old smokehouse. At the mansion site I found traces of the terraced woodland garden where daffodils still bloom, and the masonry steps leading down to the cup of a fish pond or fountain.

There is another short piece of Fraser Road on the other side of the grounds; these form parts of the oldest road of the area, described on page 52. It led from Cameron Mill on Hunting Creek to Chubb's Mill on Four Mile Run, through the grounds of Green Valley Manor to Awbury Ferry at Rosslyn. One can trace the route on present-day maps by Cameron Mill Road, jumping to the two segments of Fraser Road, then using parts of Army-Navy Drive to reach the lowlands along the Potomac.

Green Valley Manor descended from Anthony Fraser to his daughter, Presha Antonia Fraser (1838-1919). She married Jackson E. Sickels, a famous civil engineer from New York. The home was then inherited by their daughter, Frances Lee Sickels who was born there about 1878. She was a true cosmopolitan who divided her time between her homeland and the various countries of Europe. An individual of dynamic personality, charm, and unconventional decisions, she retained her maiden name through two marriages (Anderson and Carter). Mrs. Frances Lee Sickels died in England in 1956. She is survived by a married daughter, Mrs. David dePackh, and granddaughter, who live in Washington.

The Fraser estate was the scene of considerable activity during the Civil War. The first troops to cross into Virginia on May 24, 1861, having secured the bridgehead of Long Bridge, marched down Green Valley enroute to Alexandria, and camped on the banks of Four Mile Run.

Following the First Battle of Manassas, an emergency hospital was established on the Fraser estate, on the future club grounds on the bank of a small stream called Rapid Run. It is said to have run red with blood from amputations performed there.

This later became a convalescent camp for the care of soldiers discharged from hospitals, but not yet able to resume their places in the ranks. It was operated by the United States Sanitary Commission, though not directly under its control. For the most part, the buildings of "Convalescent Camp" were poorly ventilated and badly drained. The death-rate in this camp was higher than at most hospitals or prisons. "Camp Misery" was the title first bestowed on it by the soldiers. At first it was badly managed and consisted of tents. Miss Amy Bradley of the Sanitary Commission did much to improve conditions; it was entirely reorganized and barracks were built. To this camp came anxious wives, mothers, sisters and sweethearts to find the soldiers whom they had not seen in months or years.

Still standing on the club grounds is a house which served during the Civil War as the small-pox isolation ward of Convalescent Camp. It is said to have also served temporarily as a residence for the commanding officer of Fort Richardson whose earthworks remain in a fair state of preservation at the top of the hill near the Club House. It is shown on the Civil War map as belonging to "Beidermann", on a map of 1878 as the property of "Mrs. Brown", further identified on the 1900 County map as belonging to "John W. Brown". It was later acquired by Charles St. John of Berryville, from whom it was purchased by the Army-Navy Country Club in 1924.

CONVALESCENT CAMP . . .

FRASER CEMETERY . . . On the Army-Navy
Country Club Golf Course.

CORN CRIB . . . Outbuildings survived the
fire which destroyed the mansion.

SPRINGHOUSE RUINS . . . Adjacent to the
stream.

Ball and Carlin Pioneers

IT is possible that the Glencarlyn area was first visited by Colonial Virginians during the days of the Potomac Rangers. They made scouting trips in accordance with the Acts of the General Assembly which authorized the Governor to appoint a lieutenant for each county, directed to assemble eleven neighborhood men with horses and arms. The journal of 1692 written by one of these Prince William County "Potomac Rangers" is preserved. He described expeditions between Accotink Creek and Sugarland Run which took them across this area, on a route probably traversed from about 1680.

The first resident landowners in the area were John and Moses Ball. They were descended from Colonel William Ball, the great-grandfather of George Washington, who arrived in Tidewater Virginia about 1650. We first find the Ball family in northern Virginia in Hunting Creek Valley below Alexandria, where John Ball Sr. patented 221 acres in 1695. He added 340 acres in 1715 including the "wading place" (ford) of Hunting Creek. He died during the 1720's. His sons, John Jr. (born 1714), and Moses (born 1717) were both land-owning voters on Hunting Creek in 1741.

The following year, John was granted 166 acres by Lord Fairfax in the future Glencarlyn area, and Moses received 91 acres nearby in 1748. Their log houses were the first in that part of Arlington, probably built soon after each acquired title. John's house is shown on Colonel John Colville's survey of 1755. Logs of the original pioneer home are within the walls of the residence of Mr. William B. Powell at 5620 3rd Street South. There is no visible sign of antiquity, for in 1915 a clapboard cocoon encased the only remaining portion of the log house, to match the two-story wing which had been added about 1885. The crumbling kitchen wing with giant fireplace was removed at that time. In the yard is a millstone which may be one of those described in John Ball's will.

Four Mile Run was the most important natural boundary for early patents between Hunting Creek and Great Falls. On its west bank at the confluence of *upper* Long Branch, a great white oak marked the common corner of John Colville's grant of 1731 and those of the Ball brothers. The tree is mentioned in George Washington's diary and in many early deeds. In the foyer of the Burdett Library of Glencarlyn is a section of the George Washington Survey Oak, on which is an explanatory bronze tablet.

John Ball died in 1766. Six years later, his house was included in a sale to William Carlin of Alexandria. He had been born in 1732 at Yorkshire, England and emigrated to Virginia where he established a profitable tailoring business. His clientelle included George Washington whose diary of February 4, 1770 related, "At home all day. Carlin, the Taylor, came here [Mount Vernon] and stayed all night."

In 1785, Moses Ball assisted George Washington in his survey of property which Washington had acquired adjacent to the Ball patents on Four Mile Run and which eventually became known as "Washington Forest". Washington was possibly a visitor at the nearby Ball-Carlin house.

William Carlin added an eight room rear wing which has since disappeared. When he died in 1820 at the age of eighty-eight, his remains were placed in the family cemetery in the home garden, in accordance with instructions of his will. It is logical to assume that this burial ground had been previously established at the time of the death of John Ball. Although no stone now marks the resting place of either, they probably both rest in the existing Carlin cemetery, next to the Glencarlyn Library.

At 5512 North Carlin Springs Road is a most attractive log house built about 1800 by William Carlin and his son, and deeded by William to his two granddaughters. Mary Alexander Carlin was born there just before her grandfather's death. She did not marry, and resided there until her death in 1905. Her burial was the last in the Carlin family cemetery. In a picturesque setting of old fruit trees, the Mary Carlin house retains its mellow charm with the exposed logs plus a harmonious addition built by Charles H. Lane, who purchased it from the Carlin heirs and later sold to Mr. and Mrs. Lester Broyles, the present owners.

Former State Senator Frank Ball, in reviewing my manuscript, added the following:—

"Mary Alexander Carlin taught school in the Ball-Carlin log house. Among her scholars was Catherine Ball Marcey, an older sister of my father—Aunt Kate to all of us. She died on New Years Eve, 1905. A few years before her death, I drove her in our buggy over to see her former teacher who was then very old—it was probably about 1900. This is the only time I recall seeing Miss Carlin; she was very highly thought of by all of my father's family."

When Moses Ball died in 1798, it is probable that his widow, son Basil, and daughters remained at the home until they lost the property by foreclosure in 1818 to Richard Kerby. No trace is left of Moses Ball's home, but evidence indicates that it stood at the crest of a gentle slope a few hundred feet north of his existing spring. It probably faced the area's first road which ran about fifty feet south of and parallel to 5th Street South, connecting the Leesburg Pike with the mills on Four Mile Run.

About 1935, Charles Stetson and Oliver King, who lived at 605 and 601 South Carlin Springs Road and owned the spring site, repaired the masonry spring walls and attached thereto a bronze plaque bearing the inscription, "Moses Ball 1717-1792". Both these gentlemen have died, and their former estates are the site of the future Doctor's Hospital. The Stetson home was built about 1874 by Howard Young. It was remodeled in 1919 and additions were made in 1926 and 1927. This house will probably be used as a dependency building of the hospital. Mr. Stetson was the historian of the Glencarlyn area, and the author of two books on local history.

THE BALL HOMESTEAD . . . As it appeared about 1900.

"MARY CARLIN HOUSE" . . . Built about 1800 by George Washington's tailor, William Carlin.

Carlin Springs and Glencarlyn

GLENCARLYN PARK, Arlington County's largest public park encompasses within its sixty-six acres, the heavily timbered dell of Four Mile Run including the sites of the early mills and the survey oak described in previous chapters. In the early 1900's the Glencarlyn Citizens Association erected a monument at the junction of the streams bearing this inscription, "On this spot stood an old tree bearing the survey mark made by George Washington." As the years passed, vandals defaced and toppled the shaft. In 1954 the Daughters of the American Revolution, working with the County, placed it on a new base and put a protective metal fence around it.

Shaded by ancient oaks and sycamores in the glen are two famous old springs. After the Carlin family acquired this beautiful wilderness tract from the Ball heirs, the springs became known as Carlin Springs. In the early 1870's the Alexandria, Loudoun and Hampshire Railway Company erected a station on the Carlin property. John E. F. Carlin decided to develop the woodland dell near the station into a picnic and excursion resort. He bricked in the two springs, and in 1872 built an ice-cream and restaurant pavilion to accommodate 250 guests, and a dance pavilion. Nearby was a small bar which was closed when the grounds were rented to Sunday school or church groups. He also laid out a tournament course in a meadow at the top of the hill near what is now 5th Street South.

All major political meetings of the area were held at Carlin Springs. Of great appeal to the young people was "round hole" for swimming at the junction of Lubber and Four Mile Runs. Sediment has since filled its seven foot depths. Patrons came by train from Washington and Alexandria. Carlin Springs remained a popular resort for about a dozen years until the excursion resorts along the Potomac River which were accessible by boat drew its patrons away.

In 1887 Carlin Springs was included in a sale of 132 acres to William W. Curtis and Samuel S. Burdett, who the next year founded the Carlin Springs Cooperative Association. This was the County's first preplanned cooperative residential community. Each purchaser of a lot received a share of stock. Funds were available on loan for home construction. Streets were laid out and thirteen acres of the woodland glens were set aside for park purposes, dedicated in 1891. The name of the village was changed in 1896 from Carlin Springs to Glencarlyn.

William Curtis of Ohio, had come to Georgetown in 1861 as a special correspondent of the New York Times. He wrote an eye-witness report of the encounter of the *Monitor* and *Merrimac*. He was one of the Guard of Honor at the Lincoln bier at the Capitol. As President of the Board of Trustees of the Public Schools of the District of Columbia, his memory is honored by the name of Curtis School in Georgetown. His wife was Jane Backus, whose brother and family have been community leaders of Glencarlyn. The Backus family lived in the Ball-Carlin house while their own was being constructed at 5500 5th Street South. Perhaps it was their childhood memories of this pioneer home which inspired the Backus sisters to become authorities on Glencarlyn history.

Samuel S. Burdett was born in England in 1836 and came to America when twelve. He worked on a farm to finance his law course at Oberlin College. His three years as a cavalry captain in the Union Army were followed by his rise as a prominent lawyer. He was a congressman from Missouri 1869-73, Commissioner of the General Land Office 1874-76, and Commander-in-chief of the Grand Army of the Republic. He resided in Glencarlyn for twenty-five years, until his death in 1914. He had devoted his energies to his community, and to it he bequeathed his land, his fine personal library, with an endowment fund for a public library which bears his name. It is situated at the southwest corner of Kensington and 3rd Streets South.

The Burdett Library of Glencarlyn was absorbed into the Arlington County Library system on April 12, 1959, at which time Miss Constance Backus and Mrs. Charles Stetson, Trustees, presented to the County a deed to the Library, together with the trust fund.

The first religious services of the immediate area were conducted at the dance pavilion in the park, until the erection of the existing Carlin Hall in 1892 at 5711 4th Street, South. St. John's Chapel was built 1910 and its tower added in 1921. Services were conducted by seminary students until 1954 when an ordained minister was installed.

The Carlin Springs resort buildings were demolished in 1893. The Glencarlyn Cooperative Association was dissolved in 1923 at which time the park with additional acreage was offered to Arlington County. The offer was declined as the County had neither an appropriation nor administrative system for park projects. In 1935, through the efforts of Emery N. Hosmer, an Arlington attorney, the State of Virginia became interested. However, litigation required to clarify the title was not completed until February 10, 1936. The State had intended to develop the park with Civilian Conservation Corps labor, but decided that it was too small for a C. C. C. Camp. Years later Arlington County took steps to acquire it, and the transfer was made in December, 1943.

The beauty of the wilderness is similar to Washington's Rock Creek Park, with deep ravines, wooded bluffs and tumbling streams, besides the famous springs. It is now the nucleus of a proposed extensive system of Arlington County Parks.

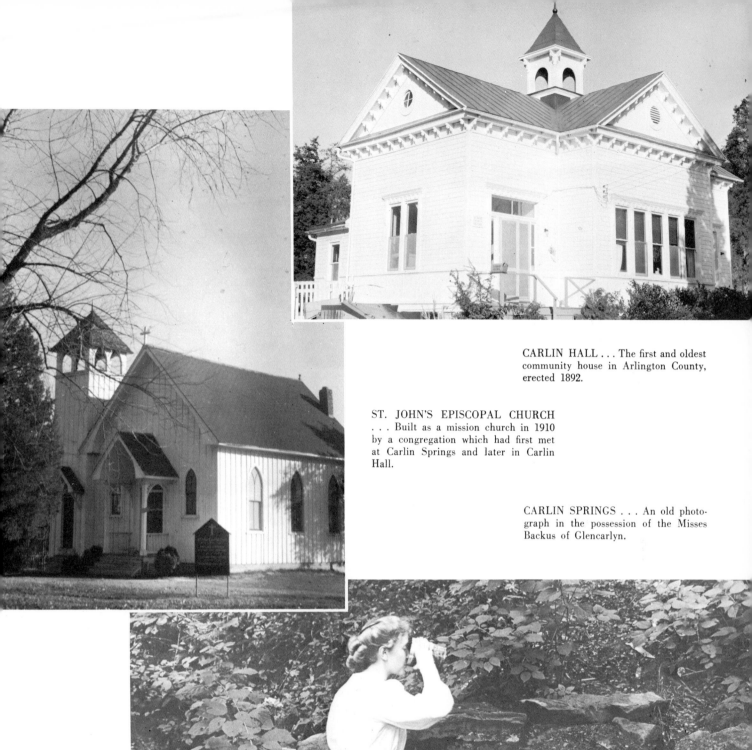

CARLIN HALL . . . The first and oldest community house in Arlington County, erected 1892.

ST. JOHN'S EPISCOPAL CHURCH . . . Built as a mission church in 1910 by a congregation which had first met at Carlin Springs and later in Carlin Hall.

CARLIN SPRINGS . . . An old photograph in the possession of the Misses Backus of Glencarlyn.

Roosevelt Island, Formerly Analostan

BETWEEN Key Bridge and Arlington Memorial Bridge near the Virginia shore lies a wilderness island nearly a mile long and a half mile wide. A hundred years before Captain John Smith saw the island, Spanish explorers recorded that an Indian tribe, taking advantage of the natural protection afforded by it, had built a village there.

A map drawn in 1670 by August Herrmann shows it as "Anacostie's Ile", derived from the local Indian name, Necostin. Lord Baltimore acquired it in 1638 as part of his Maryland grant to the Virginia shoreline; hence it sometimes was called "My Lord's Island". Captain Randolph Brandt of Indian War fame acquired title in 1681 and named it for his home in the West Indies, "Barbadoes". He died in 1698. In 1717, his son-in-law, Francis Hammersley sold it to George Mason III, father of the builder of Gunston Hall.

Neither George Mason III nor his famous son George Mason IV, who inherited the island in 1735 at the age of ten—(when his father drowned in a boating accident)—developed the seventy-five acre island's fullest potentialities. In 1748 George Mason of Gunston acquired the rights of the ferry previously owned by Awbury. The first ferry had operated below the tip of the island to the mouth of Rock Creek on the Maryland shore, but by this time had moved to the future site of Rosslyn, crossing to Georgetown. The island, then known as "Mason's Island", remained undeveloped until inherited by George Mason's son John in 1792. The estate included about two thousand acres along the Virginia shore extending almost to Little Falls.

John Mason, a Brigadier General in the District of Columbia Militia, was president of the Bank of Columbia in Georgetown. He numbered the great of this country and of France, where he had received training in the mercantile business, among his friends. Thus it was that Louis Phillipe, destined to be the last King of France, is said to have been his guest at the imposing stone mansion General Mason built on the island shortly after he inherited it.

The house was probably designed by George Hadfield, who is credited as being the architect of Arlington House. Situated fifty feet above the Potomac River, on the island's highest site, the Mason house afforded an unobstructed view of the new Federal City where work on the Capitol and the President's House was in progress.

The island, with its connecting ferry to the Georgetown mainland and the causeway General Mason had built to the Virginia shore, was strategically situated for those who had to cross the river to reach the new Nation's Capital City, so much so, that in 1807 Congress appropriated funds for the maintenance of the causeway which General Mason had been rebuilding at his own expense after each spring flood.

Washington and Jefferson, travelling to or from Mount Vernon and Monticello, would stop to rest and visit with General and Mrs. Mason. Young George Washington Lafayette, a member of General and Mrs. Washington's party on their way from Philadelphia to Mount Vernon after the last session of Congress to be held there, crossed the Potomac via Mason's Ferry.

The ferry produced some income, but General Mason also took a businessman's attitude towards the island itself and tried to make it self-supporting. He cultivated it extensively, irrigating it with river water, and put prize stock to graze in its pastures.

Since the house was a summer residence for General and Mrs. Mason and their large family, picnics in the beautiful gardens were a pleasant feature of island life. Diversion was offered by boating and fishing. Fifty pound turtles were often caught offshore. In the evenings, however, elegance prevailed. Then the mansion ballroom and its terrace were filled with dancing couples.

General Mason hoped to develop a town by the name of South Haven on the site of present Rosslyn. The Virginia Acts of Assembly of 1798 approved its establishment, with a Board of Trustees. A plat of lots already laid out was to be recorded in Fairfax Court House. South Haven did not materialize and John Mason became financially insolvent. He lost his inheritance, including the island, by foreclosure of the Bank of the United States in 1833. The Bank ordered the famous Lewis Carberry survey (1836 and 1837) of the lands thus acquired.

The neglected mansion, exposed to the elements and apparently the victim of fire, too, finally succumbed to the ravages of time. Thus was lost what is believed to have been one of our earliest examples of residential classical architecture. However, the name "Mason's Island" persisted for over a century. It was subsequently owned by the Bradley family of Georgetown, the Columbia Athletic Association, the Analostan Boat Club, and the Washington Gas Light Company. It was acquired in 1931 by the Theodore Roosevelt Memorial Association, which transferred title to the National Park Service as a living memorial to this great conservationist President.

During his term at the White House, "Teddy" Roosevelt spurred thoughtful Americans to a new evaluation of the natural resources of our Nation. Largely through his efforts, 234 million acres of land were reserved for posterity, under the administration of the United States Forest and National Park Services.

He had always been close to nature, and frequently sought the solitude of the forest to ease the tensions of urban life. This unique wilderness refuge in the midst of a large urban community is therefore a most appropriate memorial where others can gain a deeper appreciation and understanding of man's relationship to his natural environment. From its marshes to its fifty-foot elevation at the center, it offers a great variety of wild life, thirty species of trees, and 135 kinds of plants.

THE MASON MANSION
. . . Sketch of the house
as it appeared during the
residence of the Mason
family.

MANSION RUINS . . .
As the ruins appeared in
the 1930's.

DESERTED . . . A photo-
graph taken about 1900.

HOME OF GEORGE MASON (1725-92) . . .
Author of the Virginia Declaration of Rights. In
1755, he brought Wm. Buckland from England
to design and erect his home, completed in 1758.
Restored and furnished by the National Society
of Colonial Dames of America; open daily 9:30
to 5 except Christmas. *At Lorton, 14 miles south
of Alexandria, off U. S. No. 1.*

GEORGE MASON'S

PALLADIAN DRAWING ROOM . . . The portrait is of Ann Eilbeck, beloved first wife of
George Mason and mother of his nine children.
The furniture and decorative accessories are all
superb mid-18th century originals; some pieces
belonged to George Mason.

"GUNSTON HALL"

GARDEN . . . The famous boxwood gardens were planted by George Mason around 1758. The house looks out across its terraces to the Potomac. George Washington often came here in his barge from nearby Mount Vernon. These gardens were restored to their 18th century perfection by the Garden Club of Virginia in 1953.

CHINESE CHIPPENDALE ROOM . . . The portrait of George Mason hangs above the fireplace. This was the first room in America to be decorated in the "Chinese taste" which was then (1755) popular in England.

The Aqueduct Bridge

THE retrocession of the Virginia portion of the original District of Columbia is directly related to the history of the Alexandria Canal and the Aqueduct Bridge. These brought the waters of the Chesapeake and Ohio Canal on the Maryland side across the Potomac, to connect a continuous waterway from Cumberland (gateway to the Ohio settlements) with the important world seaport of Alexandria.

The financial crisis which climaxed the retrocession movement was due to delays of construction of the Chesapeake and Ohio Canal near Cumberland, which made the Alexandria investment unprofitable, and changes in the plans for the Aqueduct Bridge from wooden piers at a cost of $300,000, to masonry, costing an additional $950,000.

The Aqueduct and Alexandria Canal was chartered by Congress in May 1830; actual construction began in 1833 with impressive ceremonies. Alexandria's Mayor, John Roberts, who had been the official host of General Lafayette during his visit to America in 1824, turned the first spade of earth.

Because of the delays at Cumberland and the costly changes in specifications of the Aqueduct, both Federal allotments and funds raised in Alexandria were exhausted before completion. Although Congress had enthusiastically encouraged the project in its early stages, it was unwilling to appropriate additional funds for the completion. In fact, it had made no other monetary contribution to the portion of the District of Columbia which lay on the Virginia side of the river, except to erect a Federal jail.

The desperate Alexandrians finally appealed to the State of Virginia for aid. Virginia promised to come to the rescue if Congress would restore Alexandria County (as Arlington County was then termed) to State jurisdiction, in accordance with a vote of the inhabitants. This was granted in 1846, fifty-five years after the area had been made a part of the District of Columbia.

The Aqueduct Bridge was completed in 1843. Eight masonry piers supported a wooden flume for the canal boats; above was a plank bridge for vehicles and stock. A Washington newspaper of May 29, 1835, gives an interesting description of the construction of the piers: "We have never had an opportunity of inspecting a more remarkable triumph of art than the operation of building massive stone piers in the bed of the River Potomac, now going on near Georgetown, at the expense of the Alexandria Canal Co. We . . . found it to surpass our previous conception of it as well in regard to the magnitude of the enterprise as to the ingenuity with which very formidable obstacles have been overcome. It is truly a stupendous undertaking, with no parallel in this country, and, we believe, scarcely equalled in any other. The foundation of this pier, which is begun, is on bare rock, and the structure is solid masonry, formed of very large blocks of excellent stone from The Falls Quarries, skillfully laid in water-cement. To accomplish this object, a vast cofferdam has been constructed, the interior of which is about 80 feet long and nearly 30 feet wide. The depth of water to be shut out by this dam is 18 feet, and the depth of mud below, which it was necessary also to remove, was more than 17 feet, so that the building was begun at a depth of 37 feet below the surface of the water. Notwithstanding which, so successful has been the preparation for resisting the vast external pressure of water, that the rocky bottom was laid bare to the whole extent of the area inclosed, and even swept clean and dry with brooms before the cement was applied, in which . . . the first course of stone was laid. The length of the pier building is, at the base, 66 feet, running in its length with the current and the tide; its precise breadth we do not remember, but it must be something over 15 feet. We have given this sketch of a very remarkable work in our immediate vicinity, first because it is remarkable; secondly, to express our admiration of the spirit of the town of Alexandria in persevering in this undertaking in defiance of all obstacles; and thirdly, that we may give the credit due to the accomplished engineer who has labored so untiringly in carrying on this operation and has now the gratification of rejoicing in its success."

Maintenance was heavy, and shortly after completion, the railroads successfully competed for the trade, so the company eventually became bankrupt. However, the toll-bridge and canal operated until May 23, 1861, at which time the Federal Government seized the bridge; the flume was drained and both decks used for transportation of Union troops and munitions. After the war it was returned to the Aqueduct Company in bad condition. The superstructure was torn down sometime between 1879 and 1888; the limits are set by landmarks in existing photographs. In the meantime Congress had appropriated $125,000 to purchase it— an offer which was accepted in 1886. In 1888 a new superstructure was built. The Aqueduct Bridge was not demolished until nine years after the completion in 1923 of the adjacent Francis Scott Key Memorial Bridge.

The old masonry piers remain in the river and act as ice-baffles for the Potomac bridges downstream. One span of the old iron superstructure still crosses the Chesapeake and Ohio Canal at Georgetown. Traces of the old canal grade are still used near Rosslyn for a railroad bed. A beautiful masonry culvert beneath this grade near the George Washington Parkway is still in use to convey the waters of Rocky Run to the Potomac opposite Analostan Island.

AQUEDUCT BRIDGE . . . As seen from the George-town side of the Potomac. The bridge was dis-mantled after the completion of Key Bridge, but the stone piers remain today.

AQUEDUCT BRIDGE . . . View from the Virginia shore.

The Aqueduct Underpass

HIDDEN beneath Griffith Consumers' coalyard in Rosslyn is an old tunnel of historical interest and architectural value. Its arched ceiling is a fine piece of masonry engineering. The exact explanation of its construction has remained undocumented.

I could not accept the theory published in 1946, that it was a lock of the Alexandria Canal. Its grade is too low. We know the approximate water-level of the canal, because the present Rosslyn branch of the Pennsylvania Railroad uses the old canal grade along the first part of the parkway below Rosslyn as its railroad bed.

The tunnel entrance is in a steep embankment which divides the county-owned extension of Lee Highway into two driveways at different levels. The upper portion leading into Griffith Consumers' coalyard is at the same elevation as the railroad. The tunnel opens on the lower driveway which is some feet higher than the tunnel floor.

To support the theory that water flowed through the tunnel, it would have been necessary to get it to the higher level of the canal. Syphoning would have been impossible with barges floating on the water's surface, to say nothing of the restriction provided by the tunnel ceiling. Furthermore, the tunnel was at a right angle to the logical course of the canal, which parallels the river after leaving the aqueduct.

I determined to wrest the secret of its purpose. I obtained a copy of a photograph taken by county employees the previous year, in their attempt to decide if the tunnel was County-owned. At least part of it is beneath the county right-of-way of a possible extension of Lee Highway to the lands owned by the National Capital Parks. At the time the picture was made, the entrance was blocked by a cinder block wall into which was set a locked metal door.

The tunnel was then being used by W. H. Wolowitz for storage of surplus government office equipment which he had purchased. At the time, he was renting the old building adjacent to the parkway, since renovated into the "1101 Lee Highway Office Building". Since then Mr. Wolowitz has removed truckloads of equipment from the tunnel.

Prompted by my recollections of a similar tunnel I had walked through at Fletcher's Boat House across the Potomac, I considered the probability of this tunnel having been constructed for the same purpose. The other tunnel carries a roadway beneath the Chesapeake and Ohio Canal.

By a careful on-site study of the grade-levels and structure angles at Rosslyn, supplemented by scrutinizing many early maps, the tunnel's history began to unfold in support of my theory. On the Civil War Military Map of 1864, I found what I sought! The cartography clearly shows that the canal line goes over a roadway leading from farther back in Rosslyn to the then existing causeway to Analostan Island. Many years ago, the other exit of the tunnel was buried beneath tons of earth fill. It now lies under the coalyard.

The tunnel's existence was evidently known to the operators of Rosslyn's gambling and vice dens during that area's infamous period of gangsterism (see pages 74, 76, and 78). One could speculate endlessly upon what bizarre uses they may have made of this huge underground vault.

Let me warn would-be explorers that at the present time, nothing of interest can be seen by visiting the spot. The door has been wrenched loose from its hinges and the entrance is completely blocked with junk. Noxious fumes were present when the photographs were made and gas masks were used by the county employees who entered the vault. It would be extremely hazardous to attempt any exploration.

The area should be cleaned, the tunnel cleared, and the cinder block wall torn away to expose the fine masonry entrance. As a safety precaution, its recesses should be made visible through steel bars and a locked gate. It seems that this is a responsibility of the County, and I am assured that steps will be considered for some such action, now that the situation has come to the attention of proper officials. This sub-canal roadway has the potentials of becoming a very attractive historic site. It is quite possible that this tunnel and the one shown on the opposite page were constructed by the Roach Brick and Masonry Company (see page 58).

ROCKY RUN ON THE PARKWAY . . . The beautiful old masonry culvert
beneath the Alexandria Canal (now filled and used for the railroad at this point)
is similar to the hidden Rosslyn tunnel to the Analostan Island causeway.

Jackson City — Dream to Nightmare

THE area at the south end of the Fourteenth Street Bridge has had a varied history. No landmark has survived from its early days. Even the shape of the land has been changed by dredging and filling; what was once water is now Columbia Island; what was once land is now the Pentagon Lagoon.

This area was the probable site of Namerough-quena, the Necostin Indian village noted by Captain John Smith on the map which he drew after his visit there in 1608. In early records it was called Holmes' Island. It became part of the Alexander estate, and was later known as Alexander's Island. This land was farmed by generations of Alexanders and their tenants, and eventually came into the possession of one Richard Mason.

In 1836 a group of New York speculators promoted on paper a dream industrial twin-city to Washington. It was to be at Bridge Point, a small settlement on the Virginia end of Long Bridge which had been completed the previous year, replacing the first bridge of 1808. A seaport was to be excavated in the marsh of Roach's Run. The name was to be Jackson City in honor of the President. Alexandria and Georgetown men were not enthusiastic, as its success would take business from their own ports. Hence, their newspapers threw sarcastic and caustic jibes at what they termed a speculative hoax.

The great celebration which accompanied the laying of the cornerstone January 11, 1836 by "Old Hickory" was described in the following terms:

"It was certainly a capital hit to Christen their bantling by the illustrious name they gave it, and a still better one to enlist in its behalf . . . the Chief Magistrate who never refuses to do a generous act. The respect and esteem in which the President is held, and his great personal popularity, made everyone, no matter what they thought of the occasion, unite to do him honor . . . A bright, bracing January morning, the prospect of a 'show', drums beating, cannon firing, plates clattering, and corks drawing made high and low turn out and filled the mud bank . . . with a greater crowd than it ever bore before or ever will again. . . .

"The 'foundation stone' consisted of two seats of perishable freestone, one sunk in the earth, with a hole cut for the reception of the box, and the other slung by pulleys above. A lithographic print was circulated representing the intended monument . . . most ominously like a tombstone enclosed in a railing, inscriptions on each side to indicate the date together with some highly eulogistic references to the illustrious founder. The box was deposited and the slab let down; the general gave it three knocks with a small gilt hammer, the Masons gave nine claps with their hands, the artillery thundered in the air, and 'Humbug City' unlike Rome, was built in a day!

"After the stone was laid, the President and the gentlemen by whom he was accompanied were conducted to a platform from which G. W. P. Custis addressed the crowd. After the collation, at which appropriate toasts were drunk, the company soon dispersed. . . . After the close of proceedings the usual quantum of drunken riot and disturbance attendant upon such congregation took place, which required the interposition of the police."

Except in name, the life of Jackson City was brief. The tract of approximately 500 acres was offered for sale at public auction August 28, 1841 by the trustee of the late Richard B. Mason. It was glowingly described as fertile farm and garden land, suitable for dairy and as a cattle stand for beef brought in to supply the cities of Washington and Alexandria, and one of the finest fisheries of the Potomac. It was still farm land at the start of the Civil War although a race track had been developed at the site of the Pentagon Lagoon. Fortifications were speedily built for the protection of the bridge to the Federal City.

After the Army vacated it in 1870, the area became an infamous gambling resort. New Jersey promoters moved in after gambling and racing were outlawed in their own State. Many a gay blade from Washington lost his fortune there, to walk home over Long Bridge with empty pockets. Lawless elements ruled local politics. A nearby gulch became known as "Hell's Bottom". It was the execution spot for those who did not cooperate with the gang leaders; hangings took place on an average of one every week.

The same situation developed up-river at Rosslyn, readily accessible to the undesirable element from Georgetown via the Aqueduct Bridge. Numerous saloons and gambling houses sprang up. Between Mackey Hill and Rosslyn was "Dead Man's Hollow" to match Jackson City's "Hell's Bottom". Killings were commonplace, and never was a case brought to trial. It was alleged that local officials received weekly "pay-off" envelopes at The Klondike, a Rosslyn dive.

Saturday nights were particularly hazardous for the few law-abiding citizens who traversed the area enroute home. They organized into armed groups in Georgetown and crossed the bridge and continued through Rosslyn in a closely knit cavalcade of horses and carriages.

Around 1890, the reputable residents organized the "Good Citizens' League" to clean up local politics and drive out the undesirables who had caused the area to become known as "The Monte Carlo of America". It was a long and hard fight which did not bear results until the raids of 1904, related in the following chapter.

During the 1920's, the abandoned race track was used as Hoover Airport, later excavated for the Pentagon Lagoon. Today there is serene beauty at the site of Jackson City. The George Washington Memorial Parkway skirts the river, passing the Roach's Run Bird Sanctuary lagoon. Nearby up the river, the inspiring monument to the Men of the Sea raises its foam crested waves and sea gulls against the Washington skyline (see page 49). Where is the Jackson City cornerstone of 1836?

GEORGETOWN WHARVES . . . Vessels from all over the world docked at
Georgetown.

LONG BRIDGE . . . Civil War scene at Jackson City.

The Good Citizens' League

LOCAL residents organized the Good Citizens' League to combat the influx of gambling interests who established infamous resorts along our Potomac shores. This resulted from lax law enforcement coupled with political collusion and bribery. In order to bring the facts to the public, Frank Lyon bought the local newspaper, the *Monitor*.

Mr. Lyon had come to Virginia in 1889 and first lived west of Kirkwood Road near the William Ball house, which is now in back of the American Legion Headquarters. That Lyon home was purchased in 1946 by the Young Men's Christian Association and demolished in June 1956 to make way for a new recreation center. (See page 99).

Frank Lyon pioneered in the establishment of this County as a residential community. Both Lyon Park and Lyon Village, which he later developed, perpetuate his name. Throughout northern Virginia his series of handsome residences, including Lyonhurst at 4651 25th Street North are monuments to his versatile architectural taste.

In the autumn of 1903, a group of about twenty representative citizens met secretly at the home of William Ball to nominate a Commonwealth's Attorney who would fight corruption. The choice narrowed to three, who retired to the oak grove until the choice was made—that of Captain Crandal Mackey.

Crandal Mackey's family background reads like a resumé of early Americana. He was born in a Confederate ambulance at Shreveport, Louisiana, in 1865. He was the son of Thomas Jefferson Mackey of the Confederate Army Engineers (who later served three terms as a Circuit Judge in South Carolina) and Rosina Lloyd of Maryland. Young Crandal was graduated from the South Carolina Military Institute and Pionona College in Georgia before his family moved to Washington, where he received degrees in law.

In 1897, Crandal Mackey moved into Virginia and erected his home at 1711 22d Street, North on Rock Hill above Rosslyn. The section eventually became known as Mackey Hill. He built on two acres purchased from his mother, who had inherited a large tract which her father, Richard Bennett Lloyd of Maryland, had received as a fee. The Lloyd family provided Maryland with six early governors.

Crandal Mackey served as a captain in the Spanish-American War. Soon after return from service, he started crusading for civic betterment.

Upon his nomination for Commonwealth's Attorney, he campaigned by horse and buggy and won the election by two votes. The incumbent employed nine high-priced attorneys, including the Attorney General of Pennsylvania, to contest the election, without success. Crandal Mackey took office the first Monday of January 1904. He called in the law enforcement officers to demand a clean-out of the gambling dens; the sheriff asked for time. When no action had been taken in four months, Captain Mackey addressed letters to thirty citizens asking them to meet at four o'clock on May 30 at his law office in Washington to form a posse to accompany him in raiding the dens. Constable Lem Marcey swore the volunteers in as deputies.

Armed with pistols, axes, and sledge hammers, they boarded the southbound train, having instructed the engineer to let them off at Jackson City, which was not a regular stop. They literally wrecked every establishment, from St. Asaph's near Alexandria, on up the river through Rosslyn. Furniture, fixtures, slot machines, barrels, and bottles were smashed. At Jack Heath's, the largest and most elaborate, on the waterfront near the Mackey home, the raiders were met at the door by the owner armed with a double-barrel shotgun, and a threat to kill the first man to try to enter. Six years before, Lem and William Marcey with four others had raided Heath's, and Lem had been felled by a club and beaten unconscious with a pistol butt. Crandal Mackey rushed up to the astonished Heath, unarmed him and sent him off to jail.

St. Asaph's reopened, claiming that it was operating legally. The Grand Jury was then in session. Crandal Mackey suggested that the judge adjourn temporarily with instructions to the jurymen to seek their own evidence. The jurymen played the horses at St. Asaph's, resulting in nineteen indictments against three proprietors and sixteen employees, one of whom turned out to be a special officer of the County. He and five justices of the peace were removed from office. One of the strongest opponents to the elimination of gambling was the Alexandria and Mount Vernon Railroad (12th Street and Pennsylvania Avenue to Mount Vernon), in which the Pennsylvania Railroad Co. held stock. Strong pressures and tempting offers were made to Colonel Mackey, without avail, to call off his crusade, for this line averaged hundreds of riders daily to St. Asaph's gambling houses.

Elections in those days resulted in opponents labeling each other with rather pointed nicknames and sometimes using gunfire. In one election the defeated candidate for sheriff announced that he was going out to kill Mackey, whom he felt had worked against him. With calm courage, Mackey ignored the threat.

Even in the courts of law, trials sometimes led to scenes of violence, and some colorful language was in common usage. During one case, an attorney shot at his opponent but missed his target. The intended victim wrested the revolver from him and pistol-whipped him over the head. This episode led to another suit, wherein the defendant's attorney stated, in his closing arguments, "_____ _____ is suing _____ _____ for $30,000 damages to a thirty cent brain!"

Arlingtonians owe a great debt of gratitude to Crandal Mackey and his group of civic crusaders. The only member still living is former Judge Harry Thomas; the sons of the others are among our outstanding citizens today.

PARKWAY SCENE . . . View
of Georgetown University spires
above Key Bridge, as seen from
the Virginia shore below Rosslyn.

THE ARLINGTON SHORE . . .
Key Bridge at Rosslyn in foreground, Arlington Memorial
Bridge in center, and Highway
Bridge in the distance at site of
Jackson City. Virginia shore at
right, Georgetown in left foreground, Washington in left background.

Rosslyn — Gateway to Virginia

THROUGHOUT its history, Rosslyn has been more of a gateway than a destination. Early water transportation included boat, ferry, and aqueduct. Then there were Potomac River crossings by causeway to Analostan Island, to supplement the ferry. Pontoon bridges were used there in the 1860's and again during World War II. Rosslyn has had two bridges—the Aqueduct and since 1923 the Francis Scott Key Bridge.

Two early roads led from Awbury's Ferry at Rosslyn to Alexandria and to Falls Church (via Clarendon). They are described on page 52. After the Civil War, the Georgetown-Fairfax Road from Rosslyn was extended through Cherrydale to eventually become Lee Highway.

Although none exist today, Rosslyn was the terminal for three trolley lines and is still the terminal of two railroad lines described on page 160.

The earliest land records of Rosslyn are the 1657 and 1658 grants "in the freshes of the Pawtomack above Anacosta Iland." These grants by the Protectorate Governors lapsed, hence the land came under Lord Culpeper and descended from him to Lord Fairfax who issued proprietary grants. The earliest of these was the Struttfield patent of September 7, 1709.

On page 66, we learned of the unsuccessful attempt of John Mason of Analostan Island to establish South Haven at the Virginia end of his ferry. In 1860, Joseph Lambden purchased a substantial portion of the property and subsequently deeded it to his daughter Caroline (sometimes spelled Carolyn) and her husband, William Henry Ross. They named it "Rosslyn Farm".

They were living in France when the farm was sold in 1869 to the Rosslyn Development Corporation. The disturbances attendant upon the Civil War and the consequent occupation of Arlington by Federal troops are hinted in the deed whereby Ross reserved to himself the benefit of claims for damages done by the United States Forces. Forts Corcoran, Haggerty, and Bennett were nearby.

Then followed the infamous period when Rosslyn was considered again a gateway, one to perdition . . .! No western mining town was ever wilder, until the gambling interests were driven out in 1904. (Refer to two preceeding chapters.)

In 1896 a huge red brick building was erected for the Consumer Brewing Company just above the bridge. It closely resembled the Court House which was designed by the same architect, Albert E. Goenner. Its tall Victorian tower with a clock which long ago ceased to mark the passage of time, dominated the Rosslyn skyline until May of 1958 when it was demolished to prepare a site for a two million dollar motel.

Through Mrs. Stella May Buettner of 1716 North 22d Street, I learned much about the construction of the brewery. Her father, Phillip M. May, had a drayage business during the 1890's, with contracts to haul trash and cinders from the Treasury and other Federal buildings. The cinders were used on local roads; it was horse and mule power in those days.

The Mays moved to Virginia in 1895. They bought land on Rock Hill at five cents per foot from Rosina Bennett Lloyd, mother of Judge Crandal Mackey. The general contractor for erection of the brewery, Mr. Foster of Chicago, brought his wife and son with him and boarded at the Mays' home. May subcontracted to haul the bricks for the brewery.

When the brewery's 125-foot smoke stack was nearing completion, Phillip May took some of the steel shoes off his horses and mules used on this contract and sent them up to be fastened near the top of the stack for good luck!

I quote from a letter of Carroll J. McGuire's, the son of an original stockholder and official:

"My Dad, William McGuire, was president of the Arlington Brewery at the time it closed, due to prohibition. Mr. Abe King was secretary-treasurer and Mr. Edward L. Jordan was vice-president. Dad was one of the original stockholders of the Consumer Brewery, which was founded in the late 1890's and was reorganized about 1904 when its name was changed to the Arlington Brewery. . . . Mr. Richardson was the first president. . . ." A Mr. Jacobson owned the Arlington Bottling Company, built next to the Brewery about 1905. The stables were between. Adjacent was the Rosslyn Packing Company. As a boy, Mr. McGuire kept a riding horse at the brewery stable and enjoyed hunting small game along the river.

The building served a variety of purposes: as a brewery, winery, lithographic print shop, the Cherry Smash Bottling Company, and finally as a warehouse. The proximity of a packing plant with its abattoir caused the erroneous assumption that the brewery building was once used as a slaughter-house.

When the brewery building was being demolished, I climbed through the rubble to ask Mr. Elmo Rausch, superintendent of the Roland Larkin Company, if he would save for the Arlington Historical Society any of the horse or mule shoes found in the debris. He was intrigued with the tale. He phoned me the next day to tell me he could see the shoes near the top of the 125-foot stack, and offered to retrieve them before the chimney was blasted. The Arlington Fire Division cooperated by lending its 100-foot ladder. There was great excitement, with fire trucks, police cars, Washington reporters and photographers, and officials of the Arlington Historical Society. I brought Mrs. Buettner, to whom we gave one of the shoes when Elmo Rausch presented them to the Arlington Historical Society. A few days later, when the chimney was blasted, traffic was temporarily halted on nearby Lee Highway as a safety precaution. We find no record of fanfare regarding the erection of the brewery, but its destruction caused more excitement than Rosslyn had experienced since the raids which broke up the gambling dens in 1904!

BREWERY CHIMNEY . . . after the building was demolished.

A LAST SMOKE . . . As the chimney shattered and dropped when dynamited, loosened soot rose as if from a phantom fire from a long-dead furnace.

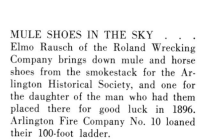

MULE SHOES IN THE SKY . . . Elmo Rausch of the Roland Wrecking Company brings down mule and horse shoes from the smokestack for the Arlington Historical Society, and one for the daughter of the man who had them placed there for good luck in 1896. Arlington Fire Company No. 10 loaned their 100-foot ladder.

Fairlington on Site of Hampton Farm

FAIRLINGTON Community in the southwest corner of Arlington County (extending into Alexandria), was developed in 1943 under the charter of Defense Homes Corporation with funds from the Reconstruction Finance Corporation. At the time, with 3,439 units, it was the largest housing development of the Nation. It was built at a cost of over thirty-five million dollars. The march of progress destroyed "Hampton Farm" and its mansion, which was probably built shortly after the Revolution. A few spruce trees remain marking the lane which led to the house at the crest of the hill on the Alexandria City-Arlington County line. The water tower at South Columbus and 30th Streets marks the site of the house. The barn and stables were at the present location of the Fire Station on South Abingdon Street at 31st Road.

Hampton Farm included 543 acres patented by William Struttfield on January 21, 1705. A series of four transfers brought it in 1756 into the possession of Colonel John Carlyle of Alexandria. He had come from Scotland to Dumfries, Virginia, about 1740, at the age of twenty, and had been one of the founders of Alexandria. His home at 121 North Fairfax Street is well known as a museum of those times. (See page 10.)

By his first wife, Sarah, the daughter of William Fairfax of "Belvoir", John Carlyle had two daughters: Sarah Carlyle, who married William Herbert, and Ann Fairfax Carlyle, who married Henry Whiting. His second wife bore him a son, George William Carlyle, who became an officer in the Continental Army at the age of seventeen and was killed at the Battle of Eutaw Springs in 1781. The estate inherited from his father the previous year was divided between his nephews, John Carlyle Herbert and Carlyle Fairfax Whiting, the Struttfield patent going to the latter.

Young Whiting lived on the estate and probably built the large white frame house that stood near the Alexandria-Leesburg Turnpike. Upon his death in 1834, his estate of 640 acres was partitioned. The mansion with 200 acres was assigned to his son, Charles H. Whiting. About 1870 this property was sold to Courtland Hawkins Smith I, a kinsman of General Robert E. Lee. Smith also purchased the adjacent Whiting acreage and the Daingerfield estate called Malvern. He remodeled the Whiting mansion and named the place Hampton. The Smith family divided their time between this country estate and their town house in Alexandria at 510 Wolfe Street.

Courtland Hawkins Smith II (born in 1878) established one of the largest and finest stock farms in the nation, raising hunters and show horses. He was reputed to be the richest man of the area, and had as many as ninety thoroughbred broodmares at a time. At the turn of the century he organized The Hampton Hounds, which soon merged with The Chevy Chase Hounds to form The Cameron Run Hunt Club. Their fox hunts, steeplechases, and horse shows were among the finest and attracted a fashionable group from far and wide.

In 1899, young Smith married Carlyle Fairfax Herbert, a descendant of John Carlyle. Courtland Smith II moved about 1908 to the more open hunt country in the Warrenton-Middleburg area, where he died in 1952. His two sons are now prominent residents of this area: Colonel Mark Alexander Herbert Smith, an official of the Burke and Herbert Bank, and Captain (USNR) Courtland Hawkins Smith III, an executive of the Chesapeake and Potomac Telephone Company.

Hampton Farm was broken up into several small holdings after it was sold by the Smiths in 1926. A portion was used for a time as a landing field for private planes and a flying school, but the residents of nearby Seminary Hill banned local flying activities after a fatal crash.

Adjacent to Fairlington was one of the finest Civil War fortifications, Fort Reynolds. Until 1955, its earthworks could be found in a wooded area north of 31st Street and back of the Arlington County Property Yard, across the ravine from Abingdon School. With ramparts which measured 360 yards in perimeter, it was erected in the autumn of 1861 to protect the valley of Four Mile Run. It was first named for General Blencker, whose German-American troops helped erect it. Two years later it was renamed in honor of Major General John Fulton Reynolds, a West Point graduate from Lancaster, Pennsylvania. He was a veteran of the Mexican and Indian campaigns who fought ably in the Federal army until his death in the battle at Gettysburg.

This well-preserved fort was offered to Arlington County in 1954 by Mark Winkler at less than half the sale price finally accepted from the Park Shirlington Apartment developers. The offer was rejected and another important historical landmark vanished before the bulldozers. About 200 yards west of Fort Reynolds near the water tower was Battery Garesche.

THE HAMPTON HOUNDS . . . Courtland Hawkins Smith II in center front was Master of the Hampton Hounds. Picture taken about 1905 on his Hampton Farm.

FORT RICHARDSON . . . Earthworks as they appear today on the grounds of the Army-Navy Country Club.

The Corbett Clan

AROUND the middle of the 1800's, New Yorkers were attracted by our milder climate and the proximity to the National Capital, which promised increasing land-values, with rumor of a railway line through the area. Among those interested was Sewell B. Corbett of Corbettsville, New York, whose ancestors had obviously pioneered that region. He was born in 1819, and when nineteen years old had married his seventeen-year-old sweetheart, Jane Ann Watruss. In 1849, they came here seeking a homesite. On April 1, 1850, they purchased 282 acres from Orlando Fairfax, and three years later bought the Joseph H. Bradley farm. The Fairfax purchase was made with three thousand dollars in gold which had been Jane's dowery.

They were so pleased with Virginia that Sewell's father and brothers decided to follow. Sewell continued to buy acreage along Columbia Pike and on the west side of Glebe Road almost to Ball's Crossroads. In 1854 his father, Cooper Corbett, and mother, Cornelia, purchased two parcels from Sewell, and in turn deeded these to his brothers, Virgil P. Corbett in 1858, and Frank E. Corbett in 1864.

The Berry homestead had been on part of Sewell's land. The Sewell Corbetts lived in the Berry home until the Civil War, when it was seized by the Federals for the erection of Fort Berry, to guard the south end of Glebe Road as it approaches Four Mile Run. The present address of the site is 3525 17th Street, South, between Monroe Street and Glebe Road. The Berry-Corbett house was finally destroyed by the troops, and all that remains of the original property is an ancient gnarled cherry tree. However, across 17th Street at 3520 in the center of the block to the south, is a large old house reputed to have been used during the war as a hospital, now the Kollmeyer home. It was probably an overseer's house on the plantation, and is reported to have later been the residence of Fred Corbett. It certainly was built long before any thought of streets, as it sits at a strange angle, akimbo to the streets and houses of the community, but on the line of earthworks shown on the map of 1864.

The Civil War map also shows a large cemetery north of Fort Berry, running along the east side of the present 1300 block of South Monroe Street. It appears on the map as about 100 feet by 500 feet, but during the years the sides of the cemetery have been encroached upon until only a tiny plot remains. This is in front of 1309 South Monroe Street. A giant holly tree stands guard over the remaining tombstones which date back to deaths as early as 1837. The names are mostly Travers, Dyer, and Whitehead. The latter family operated a blacksmith shop nearby on the southwest corner of Glebe Road and Columbia Pike.

Many years after the war, a Yankee veteran returned to this area for a visit, and told members of the Corbett family that he recalled that the barracks' bakers raised their bread on the sun-warmed tombstones. Many a loaf's bottom was imprinted with the dates and names of the departed. The mess unit of Fort Berry was closer to the cemetery than to the fortification.

Another veteran from Vermont, Charles Spaulding, had become so attracted to this particular area while assigned to guard duty at Fort Berry, that he returned in 1902 to buy a home built by Charles Corbett about 1882 at what is now 1314 South Monroe Street. Spaulding had been wounded in the Battle of the Wilderness and walked from Fredericksburg to Washington before being assigned to Fort Berry. The present occupant of the home is Clayton Warner, a grandson.

When the Sewell Corbetts had lost their home at Fort Berry, they built a house at the northwest corner of Columbia Pike and Walter Reed Drive. This was eventually acquired by their son-in-law, Sanford Bradbury. It was demolished about 1948. It had been rented for about three years in the early 1910's to Colonel Mosby, who died in 1916, following a diplomatic career after his spectacular service in the Confederate Army.

One of the most beloved men of our county in the horse-and-buggy days was Sewell Corbett's son, Dr. Henry Clay Corbett, born November 4, 1858. He married his neighborhood sweetheart, Virginia Munson, in June 1883 upon his graduation from Columbian University (now George Washington). His bride was the daughter of Miles C. Munson, whose pre-Civil War home is still standing on the northwest corner of South Irving and 13th Streets. For many years, Dr. Corbett was the only resident physician in the area. He passed away in 1955, some years after his retirement.

When the little village of Corbett was changed to Barcroft soon after 1900 as related in the next chapter, the Corbett Cemetery was the only remaining landmark to bear the family's name. The cemetery measures about 477 feet long and 116 feet wide. It runs through the center of the block between 16th and 17th Streets South, extending from South Quincy Street to the dead-end of South Randolph Street. Here are buried both Mr. and Mrs. Sewell Corbett and many others.

Mrs. Henry Clay Corbett's brother, Reginald Munson was also a physician, and another brother, Charles Munson was a dentist, but neither practiced locally. Charles' twin sister, Margaret Anna, married Thomas Jarboe De Lashmutt who had come to this area in 1880. Their descendants have taken a prominent part in the affairs of Northern Virginia. His son, Thomas Newton De Lashmutt is the present owner of "Oak Hill", the James Monroe mansion in Loudoun County.

In the 1870's, Henry W. Smith of Canada came to Virginia to visit relatives. He fell in love with a local damsel, Julia Margaret Shreve of Ballston. They were married about 1880 and bought a pre-Civil War house at the northwest corner of Columbia Pike and South Court House Road. It burned down in 1902, and they rebuilt a handsome residence which stood until 1958 when it was demolished for a commercial venture.

CORBETT-BRADBURY HOUSE . . . Etching of the home which formerly stood at the northeast corner of Columbia Pike and South Fillmore Street in a grove of oaks.

HOLLY GUARDS

ANCIENT GRAVES . . .

Barcroft Beginnings

BARCROFT, a little community which originally extended along Columbia Pike from George Mason Drive and South Taylor Street to the Fairfax County line takes its name from Dr. John Woolverton Barcroft of Rosemont, New Jersey, a graduate of the Philadelphia Medical College. Most of my information on this area came from Mrs. Milton Barcroft Payne, wife of Dr. Barcroft's grandson.

Dr. Barcroft came to Virginia in 1849 and first settled on Columbia Pike beyond our County line at Holmes Run, where he built and operated Barcroft Mill until the Civil War. The residence he had built nearby stood until demolished in 1957 in order to widen the road. The Federal troops returning from the Second Battle of Bull Run damaged the mill property so badly that Dr. Barcroft returned to New Jersey and abandoned the enterprise until after the war. The ruins of this early mill are still visible.

On Dr. Barcroft's return to Virginia he built a home on Barcroft Hill, the ruins of which are back of Magnolia Gardens Apartments on Columbia Pike between Dinwiddie and Greenbrier Streets. In 1880, he bought from George Washington Custis Lee the Custis Mill Tract of Washington Forest. This included the site of the war-wrecked Arlington Mill where Columbia Pike crosses Four Mile Run. Dr. Barcroft rebuilt the mill, which he operated personally for many years, then rented it to various other millers. One was John Newlon, who had been head miller for Herr and Cissel of Georgetown, which is now operating as the Wilkins-Rogers Company. Mr. Newlon operated the Barcroft mill at intervals between 1885 and 1906.

The thirty-six foot waterwheel was the largest on the eastern seaboard. After the mill burned in the early 1920's, neighborhood children used it as a ferris-wheel. It is to be regretted that the County did not purchase the stream valley at that time, when it was offered at a most reasonable price. The dam up Four Mile Run, and the race, eight feet wide and four feet deep, were intact until a few years ago. The mill could have then been restored as a museum type tea house. The mill site was purchased by a company which built an ice plant on the foundations, and the dam and mill-race were destroyed in the development of Glen Park apartments. The County is now negotiating to acquire the strip on each side of the stream to connect Glencarlyn Park, upstream, with Four Mile Run Park downstream.

The mill and Southern Railway station names were changed from Arlington to Barcroft. They became the nucleus of a residential community around the turn of the century. The 1900 map shows the settlement as Corbett, but this was also soon renamed Barcroft. In 1905, the business center consisted of the general store, the blacksmith shop, and the railway shed grouped clockwise around the railway crossing of the Pike, with the mill across Four Mile Run on the downstream side. The cattle pens behind the store were about a thousand yards up the tracks. Private homes were scattered along Columbia Pike from the County line back to South Taylor Street. On the north side of the village were the S. P. Wright farm and the Kolb farm. The Kolb house was built about 1880 at the crest of a rise in a grove of fine trees. It is now the home of the Milton Barcroft Paynes at 133 South Pershing Drive. Their extensive grounds have preserved the proper setting for the comfortable farmhouse with its stone milk-house nearby.

The early store was operated by Oscar Haring and his family, who lived above it. It also served as a post office. The Harings knew their neighbors so well that they were able to recognize the handwriting and make proper delivery of a letter which was addressed only, "Mother, Barcroft, Virginia." The store had one of the few telephones in the community, shared by all. It was on a local line and subject to the moods of an operator who put calls through at her own convenience. People who waited for the rarely punctual train to Washington gathered around the pot-bellied stove to discuss crops and politics. Besides passenger service, the train brought cattle from Loudoun County and "up country" farms to the cattle pens of Barcroft. They were unloaded there and driven along Columbia Pike to the abattoir which was near the present site of the Pentagon.

Young Eddie Haring edited and printed the first and only local newspaper, the *Barcroft News,* in 1904, which was filled with items of community affairs. Milton Payne, then a very small boy, was duly thrilled when permitted to help set type.

In 1906, Mr. and Mrs. Sidney T. Marye were leaders in starting the first Barcroft School. It was necessary to include the four-year-old daughter of the teacher, Mrs. Edith Fairfax, in order to swell the number of pupils to ten, the County minimum. School was "kept" in the teacher's home. By the next year, a building boom swelled the number of pupils. The need of a school building, a church, and a place for neighborhood activities prompted the erection of the Barcroft Community House. The Barcroft School and Civic League financed the project by giving plays, lawn parties, and suppers. These funds were supplemented by rent from the County School Board until the completion of a new Barcroft School in 1925.

Lack of easy transportation in the early 1900's forced residents through a mutual dependence to fall back upon themselves for enjoyment of a type of community life which drew neighbors together. Young people provided their own local amusements, something we have lost a half-century later. The little village of Barcroft has merged its borders into those of Greater Arlington, but its name is perpetuated in many ways, and in the memories of those who grew up in its happy country atmosphere.

BARCROFT MILL RUINS . . . Both the mill, on Holmes Run beyond Arlington County's line, and the village at Arlington Mill (page 51) within the county were named for Dr. John Woolverton Barcroft.

Buckingham's Background

BUCKINGHAM Community at the time of its completion in 1940, was the largest garden-apartment in the world. Its 125 acres included most of the ninety-eight-and-a-half acre Virgil Corbett estate plus some smaller holdings.

On the north side of Henderson Road lay the Cathcart Estate. Seeking data on these two pre-Civil War farms, I found myself in the home of the Paden family at 440 North Park Drive, on the remaining acreage of the Cathcart Estate. I talked with Mrs. Paden and her charming mother, ninety-two years young in spirit, who was Virgil Corbett's daughter. In 1886 when twenty, she was married to twenty-nine-year-old Arthur W. Cathcart. He was an outstanding mechanical engineer whose inventions are now in the Smithsonian Institution.

When I asked Mrs. Cathcart what had brought her husband's family into this area, there unfolded a tale which could have come from the Arabian Nights! I was shown two history books about the amazing career of her husband's grandfather, James Leander Cathcart, and parchment documents signed by John Adams, Thomas Jefferson, and James Madison.

James Leander Cathcart was born June 1, 1767 in Mount Murragh, Ireland, and at the age of eight sailed for America with a group of colonists. The following year, wishing to serve his new country in the Revolution, he signed as a cabin boy on a privateer sailing from New York. Within three years, the twelve-year-old lad was a midshipman on the frigate *Confederacy*. He was taught sailing by a Portuguese helmsman from whom he learned his language. From the Spanish navigator he learned celestial navigation, mathematics, and a strong command of Spanish.

When fourteen he was captured by the British and thrown into a prison ship in New York harbor. While imprisoned he learned how to survive under horrible conditions and acquired French from some troops who were fellow-prisoners. Upon liberation at the end of the war, Cathcart chose merchant sailing as a career. His love of the sea and his knowledge of navigation and foreign languages admirably fitted him for this field of enterprise which had been previously monopolized by the British. In 1785 the eighteen-year-old lad signed up in Boston as second mate of the schooner *Maria,* bound for Cadiz, Spain, with a trade-cargo of furs, lumber, and dried codfish.

As the broad, dumpy *Maria* reached the southwest tip of Portugal in a thick fog, it was attacked and captured by Barbary pirates. The men were stripped and taken aboard the stream-lined Corsair, where the filth and brutality of the prison-hold contrasted with the silks and rugs of the luxurious quarters of their English-speaking captor, Yusuf Rais. The Barbary pirates were the true rulers of the sea, extracting "tribute" from the nations of the world for "protection". Otherwise, their ships were preyed upon and captives held for heavy ransom. Our new nation was unable to pay either, so Cathcart realized that his only chance to free himself and his fellow prisoners was to ingratiate himself with the pirates until such time as he could personally build up a fortune by his wits, toward their eventual ransom.

Cathcart's capabilities were recognized immediately by his captor who gave him an opportunity to sail the slim swift vessel Yusuf Rais had designed.

For eleven years, Cathcart was held prisoner in the walled city of Algiers. Here he found favor with the High Dey who appointed him overseer of the Americans. According to their plan, they made themselves indispensable around the palace and grounds as masons, carpenters, painters, and gardeners. Cathcart learned to speak Arabic and Turkish. He was put in charge of feeding the Dey's pet lions, whose choicest meats he smuggled to his fellow captives. The British Consul of Algiers offered to arrange for their freedom in exchange for lifetime service to Great Britain, but they vetoed this opportunity as traitorous.

Captain O'Brien, a later captive, who became the Dey's secretary, smuggled Cathcart's letters to American authorities, whose attempts to raise ransom were futile. It was finally through Cathcart's carefully arranged political moves and hoarded funds that he and the remaining twelve of his crew (ten had died) were eventually freed. On May 22, 1796. Cathcart sailed for America on his own ship, the *Independent.* When he reached Philadelphia, he joined others in persuading Congress to create a Navy and he influenced the design of the famous frigates which were then built: the *United States,* the *Constitution,* and the *Constellation.*

In June 1798 Cathcart married a Philadelphia belle, and by December was enroute to the Barbary States where he held the highest positions in our consular service. Backed by our new naval power, he was able to negotiate important treaties at Algiers, Tunis, and Tripoli.

In 1800, the Cathcarts came to Georgetown when the capital was moved to the new Federal City. They moved to Madeira in 1807 where he had been assigned as Consul General; later to Cadiz, his youthful destination before capture by the pirates. The Cathcarts returned to Washington in 1817, where he continued to hold important offices until his death in 1843. His descendants treasure a note from Thomas Jefferson to the Senate, which reads in part, ". . . Cathcart, who was appointed by Mr. Adams and confirmed by the Senate as consul to Tripoli. He is personally known to me; he is the honestest [sic.] and ablest consul we have with the Barbary powers; a man of sound judgment and fearless. . . ."

The Virginia farm was bought by the son (named for his friend) Thomas Jefferson Cathcart, as a summer residence. His son, Arthur, courted the lass on the adjoining farm, and their marriage brought the Virgil Corbett and Cathcart estates into one family. They resided on the farm, in a series of homes including the Paden residence built in 1922.

John Adams President of the United States of America.

To all who shall see these Presents — Greeting.

Know Ye, That reposing special Trust and Confidence in the abilities and Integrity of James Leander Cathcart, a citizen of the United States, I have nominated and by and with the Advice and Consent of the Senate do appoint him Consul of the United States of America for the City and Kingdom of Tripoli, and do authorize and empower him to have and to hold the said Office according to Law, and to exercise and enjoy all the Rights, Pre eminences, Privileges and Authorities to the same of right appertaining during the Pleasure of the President of the United States for the time being. And I do hereby enjoin all Captains, Masters, and Commanders of Ships and other vessels armed or unarmed, sailing under the flag of the said United States as well as all other of their Citizens to acknowledge and consider him the said James Leander Cathcart accordingly: And I do hereby pray and request the most Illustrious the Bashaw, Lords and Governors of the City and Kingdom of Tripoli to permit the said James Leander Cathcart fully and peaceably to enjoy and exercise the said Office without giving or suffering to be given unto him any molestation or trouble, but on the contrary to afford him all proper countenance and assistance. In Testimony whereof I have caused these letters to be made patent and the Seal of the United States to be hereunto affixed. Given under my hand at the City of Philadelphia this Tenth day of July in the year of our Lord one thousand seven hundred and ninety seven, and of the Independence of the United States of America the Twenty second.

John Adams

By the President of the United States

Timothy Pickering   Secretary of State

"Alcova" and Jenks-Bailey Homestead

IN a setting of spacious lawns and stately trees is the gracious residence, Alcova, at 3435 8th Street, South. The former lane to Columbia Pike is now Lincoln Street, terminating at the present Alcova grounds. Mr. and Mrs. Douglass Wallop III are the current owners. Since they acquired it in 1950, they have added brick walks, a small formal garden, and a garage with parking lot enclosed by a wrought iron medallion fence. Both Mr. and Mrs. Wallop have achieved fame in the literary world. He is the author of *The Year the Yankees Lost the Pennant,* which was staged under the name of *Damn Yankee.* She wrote *Sorry, Wrong Number.* In the peaceful setting of Alcova, they both continue their writing careers.

How much of the original farmhouse remains incorporated within the nautilus-like present structure we do not know. The core may have been erected as early as 1836 when John M. Young, a pioneer wheelwright and carriage maker of Washington, acquired the farm from Thomas Hodges. His Virginia property was operated by a resident manager, and he used the farmhouse as a summer residence. The Civil War map shows the house with a mature orchard.

On June 1, 1875, John M. Young deeded the property to his son, William N. Young. At a ripe old age, wealthy William N. Young married Mamie Bailey, whose family's farm was just across Glebe Road. When he died, his widow married Thomas Gray. He had been her husband's farm superintendent. Upon becoming a widow again, she moved to Ballston to be nearer friends and the First Presbyterian Church, in which she was very active. When the church was renovated in 1931, Mamie Gray completely redecorated the sanctuary at her own expense and put in appropriate lighting fixtures throughout.

She sold the farm in 1915 to former State Senator Joseph Cloyd Byars of Bristol, Virginia. In 1923 Senator Byars made extensive improvements with the assistance of an able architect, Edward St. Cyr Barrington. Tall white pillars and a wrought-iron balcony were added to the east side, making the new entrance toward Glebe Road. Massive pillars flanked the new driveway entrance and also the original lane gateway on Columbia Pike. To these pillars were swung two handsome sets of wrought-iron gates formerly used at the U. S. Capitol grounds. What became of one pair of these gates is a mystery, but the other pair now graces the entrance to the home of Senator Byars' daughter at Blountville, Tennessee.

For the renovation of the farmhouse, handsome paneling, mantels, flooring, and shutters were brought from old Georgetown houses which were being demolished. The overseer's house to the west was turned on its foundation, and the carriage house attached as a rear wing. A mantel and staircase from the James G. Blaine house in Washington were added. The overseer's house is now the residence of the Carpenter family.

Senator Byars subdivided the farm into building sites and developed a residential area called "Alcova Heights", a contraction of Alexandria County, Va. This name was also given to the mansion house, which was sold in 1932 to Allen Coe.

While Senator Byars was completing his real estate transaction, the barn was temporarily turned into living quarters, and was later sold to Major General Paul W. Carroway. During the General's subsequent absence, vandals broke into the barn and it became the reputed "haunted house" of the neighborhood. To fire the imagination of the superstitious, old timers recalled that William N. Young had kept a supply of caskets stored in the barn. These, I have learned, were connected with one of his many charities. They were given to neighbors, many of whom had been greatly impoverished during the Civil War and were unable to buy them when needed. When the Carroways returned a few years ago, the barn was demolished and an attractive modern home erected on the site, their present residence.

Another pre-Civil War home, linked to the history of Alcova is the Jenks-Bailey house at 3219 7th Street, South, half a block east of Glebe Road. Great trees shade it, and giant boxwood attest to the age of its garden. The house is in a fine state of preservation and has remained in the same family for more than a century.

William Jenks of Lynn, Massachusetts, invented the breech-loading gun and came to this area in order to be near the patent office in clearing his patents. On December 10, 1850, he purchased 100 acres from Samuel D. King. This lay east of Glebe Road and north of Columbia Pike. While making plans for the construction of a home, the Jenks and their children lived in the neighborhood. During this period, their only daughter, Sarah Elizabeth, was courted and won by Harvey Bailey, a young man of local background. He was one of ten children (nine boys and one girl) of Lewis and Maria Bailey of "Bailey's X Roads" [sic.] He was born June 26, 1829. He and Sarah Elizabeth Jenks were married on November 8, 1853.

William and Elizabeth Jenks erected their home in 1854-1855. They developed a forty-four-acre berry and fruit farm. They resided here until his death in 1859 and hers in 1863.

The farm went to their daughter, Sarah Elizabeth Bailey. They moved to the house and lived there for the rest of their lives. He died first, and his widow and son, Francis Hood Bailey, continued to operate the farm until her death in September 1909.

Sarah Elizabeth Bailey deeded parcels of the farm to her older children, including Mamie, who married William N. Young. The remaining land and the house were deeded to her youngest son, Francis, who was born there January 8, 1873, and died December 1, 1952. He was the former husband of the present owner, Mrs. Emily G. Lapham of Denton, Maryland.

THE JENKS-BAILEY HOMESTEAD
. . . Built in 1854-55 by William Jenks,
an inventor from Massachusetts whose
daughter married Harvey Bailey of
Baileys Crossroads.

ALCOVA . . . The core of this home
may have been built as early as 1836
by John M. Young, a carriage maker
of Washington.

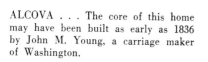

Ballston and Its Early Families

THE area around the intersection of Glebe Road and Wilson Boulevard is named Ballston. It is the site of the County's earliest hamlet, which was first called Birch's Crossroads and later, Ball's Crossroads. This was a part of the tremendous acreage which was acquired by Joseph and Janet Birch in the 1700's, as related on pages 148 and 150. That portion of their estate which included the crossroads and extending easterly through Lyon Park was inherited by the son, John Thornton Birch.

Another early resident of Ballston was Samuel Shreve (1750-1815), a Revolutionary officer from New Jersey who settled in Virginia in 1780. In 1791 he secured title to nearly 260 acres adjacent to the west boundary of the Birch tract, extending roughly from Lubber Run to Four Mile Run, and between Wilson and Washington Boulevards.

This tract was first owned by Colonel John Colville of Newcastle Upon Tyne, in England. By 1755 he had become a resident of Fairfax County and drew his will in May of that year. He bequeathed to "the present Earl of Tankerville", further described as "son of my Father's Brother's Daughter", among other tracts, the one later purchased by Samuel Shreve. John Colville's will was probated in Fairfax January 20, 1756, with Thomas Colville and the Earl of Tankerville as executors. The Earl himself drew a will on August 13, 1762, and devised the property to his eldest son, Charles, the "present Earl of Tankerville", and an interest to his second son, the Hon. Henry Astley Bennett. A deed was drawn October 1st, 1791 by "The Right Honourable Charles, Earl of Tankerville, and the Honourable Henry Astley Bennett, both of the Kingdom of Great Britain", confirming the title to the tract of land in Samuel Shreve, reciting as consideration 340 pounds, 11 shillings, 10 pence, half-penny.

Samuel Shreve's granddaughter Julia married William Randolph Birch (1816-1916), who enlisted when eighteen years old to fight the Indians in the Southwest. Both Samuel Shreve and William R. Birch are buried near their homesites, in the family graveyard between 829 and 839 North Abingdon Street. William Birch's son-in-law, George Washington Veitch, was a Lieutenant of the 6th Virginia Cavalry during the Civil War. His forebears are documented in the County records as early as 1805. Of these early families, there is not one original homestead still standing.

However, the gracious residence built in 1904 by Judge Harry Randolph Thomas at 920 North Jefferson Street is on land inherited by Mrs. Thomas. She was Julia Veitch, the daughter of George Washington Veitch, and directly descended from John Thornton Birch and Samuel Shreve. Judge Thomas recently retired as President of the Arlington Trust Company.

His great-grandfather, John Birch acquired the farm where the Iwo Jima Marine Memorial now stands, from the bankrupt Mason estate in the 1830's. This was the birthplace in 1877 of Judge Thomas. He recalls that when he was a boy and his grandfather was farming Analostan Island, he saw beautiful frescoes on the walls of the ruins of John Mason's mansion. Judge Thomas' paternal great-grandfather, Henry Lee Thomas of Forestville, Fairfax County, had moved to Capitol Hill as a federal employee.

In the early 1800's, one of the Ball family, probably a grandson of either John or Moses Ball, erected a two-story log inn, "Ball's Tavern" at the southwest corner of Birch's Crossroad which soon became known as Ball's Crossroads. The tavern was an important gathering place for the community. After recession to Virginia in 1846, it was used as a voting precinct. It later became a general store, and by 1896 a branch of the Georgetown Post Office was located therein. Across the road was Mortimer's Blacksmith Shop. Meanwhile, the settlement had become known as Ballston.

Nearer to the site of Clarendon, John Ball (1748-1814), son of the pioneer Moses Ball, erected a sturdy log house at the time of his marriage in 1773, and then went off to fight in the Revolutionary War. The house stood on the south side of Washington Boulevard until 1955. Directly across the boulevard, back of the present house numbered 3427, is the old Ball family burying ground. Ensign John Ball is buried there, and also his son, Horatio Ball (1785-1872). Horatio's son, William Ball (1842-1920) erected a home about 1890. It is behind the new American Legion Headquarters.

Among the children of William Ball who have had particular influence locally were E. Wade Ball, who died in 1954 and who had been County Treasurer for about twenty years; and Frank Livingston Ball, Senior. The latter, born October 4th, 1885, was Commonwealth's Attorney 1916-1924, State Senator 1924-1932, and served on the Constitution Convention 1946 and 1956. He was an active leader in Arlington County's civic and historical groups until his death April 29th, 1966.

The Central Methodist Church at the northwest corner of Fairfax Drive and North Stafford Street was erected close to the Robert Ball, Senior (1776-1861) family graveyard. Five stones are beside the east wall, and Stafford Street makes a slight curve in order to leave the graves undisturbed.

There is a Donaldson family burial ground on the south side of 1012 North Quincy Street. Beneath a lone tree are two stones. One is inscribed, "H. F. Thompson, Co. D, 3 Pa. Cavalry, born Feb. 22, 1843, died Jan. 16, 1864 at Warrenton, Va." The other is to Robert R. Skinner who died July 11, 1872 at the age of three months and three days. A number of burials are unmarked.

The John Mills family cemetery was on Glebe Road opposite Carlin Springs Road, in a grove of trees. It disappeared during construction (1949-1951) of the Parkington Shopping Center.

THE THOMAS GARDEN . . . The fine trees in the grounds of the home of Judge Harry Thomas at North Jefferson Street and 9th Road are older than the charming home which was built on land inherited by Mrs. Thomas.

Southern-Shreve Cemetery

IN a small well-kept family cemetery on the north side of Fairfax Drive, between North Frederick and North Harrison Streets, are gravestones which tell a story of sunshine and shadow in the lives of the Southern and Shreve families during the early 1800's. As I stood there under the oak trees, I thought of the daily lives of these people. Two of them were born near Newcastle, Durham County, England; the others, in Alexandria County, Virginia, in what their family records term "Georgetown", our present Arlington. Local mail came through the Georgetown Post Office of Washington; hence the name was used on our side of the river in those days.

The story begins with Richard Southern, born in 1795, and his wife, Mary Rutherford Southern, both natives of England. In 1820 they landed in Baltimore with their two-year-old daughter, Mary.

Richard Southern was a landscape architect and horticulturist. For two years he rented a farm on the outskirts of Baltimore. In the meantime, he met John Mason of Georgetown and Mason's Island. Impressed with Richard Southern's capabilities, John Mason leased the island with the servants and "farm hands" to him, which resulted in the beautiful gardens and splendid horticultural development of the fertile soil.

While there, Richard Southern became famous for his experimentation and propagation of the tomato, or "love apple" as it was first called. It had previously been used for decorative purposes only and had been considered poisonous. Southern was probably the first person in this area to place the tomato on the market as a food.

Little Mary Southern attended school in Georgetown, commuting each morning and evening by boat, rowed by a trusted servant. She attended Sunday school classes at Arlington Mansion, the home of their friends and neighbors, the Custis family.

It is hoped that the little English family enjoyed great happiness during their four years on the island paradise, for at the end of that time the young mother died. She was buried in a little graveyard on the Virginia shore. The exact site seems to have become lost in the network of parkways in recent years, but it was approximately across Ridge Road from the northeast corner of Arlington Cemetery.

The young widower, Richard Southern, married Frances Redin of Georgetown. From the land records, it appears that her brother, a prominent Georgetown attorney, presented a dowery of the Mulhall tract of land in Arlington, where the couple then made their home. The present location of their house site is in a wooded area north of Wilson Boulevard between North Greenbrier and Harrison, 8th and 9th Streets. The bride's brother purchased the tract, and that same day deeded it to Richard Southern. A factor of the brother's generosity may have been that the Southerns assumed the care of the elderly father, John Redin, who was buried in the garden of their home in 1832 at the age of eighty. His gravestone is the oldest and apparently was the first of many family burials, spanning at least five generations.

The Southerns were neighbors of the Shreves, Birches, and Balls, all living along the north side of the present Wilson Boulevard and west of Glebe Road. These families intermarried and produced many of Arlington's current civic leaders.

Mary Southern was successfully courted by William Henry Shreve, and on December 13, 1838, the twenty-year-old English girl married the twenty-six-year-old Virginian. For their home, William Shreve purchased Mt. Pleasant Plantation at Idylwood near Dunn Loring, north of Falls Church on the west side of the Leesburg Pike. He bought it from his mother's sister-in-law. He enlarged the house which was built in 1770. It remained in the Shreve family until 1904. It is still in a good state of preservation and is now owned by Mr. and Mrs. Lindeman.

Mary Southern Shreve's stepmother, Frances Redin Southern, died in 1874 followed by her father, Richard Southern, three years later. Their remains rest in the Southern-Shreve burying ground.

SOUTHERN-SHREVE CEMETERY
. . . Adjacent to Fairfax Drive at North Harrison Street, the first burial was in 1832.

THUNDERBOLT FROM HEAVEN
This stone records the tragic fate of a young minister and his wife.

The Shreves at "Mount Pleasant"

THE Lindsays, originally from Scotland, settled in the 1600's in Northumberland County, Virginia. Upon moving northward into this area, Colonel Robert Lindsay secured a 400-acre tract upon which he built "The Mount" in 1745.

In 1770 he built "Mount Pleasant" nearby, as a home for his son, Thomas. This home descended to Thomas Lindsay's daughter, Margaret, who married William Swink. His sister, Barbara Swink Shreve, was the mother of the William Henry Shreve who bought the place in 1838 as a home for his bride, Mary Southern (see previous chapter).

Located on an outstandingly beautiful site on the edge of a plateau facing southwest, Mt. Pleasant affords a sweeping view of a large portion of Fairfax County, with the Bull Run Mountains in the distance. It is surrounded by fine old trees. The boxwood was planted by the Shreves about 1838 and the lilacs before the Civil War.

The original house of 1770 had four rooms, two upstairs and two on the ground floor, with chimneys at each end. The kitchen and a spinning-room in a nearby log building with a massive central fireplace were destroyed some years ago.

When the Shreves bought Mt. Pleasant, they extended the original house to the west, almost doubling it in size. Later a rear wing was added for their growing family.

Life at Mt. Pleasant was marked by rich fulfillment shadowed by tragedy. Nine of the children grew to maturity, but four times infant bodies were brought back to rest in the family graveyard in Arlington. Headstones show that William died in 1845 at seven months, Eleanor in 1851 at six months, Isabella in 1853 at thirteen months, and Frances in 1854 at five months.

The Civil War subjected the family to new anxieties. The families of Northern Virginia were in a most unfortunate position. Whereas many opposed secession, their allegiance was strongly with their native State. Their homes were often in the path of military operations. Within weeks of the beginning of the conflict Federal encampments were scattered throughout the area.

Mt. Pleasant was particularly exposed, as the view from its plateau offered military observation of a vast area and the important Hampshire & Western Railway (later the Washington & Old Dominion) tracks crossed its lower meadow. Columbia Regiment Number 2 encamped in its fields. Captain and Mrs. O'Hagan spent much time at the Shreve home.

Two of the older Shreve sons joined the Confederate Army. The youngest, Benjamin R. Shreve was only fourteen when the conflict began, but he often served Colonel Mosby as a runner or messenger. Mosby's guerrillas frequently used Mt. Pleasant as a rendezvous, arriving by a circuitous route through the forest. The Shreve family lived under the fear that the opposing forces would meet at their home. In fact, Mosby arrived one night with the express purpose of taking Captain O'Hagan as a prisoner of war, but was dissuaded by William Henry Shreve because of the revenge which the Union authorities might inflict on his family and home.

Shreve had already been suspected of aiding the Confederates. On one occasion he was taken to the Alexandria prison for four or five days. Another time he was kept a week at the old Capitol prison in Washington, but was released after taking the oath of allegiance.

The next family tragedy concerned the oldest son, Richard Southern Shreve, a Methodist minister, and his wife, as recorded on their tombstone: "Richard Southern Shreve, 34 years & 8 months. Wife, Frances E. Shreve, 32 years & 3 months. Both killed by lightning June 25, 1874.

'Struck by a Thunderbolt from heaven,
They both lay down and died.
They left three lambs whom God had given,
May He for them provide.' "

William Henry Shreve died at Mt. Pleasant on June 29, 1890, two years after the couple had celebrated their golden wedding anniversary. The widow died in 1903, at which time the old home was sold. The bodies of both rest in the family plot in Arlington County.

The son who had served with Mosby married Anna K. Ball of Ballston. He died in 1949, within a fortnight of his 101st birthday.

The present patriarch of the Shreve family, Mr. Edgar Shreve, a charming gentleman who was born in 1882, lives at Dunn Loring. For thirty-six years he commuted to Washington daily. In 1944 he retired from his position as Administrative Assistant of Foreign Service Personnel.

MOUNT PLEASANT . . . Built in nearby Fairfax County in 1770, it became the home of the Shreves of Arlington County in 1838.

The Febrey Homesteads

NICHOLAS FEBREY was born on October 3rd, 1800, in Arlington County. He became a civic leader and one of the largest landholders of the area. He married first, Belinda Ball, who bore him three sons; she died in 1858. Two years later he married her cousin, Amanda Ball, by whom he had one son who died young. Both his wives were granddaughters of Moses Ball, who pioneered Glencarlyn with his patent of 1748.

Among the tracts which Nicholas Febrey acquired was a large portion of "Washington Forest" in the Glencarlyn area, purchased in 1837 from his friend G. W. P. Custis. Through other large purchases he acquired parts of the Adams property on Leesburg Pike near Munson Hill, Minor lands toward Minor Hill, and the present Willston Shopping Center site from the widow Rebecca A. Upton of Upton's Hill, also the land on both sides of Wilson Boulevard west of Four Mile Run. Among the friends who witnessed some of his deeds were Alexandria's mayor Edmund J. Lee, and the Maryland statesman, Tench Ringgold.

Nicholas Febrey's home was probably the Febrey house shown on the Civil War map on the north side of Wilson Boulevard on the hill just west of Four Mile Run. At the time of his second marriage in 1860, the family moved to the home his wife had inherited from her father, Robert Ball, at the site of Swanson Junior High School. He died in 1868 and is buried in the family plot in Oakwood Cemetery of Falls Church. Nicholas' three sons, upon their marriages, built homes which are now landmarks.

John E. Febrey, (1831-1893), married a cousin, Mary Frances Ball, in 1855 and built a home on the crest of the hill on the north side of Wilson Boulevard across from the Willston Apartment watertower. He was a very successful real estate dealer, and some time after the Civil War built a mansion nearby. He died in 1893. The property was then sold to Alvin Lothrop of the Woodward and Lothrop Company, and became known as the "Lothrop Estate". It is now the home of Randolph Rouse.

Moses Alexander Febrey brought his bride, Caroline, to a home (since destroyed) above Powhatan Springs. They leased the springs to the Harper Company, which bottled the fine water for sale throughout Washington and included the White House among its clientele.

In 1851, Henry Wand Febrey married Margaret Amelia Payne of the prominent Adams and Payne families of Fairfax County. They built a handsome farmhouse at what is now 2230 North Powhatan Street, two blocks south of Lee Highway. The lane which led to their gate became Powhatan Street, which ended at their property line until October 1957. Henry Febrey received the title of Captain from a commission in the 175th Regiment of the 2nd Division of Virginia Militia in 1849. He was a Justice of the Peace of Alexandria County, a trustee and steward of the Dulin Chapel M. E. South Church of Falls Church, and Superintendent of the Sunday School. Their eleven children and their first cousins married into the most prominent families of the area—the Talbott, Adams, Bailey, Wright, Shreve, Hughes, Schaaff, Walters, Payne, and Simmonds families. Among their descendants are many of our outstanding citizens.

Henry Febrey's home bears within its walls hidden scars of the Hall's Hill skirmish which occurred at the time of the "Battle of Munson Hill", which was the only notable engagement to take place within the boundaries of Arlington County, during the Civil War, although other scattered skirmishes occurred. One shot came through the dining room and sheared off the leg of a table set for dinner, without disturbing the meal thereon.

This home was acquired in 1919 by Albert Lee Paxton, who in 1926 completely renovated it, removing the appendages which had been added as the Febrey family grew. The entrance was reversed from the west to the east side, where a beautiful southern plantation type of veranda was added with two-story columns. The barn, which had been on that side, was taken down, and a lovely sweep of lawn gave the proper setting to the house, which was named "Maple Shade" for the stately grove of trees framing it. Its charm has been preserved by a series of appreciative owners, the Coxens, Colonel and Mrs. K. G. Hoge, and recently by Mr. and Mrs. Peter C. Logtens. Skyrocketing taxes on the five-acre lawn made it impractical to maintain the property for one residence, so it was sold for development in 1957. The lawns are now intersected by an extension of Powhatan Street, and a lateral of 22nd Road which destroyed the picturesque old stone spring house. Fortunately, the developer preserved the original house and as many of the fine trees as practicable.

Captain Henry Febrey's son, Ernest Jackson Febrey, built the house at 6060 Lee Highway which eventually became the Kincheloe family home where Mrs. Kincheloe later conducted the Crestwood Sanitarium. It is now the new Overlee Knolls Recreation Club with a fine swimming pool.

POWHATAN SPRINGS . . . Named for Chief Powhatan. Finding of many Indian artifacts nearby indicate use of area as an Indian camping ground. Water was commercially bottled for many years for wide distribution.

MAPLE SHADE . . . Built 1851 by Captain Henry W. Febrey of the Virginia Militia.

Clarendon's Early Days

CLARENDON lies along the edge of the disputed northwest boundary line of the Alexander purchase of 1669. The first record of anyone living in the vicinity is found in a lawsuit of Carlyle versus Alexander. A witness, John George Boucher, testified in 1767 that he lived in a house above Breckin's Branch, previously lived in by James Ball as a tenant of Major Robert Alexander who died in 1735. The recently culverted branch of Spout Run along Kirkwood Road appeared on early maps as Breckin's Branch, named for the Reverend James Breckin of Cople Parish, Westmoreland County who had patented 795 acres nearby. This stream eventually became known as Ball's Branch. It was not named for James Ball, whose tenancy seems to have been brief, but for descendants of his half-brother, Moses Ball, of Glencarlyn, who settled along its west bank in the late 1700's, as related on page 90.

A number of other early patents affected this area. Thomas Owsley's patent house may be the structure described on page 136. In 1709, William Struttfield received 500 acres adjacent to the Alexander tract.

The Carlyle versus Alexander suit disclosed some interesting testimony regarding two brothers, James and Thomas Going, who acquired large tracts in the early 1700's including 653 acres west of the mouth of Spout Run. They were reported to have been spending money lavishly about 1724 at the races, where they were running their own fine horses. This wealth was alleged to have been acquired by the sale of land which belonged to Major Alexander.

About 1850, William Douglas bought the south portion of the "Sisson Tract" including the site of Washington-Lee High School and campus. The Sisson home was on the north part of the estate, nearer Cherrydale, and is further discussed on page 110. William Douglas was a native of Scotland who had lived for a time in the Federal City. After his death, one son remained at the homestead and another built nearby. The only remaining early Douglas home was erected about 1900 by a grandson, "Will" W. Douglas (1861-1941). His son, Lawrence W. Douglas, formerly Commonwealth's Attorney for many years is currently the President of the Arlington Trust Company.

Annie Douglas, a daughter of the first William Douglas, married Lemuel Topley, a Union veteran. She inherited the northwest corner of her father's estate, upon which the Topleys built a home at 1700 North Randolph Street. It was inherited by Mrs. N. Nelson Parker, its present occupant.

On the present site of the Thomas Nelson Page School on the hill west of Kirkwood Road was the early Hayes home. It was built by Alonzo Hayes, a Congregational minister from Barnstable, Massachusetts. He purchased his farm in 1853 from William Ball and died six years later. His family remained in residence during the Civil War. Tents and barracks were scattered about the farm. One can still find traces of the gravel which the soldiers brought from the nearby stream to floor their tents and the stables.

Artillerymen of the nearby forts held target practice over this little valley until a faulty firing dropped a shell into the Hayes yard. It exploded and a fragment broke the leg of twelve-year-old Alonzo, Junior. The oldest existing Hayes house was built in 1893 by William Douglas Hayes and is now the Hayes Community Center at 1516 North Lincoln Street.

A fine old house at 1001 North Pollard Street causes both 10th and Pollard Streets to come to an end at its grounds. It was built in 1898 by Dr. Jonothan Richard Hagan and is the birthplace of his son, J. Foster Hagan, well-known attorney.

The village of Clarendon was named and dedicated March 31, 1900. Although the reason is obscure, this real-estate venture took the name of an English historian and statesman, the Earl of Clarendon (1609-1674). It originally included twenty-five acres on the north side of Wilson Boulevard, extending approximately to Key Boulevard. It was bounded on the west by Jackson Street a block beyond Clarendon Circle, and extended eastward to the center of the block between North Highland and Herndon Streets. This area was chosen as the site of one of the county's first planned communities mainly because of the availability of good transportation. It was at the point of convergence of the Georgetown-Falls Church Pike and the trolley line from Washington to Fairfax Court House. It was adjacent to the homes of prominent early families.

A booklet published in 1920 by the Clarendon Citizens' Association gives us an idea of the village at that time. "It now covers an area of one square mile, contains nearly six hundred homes and boasts of a population of approximately 2,500 . . . Clarendon is indeed a healthy place to live, the birth rate exceeding the death rate by more than double. . . .

"During the past two years the Citizens' Association has become the most aggressively progressive civic organization in the State, with a membership in excess of 350 men who are working together with the one idea of making Clarendon what it should and shall be —one of the most attractive spots within easy reach of the business sections of Washington.

"Under the forceful, stimulating influence of the Citizens' Association, the community has succeeded in purchasing the largest motor-driven chemical fire apparatus now operating in Arlington County . . . in securing house-to-house delivery of mail . . . and installing of water and sewer systems."

The three most important remaining early business buildings are Clarendon Elementary School (renamed Maury) erected 1910 at 3550 Wilson Boulevard, the Masonic Building on Wilson Boulevard at North Hudson Street, and the Telephone Building in 1907 on Washington Boulevard at Clarendon Circle.

Every spring, the beauty of blossoming fruit trees in the yards throughout this area remind us that many of the homes of Clarendon were built in the orchards of its first families.

TRACERY OF TREES . . . These trees are on the Young Men's Christian Association grounds adjacent to the Ball Family Cemetery.

THE HAGAN HOUSE . . . One of the few remaining 19th century homes of the Clarendon area. *1001 North Pollard Street.*

Falls Church

FALLS Church is a charming Virginia village on Lee Highway in Fairfax County just beyond the Arlington County line. In fact, part of it spills over the boundary, and is called East Falls Church. It has always been strictly residential, and even in the horse-and-buggy days, many people employed in Washington considered living in this peaceful environment worth the trouble and time of commuting. One's strongest impression of Falls Church is of its mellow homelike atmosphere. Comfortable looking red brick or white frame houses sit far back on spacious lawns upon which venerable trees paint ever-changing shadow patterns. The side streets are lined with giant maple trees which form cool green arches.

The history of the town centers about the Colonial edifice known as The Falls Church, which took its name from the Little Falls of the Potomac five miles distant, it being at the crossroads which led there. Before a church was erected, the first services of Truro Parish were held at the house of William Gunnell on the upper waters of Four Mile Run, within the present limits of the town.

The first church was built in 1733, and was known as the Upper Church (of the parish; the lower being at Pohick). It was a wooden structure. Richard Blackburn of Rippon Lodge (just south of Occoquan Bay), noted in the records as "a builder of skill" who had designed the original Mount Vernon, contracted the job for 33,500 pounds of tobacco.

An addition to the old church was undertaken in 1750. In 1763, the vestrymen finding it "rotten and unfit for repairs", resolved to build a brick church at the same place. The construction and subsequent history of The Falls Church may be found on page 174.

The two early roads which intersected at the point whereon the church was erected were from Hunting Creek and Alexandria, the other from the ferry below Little Falls. In Colonial times, the "Great Road" which passed this way connected Tidewater Virginia with the western frontier of the colony. It followed an Indian trail which had been used by the troublesome Susquehannock Indians who frequented the area.

In 1675 the Susquehannock War suppressed the Indian menace and opened much territory for settlers in the Falls Church area and other parts of Northern Virginia. During the French and Indian War, a portion of General Braddock's ill-fated expeditionary force camped in the shadow of The Falls Church. During the Revolutionary War, Colonel Charles Broadwater, one of Fairfax County's first patriots, had a recruiting headquarters in the church. From the church, Captain Henry Fairfax led a command of Fairfax volunteers to Mexico during the Mexican War.

Civil War skirmishes were fought around its walls. Both Confederate General Longstreet and Union General McClellan used it at different times as their headquarters. At one time, it was used as a military hospital. Later, Union cavalry officers stabled their horses in it, knocking out the bricks under each window for readier access.

At the south end of the town at the present convergence of Arlington Boulevard, Wilson Boulevard, Sleepy Hollow Road, and the Leesburg Pike is the present "7 Corners" shopping center, with forty specialty shops and branches of Washington's department stores. It is on the site of Fort Buffalo which was constructed during the Civil War on the defense perimeter of Washington.

Within the town, some frame houses built in the 1700's still stand. The Big Chimney House, erected in 1699 was destroyed some years ago. The chimneys on each end were eighteen feet in width. The building was made of logs held together with wooden pegs two feet long, and split at the ends. In 1720, Nelson's Inn was opened. Old Star Tavern, built in 1850 was a famous rendezvous for weary stagecoach travelers. It occupied the northwest corner of Broad and Washington Streets.

In 1702 the settlement had a private school with bars at the windows to protect the children from stray bands of Indians. The first public school, Jefferson Institute, was built in 1875. It was supported by public subscription and operated most successfully for many years. The brick building was torn down in 1958.

Three blocks west of Lee Highway on the side of Leesburg Pike as it passes through Falls Church, is a beautiful oak called Hangman's Tree. The legend of Mosby's having hung Union spies from it is apparently without fact.

On Lee Highway one mile west of Falls Church is the National Memorial Park, a beautifully landscaped cemetery without tombstones. A series of pools and fountains is the setting for the group of statuary by Carl Milles symbolizing various aspects of immortality. This is America's greatest display of the work of this world-famous Swedish sculptor.

CAMP ALGER PICKET AND SUPPLY DE-
POT . . . Established during the Spanish-American War in East Falls Church for the camp
west of the village.

THE FALLS CHURCH . . . From
which the village took its name.

FOUR MILE RUN . . . Scene at the turn of the
century, showing the stream at the Arlington
County line on present Lee Highway.

Cruit Farm and "Cedar Lane"

PERHAPS you've passed the charming old home at 1614 North Highland Street without seeing it, for hemlocks and magnolias hide its white columns. Mrs. John M. Waggaman, its present owner, helped me to discover its history through her correspondence with Miss Nina C. Mackall of Bethlehem, Pennsylvania, whose family owned it for generations.

The Virginia house was built by Miss Mackall's great-grandfather, Robert Cruit, who was born in 1795 in Washington and lived on F Street across from the Willard Hotel, in the home which became Ballantyne's Book Shop through 1956. The Cruits were the last residents of that section which is now completely commercial. They at one time owned the entire block.

Miss Mackall's mother was the granddaughter of Robert Cruit. She was a posthumous child born in 1848 and was brought up by the grandparents. She was her grandfather's constant companion on his trips to the Virginia farm, which he had purchased in 1825 as a pleasant place for his family to spend weekends and holidays. He also wished to indulge his hobby of raising thoroughbred horses and developing a fine dairy herd. He was the first person in the United States to import Jersey cows. These were tended by German employees whom he considered the most efficient farmers.

The interior framing of the Highland Street house is of sturdy hand-adzed timbers. It was used as a hospital during the Civil War. After the conflict, the Cruits found Confederate money cached in the attic. The beautiful trees bore the initials of convalescent soldiers. Mrs. Waggaman has a spur bearing the imprint of the Allegheny Arsenal. It was dug up in her garden about 1954.

Miss Mackall wrote, "The attic which covered the entire building was unfinished, but was really a treasure-trove of many lovely pieces of furniture. . . . On rainy days, we used it for scouting into trunks. . . . It has many, many happy memories for me . . . and for everyone connected with my family." Her mother when about five years old buried a gold piece in the yard, hoping to raise a gold tree as predicted in a fable. Has anyone in the neighborhood dug up this treasure?

The house with its large acreage included all of what is now Lyon Village, and was not sold until 1923 following the death of Miss Mackall's mother, who had kept it because of family associations. The purchaser, Frank Lyon, completed the second floor and added the columned portico. Until about 1930, water was piped and pumped from a picturesque old stone springhouse down the hill beneath two huge oak trees. Although the oaks were saved, the springhouse was destroyed and the spring capped about 1952 when a house was erected on the site, at 1700 North Highland Street.

Back of the Cruit home was a fine orchard, shown on the 1864 map with a lane beside it. Now, on the site of the orchard, at 1912 North Harvard Street, is "Cedar Lane", a house of authentic Colonial architecture, with a steep-pitched gambrel (hip) roof which was popular in Williamsburg in the early 1700's. The bricks are laid in Flemish bond; glazed header-bricks alternating endwise with lengthwise bricks. In the garden are six gnarled cedar trees which were on the fence line between the orchard and the lane. They run diagonally to the present property line, as the old lane was ignored when the streets were laid out. Cedar trees along the fence-rows of Virginia farms are gifts of the mockingbirds whose favorite berries are cedar, and whose frequent perches are fences.

Cedar Lane was built in 1936 by Arthur J. Porter for his son, Captain Carl W. Porter, who later sold it to the present owners, Mr. and Mrs. J. D. Jameson. During their travels, Mr. and Mrs. Porter brought back to Arlington parts of beautiful old homes which were being demolished. Their architect, Delos Smith, worked with them to adjust wall and window spaces to accommodate these treasures. The result is a harmonious blending of many fine homes.

Both the house and garden wall are of handmade bricks which were left over from the restoration of historic St. Mary's Court House in Maryland. The wrought-iron front fence is from Beaufort, South Carolina. There it had stood before a home which had burned down many years ago. The metal railings and stone steps of the porches are from an old house which stood on the site of George Washington University.

The hand-carved American-Adam style mantels, wainscot, and paneling are from a Charleston house. On the back of a piece of chair rail is the following inscription—"John L. Pizant, his home. Built by Mr. Henry, carpenter from Charleston, South Carolina." The living room and dining room mantels have fan medallions, one symbolizing sunrise and the other sunset. The metal fireplace linings which came from a Georgetown house bear fan designs which amazingly match the ones from Charleston. The stairway, balusters, rails, and newel posts are from a Georgetown house which was converted into a store on M Street near 32nd. Old oak boards found near Frederick, Maryland, were used for flooring.

The house is beautifully furnished with heirlooms from both Mr. and Mrs. Jameson's families of Roanoke and Richmond. The mellow charm of this home should inspire others to re-use the fine craftsmanship of parts of old houses which are being demolished.

The Cruit home and Cedar Lane are but two of the lovely homes of Lyon Village, a residential community developed by the late Frank Lyon. He came into the county in 1889, and edited the *Monitor* which played an important part in the crusade to eliminate gangsters and gambling interests from the river-front in 1904.

CEDAR LANE . . . Named for the trees in the rear garden, which formerly bordered the lane along the Cruit orchard.

ROBERT CRUIT'S FARMHOUSE . . . The Cruit farm is now Lyon Village.

Fort Strong Villa

FORT STRONG VILLA bears the address of 2627 Lee Highway, but this handsome house approached by an avenue of trees is set far back from the street. It is one of the largest private homes ever erected in the county. It was built in 1888 by John Walter Clark, on the site of an earlier log house built before the Civil War by the Veitch family or their predecessors.

The early land records trace the ownership of the site to W. G. Cazenove, a prominent Alexandrian who probably purchased the acreage from the Mason estate as an investment. In 1849 he sold it to Samuel Stott, who in turn sold it to Allen Pearce four years later. In August of 1860 W. C. Veitch and his wife, Sarah, purchased the property, and the map shows them as residing there during the War. On November 28, 1888, the tract was purchased by John Walter Clark, a wealthy Washingtonian whose family had originally come from New Jersey. The home of Clark's father still stands at the northwest corner of 17th Street and New York Avenue and is now The Allies' Inn, one of the famous eating places of the National Capital.

When Allen Pearce sold the property to the Veitch family in 1860, he retained one acre on the west side for his daughter Mary and her husband Antone C. Mertens. They built a home and resided there until they sold it to John Clark in 1897. On the property line between these two tracts a "common well" is shown on the old plat. The daughter of John Clark, Marie Clark Bell who resides on the site of the old Mertens home tells me that the well still exists and was used until it was capped a few years ago.

John Clark tore down the log house on his Virginia property and erected the handsome twenty-one-room residence designed by his father. He did a great deal of lavish entertaining. Food was brought to the banquets by way of a dumb-waiter from the basement kitchen. A large retinue of servants lived in a house which is now 2001 North Cleveland Street.

Mr. Clark was bothered by the condition of the "Georgetown and Fairfax Turnpike" (Lee Highway) over which lay his route to the city; it was alternately a sea of red mud or dust. Therefore, he had it surfaced from Rosslyn to his door with crushed oyster shells. His fine carriage drawn by a high-spirited pacing roan mare was a sight which is still remembered by the old-timers.

Clark owned and operated "The White House" in Rosslyn, one of the most elaborate of the gambling establishments. I have in hand a booklet published by Crandal Mackey in 1912 when seeking re-election as Commonwealth's Attorney. It contains pictures and descriptions of fourteen of the saloons and gambling dens closed under his leadership in 1904. Among them was, "the old White House . . . the only place where liquor was not sold on Sunday in Rosslyn. Above the bar room was a gambling room elaborately furnished, with all kinds of gambling paraphernalia and electric lights. It was raided by citizens and the . . . apparatus confiscated. Before the proprietor could be taken before a Justice of the Peace selected by the citizens, he was hurried before one agreeable to the proprietor, and a small fine imposed, so that a plea of former conviction would bar any subsequent prosecution. . . ." The site is now occupied by the Griffith Consumer Company.

A perusal of the County records shows that Mr. Clark was frequently approached for business loans. Most business in Rosslyn involved gambling, and a series of foreclosures eventually brought a great deal of Rosslyn property into Mr. Clark's hands. He foreclosed on Thomas Marmaduke on June 14, 1894, whose place was among those described in the Mackey booklet thus—"This was the old Marmaduke Place in Rosslyn. It flourished under different proprietors as a Sunday bar and gambling place."

John Walter Clark died in 1914. His widow, the former Julia M. Savage of Maine, sold the house and grounds in 1921 to Everlina Burlasque, the mother of the present owner, Mrs. Maude C. Heys, to whom it was deeded in 1923. For many years she took a select clientele of boarders who wished to escape the heat of the Washington summers. Among these were officials of the diplomatic service. Mrs. Heys eventually converted the interior into six apartments, retaining one for herself.

The name "Fort Strong Villa" is a bit confusing, as there was another mansion at 2013 North Adams Street, erected during the same period which had fragments of the Fort Strong earthworks in its gardens. This was "Ruthcomb Hall", lated named "Altha Hall", described in the following chapter. However, there were probably outlying earthworks of the Fort which extended across the Villa grounds.

FORT STRONG VILLA . . . Named for a Civil War Fort which was some blocks distant.

"Ruthcomb" Renamed "Altha Hall"

TWO blocks north of Lee Highway at 2013 North Adams Street stood Arlington's finest example of Southern Greek-revival architecture.

The mansion was built by Andrew Adgate Lipscomb II of Fairfax (born 1854), who became Assistant District Attorney of the District of Columbia during Cleveland's administration. Colonel Lipscomb lost his first wife, Grace Harmon, when their children were young. Later he married Lamar Rutherford of Athens, Georgia, and in 1886 started construction in Arlington of a mansion patterned after one admired by his bride in her home state. His own great-grandfather, for whom he was named, had been the first chancellor of the University of Georgia. The finest of Georgia pine was especially milled for the panelling and for the forty-foot pillars which were shipped to Washington by rail. Throngs lined Pennsylvania Avenue to see them hauled by horse and wagon to the house site. Hardware for the massive front doors came from a castle in England. Fine Italian marble for the fireplaces and crystal chandeliers were brought from Europe.

The Lipscombs moved into their completed home early in 1889. They named it "Ruthcomb" as a composite of their names, Rutherford and Lipscomb. There they entertained great statesmen with gracious southern hospitality. As related by a grandson, Captain Steuart A. Reiss:

"My grandfather was a criminal lawyer whose courtroom brilliance and remarkable legal mind caused him to be exceptionally well known. A genial host despite a sarcastic streak which was ever near the surface, he entertained frequently and on a lavish scale.

"His leather-bound visitor's book has proven a treasure-trove for bringing back those storied guests from long ago. When I looked at their signatures they seemed to come alive again and walk toward me from the pages.

"There was Senator Daniel W. Voorhees of Indiana, for thirty years a member of the House and Senate, noted for magnificent oratory.

"There, too, was Senator John Sherman of Ohio, brother of William Tecumseh, Grant's right hand. Also Henry W. Blair of the Blair family so prominent in the wartime cabinet.

"And there was Leland Stanford, the philanthropist and Senator from California who had a university named after him. And Senator Bill Teller of Colorado, the mining king of the West who built the Teller House in famed Central City, the 'richest square mile on earth.'

"With all the nostalgia of yesteryear one can see the signature of Senator George G. Vest of Missouri whose courtroom eulogy to a dog brought him world renown. Growing older, and with a tendency to shake, stretches the signature of North Carolina's wartime Governor Zebulon B. Vance, around whose sturdy and imposing frame people gathered as he led them through the evils of reconstruction.

"Also entered is the name of George Hearst, Senator from California and father of the late William Randolph Hearst. And the proud General Wade Hampton of South Carolina, one of the South's finest fighters. A man of extreme wealth and culture, a great hunter who killed upwards of eighty black bears with hunting knife alone, the South Carolinians rallied to him to stem the odious invasion of the carpet-baggers.

"And one can sense the quiet dignity of Lucius Quintus C. Lamar, who left the shaded walks of his college retreat to fight again for his native Georgia during the horror of postwar days. Sent to the Senate by a grateful people and later named to the Supreme Court, he was a frequent visitor to 'Ruthcomb,' being a cousin of Mrs. Lipscomb.

"And there, in the midst of all the names, the record shows the entire Supreme Court came to dinner on April 29, 1890.

"Men of another age, men of history, men who understood and brought resurrection to a South bitter in defeat, wined, dined and talked politics in the grand old house that will now go down to rubble before the modern titans."

After the death of Colonel Lipscomb, the property was sold in 1905 to Mr. and Mrs. Thaddeus Mathew Tyssowski of Washington; she was the former Alice Walton Green of Lewinsville, Virginia. Following the precedent of the original owners, the new owners renamed the home for a combination of their names, Alice and Thaddeus, and so it became "Altha Hall".

Thaddeus Tyssowski, a successful merchant and insurance company executive, erected the Home Life Building at 15th and G Streets, the first modern steel construction office building in Washington. His son, Colonel John Tyssowski, married Catherine Woodward. He is now Chairman of the Board of Directors of Woodward & Lothrop, and commutes from his estate at Delaplane, Virginia.

About 1921, the Tyssowski family sold Altha Hall to Dr. W. S. Benedict, who resided there for about fourteen years before moving to a country home near Sterling, Virginia. For a number of years he leased Altha Hall to Miss Anna Payne, who conducted a nursery school and kindergarten there. It was sold in February 1957 to a group of real estate investors as a potential apartment house site, having been rezoned from residential. In the meantime, it was the home of the Lance family who loved the old mansion and remained there until its destruction. Although I have no personal associations with Altha Hall, I feel a pang of loss to Arlington County for this symbol of a time when homes were spacious and life was gracious.

The remnants of Fort Strong were within the grounds, but their position made it impossible for them to be preserved in the landscaping plans for "Potomac Towers". However, Mr. Preston C. Caruthers, the developer of the property, has given special consideration to preservation of the splendid evergreen trees, an example which we hope will be followed by other builders.

PORTALS OF THE PAST . . . The hardware for these doors came from a castle in England.

RUTHCOMB HALL . . . This lovely mansion falls to the name of progress as an apartment house is erected upon the site in 1959. In recent years, it has been known by its second name, Altha Hall.

Cherrydale Named for an Orchard

CHERRYDALE was not settled until after the Civil War; the map of 1864 shows not even a single house on the site. The nearest homes formed an arc beginning west of present Kirkwood Road at 15th Street, swinging up to what is now Lee Highway at Woodstock Street. The Hayes house was built about 1853 above Spout Run. The site is between Cherrydale and Clarendon. The next house was just behind 1721 North Quincy Street, and belonged to the Sisson family. Two more houses were on the hill west of Cherrydale: the Harrisons' at the southeast corner of Lee Highway and Woodstock Street and the Osburn house to the south at about 20th and Woodstock; neither house remains. The map also shows a ruin marked "Paine" at about 20th and Upton Streets.

In those days a lane led from Cherrydale's future site to the Harrisons' house, but one could not go on past to Glebe Road, but had to go around by way of Quincy Street, which swung west intersecting a road, now about 19th Street, to Glebe. Another road swung southwest from Marceytown on 26th Street and followed parts of Randoph, Upton, and Woodstock intersecting Glebe Road south of the present intersection at Lee Highway. Mr. Wunder had a fine farm that ran back from Glebe Road to the north. When the road was finally cut directly through to Cherrydale from Hall's Hill, the intersection became known as "Wunder's X-Roads".

Apparently the first mid-Cherrydale settler was Dorsey Donaldson, who built his home just back of the present fire-house. It is still standing. He planted a large cherry orchard on his farm. His son-in-law, Robert Shreve, also planted "carnation cherries" along Quincy Street. Hence, Quincy Street's first name was "Cherry Valley Road". When Mr. Donaldson requested a branch post office at Shreve's Store at the northeast corner of Pollard Street and Lee Highway he was asked to suggest a name. The appropriate reply was "Cherrydale". Little remains now of the glory of spring blossoms, but the Women's Club of Cherrydale is sponsoring a series of drives to beautify the area again by replanting cherry trees in private yards, at the schools, and perhaps along the streets, with the cooperation of other civic groups. In 1958, the State Highway Department cooperated in setting out fifty trees along Spout Run between Lorcom Lane and Lee Highway.

What really put Cherrydale on the map was the Great Falls and Old Dominion Railway, which ran from Rosslyn through the center of the village along what is now Old Dominion Drive. Mrs. Hendree Payne Simpson, who lives at 2325 North Glebe Road, has told me many interesting things about this trolley line. Her husband gave a strip of land thirty-two feet wide and 307 feet long for the right-of-way. She recalls that it was on February 17, 1906, that the first trolley car made a successful pre-schedule "sneak" trial run to Great Falls. The scheduled *official* opening of the trolley line was March 8, but a blizzard made that celebration an anticlimax. The railway was abandoned in

1935 and its roadbed became Old Dominion Drive. However, the trackage between Rosslyn and former Thrifton Junction near Lee Highway at North Edgewood Street remains in use as it has been since 1912 for a combined freight-passenger line; the latter service was discontinued in 1951.

The first fire engine in our county was a hand-propelled affair kept in a shed behind the Cherrydale School. One of the first Boy Scout Troops, No 149, was organized in Cherrydale in 1917 by H. O. Clower, only seven years after the national organization was formed. In 1957 the Troop celebrated its fortieth anniversary in the present Fire Hall, with the organizer as guest of honor.

Cherrydale has its place in the baseball hall of fame. Mike Martin, trainer of the Washington Senators, lived in the "Shreve House", built about 1889 on Pollard Street a block north of the Highway, and Eddie Foster lived at 1920 North Nelson Street.

Entertainment sites recalled by early Cherrydale residents were the Alexandria Recreation Center in the old icehouse which stood on Lincoln Street just north of Lee Highway. Of course the name indicated its use prior to this County's being renamed Arlington. The Pottertons ran the County's first movie house, "Pioneer Hall", at 4018 Lee Highway.

The Cherrydale School is one of the oldest school buildings still in use. It was built in 1917. In the schoolyard is a bronze plaque mounted on a stone. The inscription reads: "Erected in honor of the boys of Cherrydale, Virginia, who gave their lives in the World War:—Lt. John Lyon, U.S.A.; Lt. Irving T. C. Newman, Aviator; Fred W. Schutt, U.S.A.; and Dr. Harry Vermillion, U.S.A. Francis Wallis Chapter, D.A.R., 1925."

Two blocks north of Lee Highway, at the southeast corner of Military Road and Lorcom Lane, is the site of the old Van Dorn House. It was built about 1890 and torn down in 1953. In excavating for its foundations, six bodies were exhumed; buttons identified them as Civil War soldiers, probably casualties from one of the nearby Union hospitals. The Marcey family gave permission for the remains to be buried in their private cemetery. A beautiful new Cherrydale Baptist Church now occupies this corner.

In the center of the block northeast of the Lorcom Lane-Military Road intersection is the T. Curtis Hudson home, built about 1907. Until about 1956, it had a boxwood lane leading to Military Road. With the recent cutting of Nellie Custis Drive near its north side, the house turned its face to the new thoroughfare and has acquired the added dignity of white columns as it faces the street named in honor of the mistress of Woodlawn Plantation and sister of the builder of Arlington House. The pasture which sloped away from the east of the house was called "Terrell's Hill" for the colored family of that name who grazed their cows there. It was the favorite sledding spot of the Cherrydale youngsters in bygone days.

CHERRYDALE . . . Picture made about 1906.

CHERRYDALE'S OLDEST HOUSE . . . The home of Dorsey Donaldson whose cherry trees gave the village its name. Beneath the exterior covering are log walls. This house will be destroyed during 1959 as part of a motel site.

"Ellenwood" and "Lorcom Farm"

"ELLENWOOD", the pillared cement house set in a grove far back from the street at 1906 North Randolph Street, was designed by and built under the personal supervision of a young woman. Ellen Isham Schutt was born on April 15, 1873, at "Oak Grove" nearby, the youngest of seven children of Francis Granger Schutt Sr., of a prominent Hudson River Dutch family. In 1862 he had married Elizabeth Thomas Wallis of Kent County, Maryland, of colonial Dutch, English, Welsh, and French Huguenot ancestry. In 1865 they purchased Oak Grove, which was set far back from Quincy Street at 22nd, in its estate of seventy-nine acres. It had belonged to the Sisson family, and there is a legend that John Brown visited this house just before his departure for Harper's Ferry in October, 1859. The Schutts filled the fourteen-room house with heirlooms. They entertained a great deal. Musicales were held, with Mr. Schutt playing the guitar and Mrs. Schutt singing in her rich contralto voice. Quadrilles were danced in the long dining room while a fiddler called the figures.

Parties were planned for moonlight nights to compensate for the absence of street or road lights and the inadequacy or absence of headlamps on buggies and wagons.

Early one November morning in 1900, the family awoke to the glare of flames and barely escaped from the house before it became an inferno, destroying all their treasured heirlooms. They immediately rebuilt, this time closer to Cherry Valley Road, on a gentle knoll surrounded by white oaks. The house has fine, simple lines relieved by a Monterey type of veranda on both first and second floors, festooned by a giant wisteria vine.

Meanwhile, Cherrydale was growing like a mushroom. Mr. Schutt, in a letter of September 18, 1905, to a cousin in Colorado, enclosed a very interesting map he had drawn of the area around Cherrydale. This map, now in the possession of his descendants, bears many informative notations. It shows the trolley line through Clarendon and Ballston with the names of eight stations. It also shows the Old Dominion Electric Railroad which was being constructed through Cherrydale enroute to Great Falls. At the crest of the rise west of Cherrydale is a notation: " 'Lookout Heights'. 400 feet elevation. Magnificent view of city of Washington." Another notation states: "Building up about us reminds me of Western towns fifty years ago."

The terror of fire remained vividly in the mind of twenty-seven-year-old Ellen Schutt, and she determined to build a completely fireproof house of cement blocks, to design the structure and manufacture the materials. To finance it, she secured a position as a scientific illustrator in the United States Department of Agriculture, where she worked from 1907 to 1917. Her illustrations of grasses and fruits were so outstanding that she was sent to the University of California to prepare material for class instruction.

Ellen Schutt secured bulletins on the manufacture of cement blocks, determined the best formula for her purposes, built the molds, and employed inexperienced labor to make them on the site. Under careful supervision, the house progressed, as "sound as the Rock of Gibraltar." Even the staircases and floors are of concrete, which established a precedent for home construction. The front exterior has four 18-foot columns. On the portico are four handsome marble urns which had been made for the Centennial Exposition in Philadelphia in 1876 and then were exhibited in the grounds of the Department of Agriculture. They were finally discarded and Ella Schutt bought them "for a song" from a junk dealer.

The house was started about 1907 and completed early in 1909. Ellen brought her parents with her to the new home. Three years later electricity was installed (among the first in our County), and the home was brilliantly illuminated throughout for the celebration of the golden wedding anniversary of her parents. In 1917 Ellen married her cousin, Thomas Smythe Wallis of Kent County, Maryland. He had been a frequent visitor and had assisted his cousin in building the home.

In 1921, Ellen Schutt Wallis organized the first Arlington County chapter of the Daughters of the American Revolution. She dedicated it to the memory of her mother, naming it for the mutual ancestor of herself and her husband, Lt. Francis Wallis, who had served three years during the Revolution despite his Quaker parentage. Mrs. Wallis was appointed Virginia State Chairman of the Memorial Bell Tower at Valley Forge. Her chapter erected the plaque in the grounds of the Cherrydale School, in memory of the local men who gave their lives in World War I.

Ellen Schutt-Wallis died on December 3, 1955, but both Ellenwood and the second Oak Grove at 1721 North Quincy Street remain in family possession.

On the other side of Cherrydale, we find a handsome home built in 1907 by Dr. Joseph Taber Johnson, a surgeon of note. It is on the crest of the hill just above the present St. Andrews Church. The most unusual architectural feature of the house is the chimney, which makes a spiral turn in the attic so that it emerges from the roof at a reverse angle from its interior structure. It was probably copied from "Bellevue's" chimney, shown on page 133. Dr. Johnson named his residence "Lorcom Farm", a combination-contraction of the names of his sons, Loren and Bascom. Hence the name of Lorcom Lane, an important lateral of the Spout Run branch of the George Washington Memorial Parkway, which passes the house.

Dr. Johnson also built homes nearby for his sons. One later became the summer retreat of the Washington Young Women's Christian Association. It was demolished to prepare the site for Stratford Junior High School, but Vacation Lane perpetuates the memory of happy holidays.

Chain Bridge Environs

FORT ETHAN ALLEN occupied a strong position at what is now the intersection of North Glebe and Military Roads. It was named for the commander of the Green Mountain Boys of the Revolution. The first work on Fort Ethan Allen was done by the 33rd New York Artillery, but other commands aided in completing it. It had a perimeter of 756 feet, was fully equipped with magazines and bombproofs, and had a powerful armament. Constructed in conjunction with Fort Marcy for the protection of Chain Bridge, it was of utmost importance for the operation of the Union Army in Virginia.

Fort Marcy was constructed on the crest of Prospect Hill just past the Fairfax County line about a mile from Chain Bridge on the Leesburg-Georgetown Turnpike. On the night of September 24, 1861, the troops crossed the bridge and immediately commenced construction of both these forts which were completed as speedily as possible. These works were connected with auxiliary batteries and lines of rifle trenches which also extended to the river and afforded full view and defense of the numerous ravines of the area. All trees were cut low enough for visibility, but were left with stumps too high for artillery to clear.

Fort Marcy was built under the direction of General William Farrar Smith. The men of his division first called it Fort Baldy Smith, until it was officially named Fort Marcy by Army General Order Number 18, 1861, in honor of General Randolph Barnes Marcy, a native of Massachusetts. He was a distinguished soldier and Chief of Staff of General George B. McClellan. His daughter was General McClellan's wife.

Locally, it has been erroneously assumed that this fort was named for the pioneer Marcey family of Arlington County; I had thought so. However, it is possible that when it was decided by General McClellan to honor his father-in-law, the proximity of the Marcey family homesteads may have been a factor in the choice of a fort to bear the name of Marcy though with a difference in spelling.

The perimeter of Fort Marcy is 338 feet. It is 275.4 feet above the mean low tide of the Potomac River. When completed, the fort mounted eighteen guns, a ten-inch mortar, and two twenty-four-pound Coehorn mortars. On October 23, 1865, after hostilities had ceased, Fort Marcy was transferred to the owner of the land, Gilbert Vanderwerken, who eventually sold it to the DeLashmutt family, from whom the Government recently acquired it. It is in an excellent state of preservation, the best in this area, but at present debris and brush prevent one from being able to satisfactorily examine the earthworks. It is to be restored and maintained by the National Park Service as a historic site along the George Washington Memorial Parkway.

The early road to Pimmit Run Bridge led from Walker Chapel down the west flank of the hill through the side of a little valley. This area became quite isolated after the Civil War when the route was abandoned in favor of the newer route down Chain Bridge Hill. This is where the gypsies used to camp. Here also was the log cabin of the strange old white woman who used to raise goats and tell fortunes. It is said that she was a distant relative of Clara Barton, founder of the American Red Cross, who provided for her.

On the east side of the little valley are traces of an early colored settlement and a cemetery This previously hidden valley will soon be viewed by many people for the first time, as the new segment of the Parkway traverses it.

In the early 1880's High View Hotel was erected on the crag above Chain Bridge on Civil War earthworks which were the outposts of nearby Fort Marcy and Fort Ethan Allen.

High View Hotel became a noted resort during our County's infamous period of gambling. It probably catered to a more affluent Washington clientele than did its Rosslyn and Jackson City neighbors down the river, but it shared the same fate when the county was "cleaned up" shortly after the turn of the century. The hotel was abandoned, and later burned.

This beautiful site on the Potomac Palisades had been considered by President Wilson for a home, but his declining health forestalled his wish. During World War I, Assistant Secretary of the Navy Franklin Roosevelt and his friends favored it for their oyster roasts.

The property was purchased about 1924 by William N. Doak, President Hoover's Secretary of Labor. He was born in 1883 near Wytheville in the Blue Ridge Mountains at "Rural Retreat", on the family's colonial land grant. Mrs. Doak designed their home to take full advantage of the magnificent view. Banks of windows and terraces overlook Little Falls and the chasm of the Potomac, down to the expanse of water at Georgetown. They named it "Notre Nid" (Pronounced Notra Need), which is French for "Our Nest". It was truly a haven for this couple until the end of their days. His was reached in 1933 at the age of fifty and hers in 1951. Their remains rest in a mausoleum in a churchyard near his birthplace.

The Doak's threshold was crossed by many national figures, including President Hoover and members of his Cabinet. President Roosevelt came to Notre Nid to view the flood of 1936 which flowed through the superstructure of Chain Bridge. The *National Geographic Magazine* for July 1945 illustrated its article "Potomac, River of Destiny" with a full color photograph of Notre Nid's wisteria-festooned terraces. A residential area on upper Military Road developed in 1934 by Secretary Doak's nephew perpetuates the name of the family home, Rural Retreat Park.

FEDERAL DEFENSES . . .

GUARDS
AT CHAIN BRIDGE.

MILITARY TELEGRAPH
IN "ALEXANDRIA COUNTY."

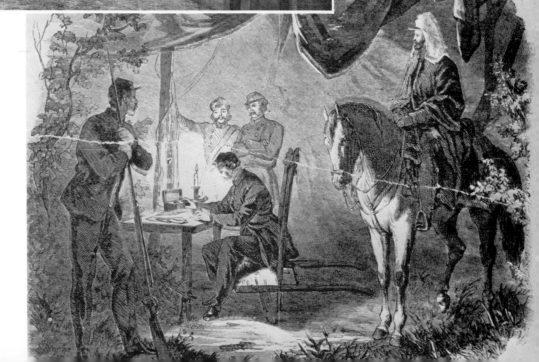

Forts Throughout the County

WITH the approach of the Civil War Centennial, our thoughts turn to Arlington County's disappearing landmarks of this important period in history. The extensive fortifications constructed locally were of great strategic importance. Their very existence prevented any serious attack on the National Capital. Most of the system has now been obliterated—some parts of it in very recent times. Those which remain are worthy of preservation for their historical interest.

Whereas most of these forts are described in detail in other chapters, as will be noted, it is well to review them as parts of a master-plan, with their relationship to each other. They were each part of a protective line which started with Fort Marcy, just over the Fairfax County line above Chain Bridge, and extended to Fort Willard on Belle Haven Heights on the south side of Alexandria. This list will stop at the Alexandria City line. The perimeter of each fort in yards is shown in parentheses.

Among the first to be established were those at and near Jackson City (page 74), for the protection of the Long Bridge to the National Capital. Fort Runyon (1,484 yards) was the largest. It was named in honor of Brigadier General Theodore Runyon of New Jersey. Fort Albany (429 yards) was constructed by troops from New York and named for their State capital. The guard post, Fort Jackson was named for its location at Jackson City.

Fort Corcoran (576 yards) was speedily constructed at the brink of the hill above Rosslyn, for the protection of the Aqueduct and of the road from Falls Church which is present Wilson Boulevard. Fort Corcoran was flanked by Fort Bennett (146 yards) to the north on the palisades (page 136) and Fort Haggerty down the hill near the Alexandria Canal. The first of these honored Colonel Michael Corcoran of the 69th New York Volunteers, the second honored Captain Michael P. Bennett of the 28th New York Volunteers. The third honored Colonel James Haggerty of the 69th New York Irish Brigade. He died at Bull Run in July 1861.

The use of the Custis-Lee Mansion as Headquarters of the Army of the Potomac was related on page 34. The adjacent military activity and installations at Fort Whipple (316 yards) are described on pages 116 and 118. Fort McPherson (316 yards) on the hill south of Arlington House was never completed. It was named for General James B. McPherson, killed in Atlanta, Georgia on July 22, 1864.

Fort Scott (313 yards) was erected at the south end of Arlington Ridge above Four Mile Run, overlooking the road from Alexandria to Long Bridge. It was named for General Winfield Scott. A good part of the earthworks remain intact, and Arlington County is presently investigating the possibility of acquiring and preserving them in conjunction with the adjacent acreage now used by the County Recreation Department.

In order to fortify the defense line of Arlington Heights, a second series of forts were hastily laid out and commenced in August 1861. These included Forts Craig (324 yards), Tillinghast (298 yards), and Cass (288 yards) back of present Fort Myer. They were named for Lieutenant Presley O. Craig of Massachusetts, Captain Otis H. Tillinghast of New York who was killed at Bull Run in July, 1861, and General Lewis Cass of Michigan.

These were connected by a line of trenches to Fort Richardson (316 yards) on the Army-Navy Club grounds (page 60), to Fort Berry (215 yards) west of Glebe Road (page 82), thence to Fort Barnard (250 yards) overlooking the railroad and the valley of Four Mile Run. These were named for Colonel Isreal B. Richardson of the 2nd Michigan Volunteers, a native of Vermont, who died of wounds at Antietam November 3rd, 1862; for General Hiram Berry, Col. 4th Maine, killed at Chancellorsville May 2, 1863; and for Major General Jonathan G. Barnard of the Engineering Corps. He was in charge of constructing most of the earthworks encircling Washington. Fort Berry was erected on the site of the Berry homestead and so named before General Berry's memory was honored.

Across Four Mile Run was Fort Reynolds (360 yards), further fortified by Battery Garesche (166 yards) about two hundred yards to the west. The naming of Fort Reynolds is told on page 80. The Battery was named for Lieutenant-Colonel Julius P. Garesche, Assistant Adjutant General, killed at the Battle of Murfreesboro, Tennessee, December 31, 1862.

North of the three forts back of Fort Myer were a line of fortifications extending to the palisades, likewise connected with earthworks. These were Woodbury (275 yards) at the Court House site, Morton (250 yards) at James Monroe School site, Strong (318 yards) at the Altha Hall site, and Fort Smith (368 yards) whose earthworks are partially preserved on the present Hendry estate (page 136). Fort Woodbury was named for General D. P. Woodbury of the Engineers, and Fort Morton for Oliver P. Morton, Governor of Indiana. Fort Strong was first called De Kalb for Major General John Baron De Kalb of the Revolution. It was later renamed in honor of Major General George Crockett Strong, born in Vermont and appointed to the United States Military Academy from Massachusetts. He died in New York City on July 30, 1863 of wounds received at the assault on Fort Wagner, Charleston Harbor, South Carolina. Some of the earthworks were preserved until June 1959. Fort Smith honored the memory of General Charles F. Smith, who was wounded at Fort Donelson, Tennessee and died April 25, 1862.

Military Road was built in three days, "mainly

through a broken and densely wooded country" to connect Forts Strong and Smith with the fortifications of Chain Bridge, described in the previous chapter. As therein mentioned, Fort Marcy is being preserved as a historic site by the National Park Service. Arlington County is planning to preserve the remaining earthworks of Fort Ethan Allen which is on County-owned land next to James Madison School.

Aside from the fortifications, there was a large reserve force stationed on Minor Hill for the duration of the conflict (pages 124 through 132, and page 146). Numerous homes throughout the county were commandeered for use as hospitals, and some casualties were buried locally in unmarked graves (page 108). Civil War artifacts are currently being unearthed throughout the County.

PONTOON BRIDGE . . . Looking toward Virginia from Georgetown, with Analostan Island in foreground. Deserted Mason home shows on island.

VIEW FROM ANALOSTAN ISLAND . . . Looking upstream toward Aqueduct Bridge, showing vehicles on ferry before installation of pontoon bridge.

Fort Myer, "Show Post of the Nation"

THE Civil War installation on the Custis-Lee plantation was referred to in the early dispatches as "Arlington Heights". It was from this site that General Amiel W. Whipple had sent up an observation balloon August 28, 1861. On June 12, 1863 it was named Fort Whipple in his honor. He had died May 7, 1863 in Washington of wounds received in the Battle of Chancellorsville.

The Fort was principally an artillery and infantry post until 1869, when it also became the first post of the Signal Service, with its school of instruction. General Albert J. Myer became the Post Commander the following year, and on June 16, 1880, became the first Chief Signal Officer. He died two months later, and Fort Whipple was re-designated Fort Myer in his honor. It was during this period that the Signal Corps began weather observations, later carried out by the United States Weather Bureau.

In 1887 cavalry was added to Fort Myer and it became a permanent cavalry post in 1902. Called the "Show Post of the Nation", it was the scene of spectacular horse shows and dress parades which continued up to the beginning of World War II, when the Army's five Cavalry Regiments were converted from horse to mechanized units.

Aviation in its infancy was considered to be a function of the Signal Corps. Fort Myer was therefore the site of the early tests of the first military plane, which led to the eventual establishment of the United States Air Force. The Wright brothers made many flights from the north area drill field. On September 17, 1908, the world's first air fatality occurred there. A plane piloted by Orville Wright plunged to earth, fatally injuring Lieutenant Thomas Selfridge, Wright's passenger.

In 1913 the Navy Department erected at the south end of Fort Myer three steel towers of the world's most powerful broadcasting station. This was named "Radio, Virginia", the first use of the term radio to replace wireless station. Two of the towers measured 450 feet each. The third was the world's tallest self-supporting radio tower with a height of 600 feet, forty-five feet taller than the Washington Monument. Only the Eiffel Tower of Paris exceeded it in height. Atop a 200 foot ridge above the National Airport, these towers were doomed in 1941 as a menace to celestial navigation.

Aside from its military and scientific fame, this is considered the founding station of the radio broadcasting industry. This station handled the first radio-telephone long distance conversation. It was between the Secretary of the Navy and the *U. S. S. Nebraska* off the Virginia Capes. The first over-seas conversation took place in 1915 with the Eiffel Tower Station, followed by one with our Navy's "Radio Honolulu". The War Department messages of World War I were sent through this station. During the years of peace, the world received its noon time signals and weather reports through it.

Since the early 1900's, "Quarters Number One" has been the home of the Army Chief of Staff. Other officers of the Department of the Army occupy quarters on the post. The "Home of Generals" has housed, among others, Leonard Wood, Douglas MacArthur, Malin Craig, George Marshall, Dwight D. Eisenhower, Omar Bradley, Matthew B. Ridgeway, and Maxwell D. Taylor.

Fort Myer is also the home of the United States Army Band and the United States Army Chorus. The Band, created in 1922 by order of General John J. Pershing, is composed of more than a hundred musicians. It has marched in inaugural parades of many presidents, and has represented our Nation with distinction throughout the world. It gives public concerts at the Watergate on the Potomac, at the Capitol, and the Departmental Auditorium.

The need of an inter-faith place of worship, and for the conducting of funeral services at the post was met with the building of Fort Myer Chapel, a Works Progress Administration project. It is adjacent to the West Gate of Arlington Cemetery. The Project Officer was General (then Major) George S. Patton Jr. The dedication service was held Easter Sunday 1935.

When the cavalry and artillery left for World War II, the Military Police were assigned to Fort Myer. After the War, the First Battle Group, 3rd Infantry was also brought in. It is our Nation's oldest active Regular Army Infantry unit. It antedates the Constitution and has participated in every war in which this Nation has been concerned. For its valiant service during the Mexican War, General Winfield Scott designated it "The Old Guard".

The 3rd Infantry furnishes specially selected soldiers as a continuous guard at the Tomb of the Unknowns. The sentinels relieve one another during an impressive guard-changing ceremony every hour on the hour. The Old Guard Infantry Regiment also furnishes military escort for Presidential Inaugural parades, other ceremonial duties, and for State and military funerals. Eight horses belonging to the Regiment are used for military burials. The flag-draped casket rests on a caisson drawn by six matched greys, led by a seventh ridden by the Command Sergeant. If the deceased was a member of the Cavalry, or an officer, the caisson may be followed by a riderless black charger carrying a pair of cavalry boots reversed in the stirrups. (At this time, a set of black horses is being trained to replace the greys, which will soon be retired to green pastures.) The impressive procession is accompanied by muffled drums of the band, and climaxed by the firing of volleys over the grave and the clear sound of "Taps" in the oak forest of Arlington Cemetery.

WHITE HORSE BATTERY . . . Cavalry racing across parade ground, with Arlington Radio Towers in background.

FIRST AIR FATALITY . . . Orville Wright was testing this plane for the Army at Fort Myer in 1908, when it plummeted to earth, killing Wright's passenger, Lt. Thomas Selfridge.

MILITARY BURIAL . . . The 100,000th burial at Arlington National Cemetery took place April 3rd, 1959. Fort Myer furnishes military escort for services.

Balloons and Quaker Guns

AFTER the First Battle of Manassas (June 21, 1861), the Confederates established a cavalry outpost line extending in part across the western end of Arlington County, in order to observe what the Federal forces in Washington and Alexandria and along Arlington Heights might be up to. This outpost line was supported by several lightly fortified positions, including one at Munson Hill (midway between Seven Corners and Bailey's Crossroads). From the Confederate signal station on Munson Hill, the Capitol in Washington could be plainly seen. The main cavalry camp remained at Fairfax, the main army at Centerville.

In late August the Federals sent up an observation balloon from Arlington Heights (later Fort Myer) and from Ball's Crossroads. The balloonists reported that the Confederates were busily entrenching at Clark's Hill (above Chain Bridge) and Upton's Hill (on Wilson Boulevard at the Willston water tower), and that an estimated thousand men were erecting formidable works on Munson Hill, with two guns already in position.

On the last day of August the Federals sallied forth from their defenses to reconnoitre this line of works and, if practicable, to break it up. The result was some confused cavalry skirmishing along Lee Highway as far as Hall's Hill, and to the north on Minor Hill. There was also a long-range artillery bombardment of Munson Hill. The Federals concluded that the works on Munson Hill were too formidable to be attacked, and withdrew to their own lines.

In the meantime, General Beauregard (Confederate Army) attempted unsuccessfully to secure an observation balloon through Richmond authorities. He finally obtained one through a private source, but defective construction prevented successful operation. It was raised, however, for a Union dispatch reported it hovering over Munson Hill on the 4th of September. At the end of September the Confederates voluntarily withdrew to Fairfax, to shorten their lines of communication in anticipation of winter weather, and the Federals came out and occupied their former outpost positions. Only then did they discover that the works which they had not dared to assault in August had been armed chiefly with "Quaker cannon"—dressed logs mounted at the embrasures to resemble artillery!

It is said that "Jeb" Stuart, the Confederate cavalry commander, received his commission as a Brigadier General while at Munson Hill during the last days of September. An historical organization erected a bronze marker there in memory of the occasion, but it was destroyed a few years ago when bulldozers sliced off the hilltop for house sites. Who can furnish detailed information on this: the donor, the date, and the text of the inscription? To make a military triumph of the unopposed occupation of the Confederate outpost line (and perhaps to offset the psychological effect of the discoveries on Munson Hill), General McClellan staged a series of spectacular military reviews on the new line. The grandest of all was held at Bailey's Crossroads on November 21 with fifty-thousand troops reviewed by President Lincoln. A young lady visitor from Boston, Julia Ward Howe, was so inspired by the sound of the feet tramping out Columbia Pike that, upon her return to the Willard Hotel, she composed *The Battle Hymn of the Republic,* to the tune of the Massachusetts Regiment's favorite, *John Brown's Body.*

The homestead of the Munson family for whom Munson Hill was named is still standing at the present address of 332 Leesburg Pike. It is the home of the Donald Wilkins family. Across the Pike was the Munson Nursery which was shown on the Civil War map. From it came the maple saplings which now, as venerable giants, shade the streets of Falls Church.

The records of the Columbia Historical Society contain an interesting account of the use of balloons during the Civil War. Thaddeus S. C. Lowe was an aeronaut, and was empowered to organize the Aeronautical Corps of the Army. In the first months of the war he made balloon ascensions at Arlington Heights and at Ball's Crossroads. On August 31, 1861, at the latter site, he was fired upon by the Confederates and narrowly escaped disaster.

The balloon was inflated in Washington where hydrogen was readily obtainable and thence towed across the river. A nocturnal crossing of Chain Bridge proved more hazardous, as related in Lowe's own report:

"Our progress was slow, the night being very dark, and we were constantly apprehensive of running the balloon against trees and other obstacles. After passing through Washington and Georgetown, crossing numerous flag-poles and telegraph wires stretched across the streets, we reached the road to Chain Bridge . . . The wind was too high to tow the balloon when elevated . . . At several points trees had to be felled . . . We arrived at the Chain Bridge about 3 o'clock the next morning, and found it filled with artillery and cavalry going to Virginia . . . My men were obliged to mount the trestle-work and walk along the stringers, only 18" wide . . . with the balloon over their heads, myself in the car directing the management of the ropes, the men getting on and off the trestle-work, with a column of artillery moving below, and a hundred feet still lower the deep strong current rushing over the rocks . . ."

Thaddeus Lowe later became a distinguished astronomer and founded Lowe Observatory in California upon the mountain which also bears his name.

FEDERAL SOLDIERS INFLATING MILITARY BALLOON . . .

CHAIN BRIDGE WITH MILITARY GUARD . . . Chesapeake and Ohio Canal in foreground, swift narrow river channel in background, with lowlands between which are inundated during high water.

Story-Book House, "Broadview"

ITS real name is "Broadview," although it is generally called The Old Lacey Place. It was hard to find; the mailbox address and that given in the phone book is 5101 Washington Boulevard, but there's nothing there except a pretty wooded lot! I kept circling around the block, and the only old place I could find was a block to the north where Evergreen Street comes to a dead end against the property on 14th Street. It seemed that this just had to be it, so I knocked at the door, and sure enough, it was! Washington Boulevard was the nearest street when the house was originally numbered, and they haven't changed it since the seventeen-acre farm was cut up into new streets; it should be 5151 14th Street North.

Mr. and Mrs. George Newland live there with Mrs. Newland's mother and sisters, Mrs. Rena Weaver and Miss Mabel Holmes. Mr. and Mrs. Ralph W. Crain, who live nearby own it. Mrs. Crain is the great-grand-niece of the builder, Major R. S. Lacey. Major Lacey was from Ohio with the Union Army in Virginia, and was so attracted to this area that he bought acreage in 1864 and 1867, apparently settled on it at the end of hostilities, and enlarged the house in 1879 when his widowed sister-in-law and her children moved here from Ohio. Ownership of the property descended to Mrs. Crain's aunt in Oregon, from whom the Crains purchased it.

I've just read a delightful children's book written in 1941 by Mrs. Margaret Leighton of California, who had lived there with her family. The book, a mixture of fact, legend, imagination, mystery, and adventure, is one that can be enjoyed equally by children from eight to eighty. To quote the author's foreword from *The Secret of the Old House* (John C. Winston Co., Philadelphia):

"This story is about a real house. When my own four children, two boys and two girls, first saw the rambling old building, they thought it quite the nicest place that they had ever hoped to live in. They couldn't decide which they wanted to begin exploring first, the funny square tower that rose so unexpectedly from the corner of its roof or the seventeen acres of woods and meadow that spread around it . . . the tall, dark hemlock trees whose branches swept the ground like ladies' party skirts, the path through the woods, the brook, the long dangling grapevines that made such perfect swings—surely other boys and girls would like to read about what my own had found so delightful!

"As for the mystery and the adventures that the young Hills found there, if those were only partly true, the other parts were what might so well have happened, given such a house, such a location, and four such lively boys and girls . . . The ingredients were all there, you see, like the eggs and butter and sugar and flour and milk for a cake. It took only a certain kind of mixing, with the addition of some imagination (like baking powder) and the story was ready to write down . . .

"I hope that the dogwood is as bright in the woods in the spring and that the honeysuckle is still as sweet when summer begins as it was when we lived there . . . The other characters, outside of the Hill family, had to be made up to fit the story. All, that is, but John Mosby . . . It would hardly be possible to make up any adventures more exciting than those that really happened to him!"

The fields around Broadview have yielded a quantity of Civil War canteens, buckles, buttons, and other relics; and from beneath the porch came an old bayonet.

I have gone all through the interesting Victorian structure and have seen the secret stairwell beside the fireplaces, extending from attic to basement. A few years ago, the ladders were removed and the spaces filled with bookshelves. I have seen the old stone cellars; they most certainly look as if they antedate the house's erection in 1879. I have a strong personal conviction, shared by the present lessors, that the house was built upon the foundations of an earlier structure. The Civil War map of 1864 does not show a house standing at that time. Could it be that some of these legends, (referred to in Mrs. Leighton's book), of people having been hidden in the cellar during the war are true, and this led to the burning of the house before 1864?

John Singleton Mosby

MARGARET LEIGHTON, who tells the story of Old Lacey House, makes the exploits of the daring Confederate Colonel, John Singleton Mosby (1833-1916) a part of its happenings. With her permission, I quote directly from her book:

"There are almost as many stories about him as there are ballads of Robin Hood! Most of them are legends, but the best of them are really true . . .

"He started as a cavalry [private] under Jeb Stuart, but [was selected] to organize his own troop of what he called 'Rangers'. He picked his men carefully. I think he only had nine to begin with, and never more than five hundred in all, chosen for their daring and skill as riders. Their horses could outrun and outjump any in the army. The troopers knew every road and mountain path in northern Virginia—knew them in the dark!

"They didn't fight pitched battles. They made sudden raids on Federal supply trains and on the railroads. They never had tents or equipment, didn't drill, carried no supplies. They ate when they could and slept where night found them . . . Local farmers helped them, and Mosby repaid them by loot from the Northern Armies.

"After every raid, they scattered and hid, to meet later at some place agreed upon. At first the Union armies called them guerrillas. But they weren't. They were disciplined and obeyed orders implicitly and really were superb fighters. His men carried six-shooters.

"About the raid he made at Fairfax Court House: in the spring of '63 he swooped down in the night on Brigadier General Stoughton who was sleeping comfortably in his bed, and took him prisoner, along with two captains, thirty-five men, and fifty-eight horses. As the story goes . . . Mosby came into the room, pulled the covers off him, and waked him by spanking him with his saber!

"Well, Mosby kept things hot for the Federal Cavalry. He did some valuable scouting in the Gettysburg Campaign, and after Lee's retreat he and his men were about the only disciplined force the Confederates had left in northern Virginia. Of course, the Union armies were in possession of all this territory; but even with a price on his head, Mosby stayed on, kept his men under orders, continued his campaign of raids and sallies. People called this section "Mosby's Confederacy". Along in the fall of '64 he made perhaps his most spectacular raid. He captured two of General Sheridan's paymasters, with $168,000 in Federal money!

"Whenever the Yankees found that a farmer or householder had sheltered any of the Rangers, they burned his house and barns without mercy . . . Mosby was afraid of nothing, so it seemed. He was wounded six times, left for dead once, hunted high and low, and was one of the very last of the Confederate officers to surrender his command.

"But he took defeat with a better grace than many who had been less dangerous as enemies . . . He lived to be a very old man . . . a fine white-haired old gentleman with a fierce hooked nose and a mighty keen blue eye."

A true tale of Mosby's Rangers concerns the family of an Arlington attorney, Foster Hagan, before his father moved here from Loudoun County. The family home was at Paeonion Springs, about four miles west of Leesburg, and an equal distance southwest of Waterford. The latter community was established about 1732 by a group of Quakers who settled around the mill erected by Amos Janney, the surveyor of Lord Fairfax.

During the Civil War, the Quakers were predominantly Federal in their sentiments. Their religion would not allow them to engage in active warfare, but they practiced the "scorched-earth policy". Under Union military guard, they harrassed the families of Confederates, destroying their crops and stock.

Operating for the Confederate cause under General Mosby was a Partisan leader named Elijah B. White, who lived near Leesburg. His men identified themselves by wearing a sprig of mountain laurel leaves in their hats, hence were called by some The Laurel Brigade. However, others termed them The Comanches, because they streamed through Leesburg screaming like wild Indians.

Benjamin Franklin Hagan, grandfather of Foster Hagan, was a member of White's Rangers. Mrs. Hagan was left at home with two small sons; Charles, about six years old who helped his mother to care for the farm, and four-year-old Jonathan (Foster's father). The Waterford Quakers, in their cold war against the Confederates paid the Hagan farm a heartbreaking visit. They burned the crops which Mrs. Hagan and Charles had just harvested. They killed the cow and pig. As a final cruelty, they bayonetted Jonathan's pet rooster!

Benjamin Hagan and his fellow Rangers retaliated with their own version of bloodless revenge. They wrapped their horses' hooves in rags to muffle their tread. Every evening for a week, these silent horsemen circled Waterford single file, and finally rode up one street and down another in the dusk. No word was spoken, no shot fired, but the uncertainty of their plans; the mounting suspense and tension completely shattered the nerves of the terrified Quakers. How appropiate the term, Grey Ghosts!

Twenty years later, the wounds were healed when the Waterford Quakers attended the Hagan's "barn-raising" enmasse, with their elder offering the benediction. This was climaxed by a bountiful feast cooked and served by Mrs. Hagan.

After the war, Mosby resumed his law practice and joined the Whig Party. He served as United States Consul at Hong Kong from 1878 to 1885. He wrote *Mosby's War Reminiscences* and *Stuart's Cavalry Campaigns* in 1887, and *Stuart's Cavalry in the Gettysburg Campaign* in 1908 when he was seventy-five years old. After retirement, General Mosby rented the Bradbury House on Columbia Pike for about three years.

JOHN SINGLETON MOSBY . . .

THE RECTORY . . . *Across from Fairfax Court House*. This is the present rectory of Truro Parish. It was from this home that Mosby kidnapped Union General Stoughton from his bed in the middle of the night and escaped with him through the lines of an army numbering 17,000.

Vandenbergs' "Reserve Hill"

THE impressive stone mansion at 5115 Little Falls Road, which is the present headquarters of the Knights of Columbus, is built on a hilltop which is believed to have been the site of an Indian village and burial ground. This seems likely because of its vantage point and nearness to excellent springs. Numerous artifacts have been found nearby. The site once belonged to John Vandenberg* of Wisconsin. His sister Jane had married a first cousin, Gilbert Vanderwerken, who had built on the adjoining farm to the east at the intersection of Little Falls and Glebe Roads. Another brother, Gilbert Vandenberg, came down from Wisconsin to visit his brother and sister, decided he preferred the milder Virginia climate, and traded his Wisconsin farm for his brother John's Virginia farm.

Gilbert Vandenberg built the original house in 1855 and prospered. The family also had a town house on the north side of I Street, N.W. in Washington near the Arts Club, but they spent much time at the Virginia farm. By the time of the Civil War, his three daughters were young ladies.

One daughter, Evaline, loved to ride her high-spirited horse about the countryside. Once when she recklessly ventured out-of-bounds without her pass, Union soldiers mistook her for the beautiful and daring Southern spy Belle Boyd, and placed her under arrest until her father arrived to identify her. The Union Army Reserve Units were stationed at nearby Minor Hill, which led to the Vandenbergs naming their homestead "Reserve Hill".

Mrs. Vandenberg took a few select boarders, three of whom married the daughters: Rudolph Reichmann, an artist and photographer, married Evaline and moved to New York; Henry Alexander Lockwood of "Easter Spring Farm" married Charlotte Eleanor and moved to another hilltop toward Chain Bridge; George Nicholas Saegmuller married Maria Jane. They remained at the homestead.

Saegmuller, a native of Germany, went as a young man to England, where he was employed by the Thomas Cook & Son Company, who subsequently sent him as their representative to the Paris Exposition. He came to America just before the Franco-Prussian War. He was given a position with the Coast and Geodetic Survey in charge of all their precision instruments. Later, with his brother-in-law, Henry Lockwood and Camil Fauth, he entered into a partnership forming the Fauth and Company, which supplied scientific equipment for observatories and various departments of the government. He invented the Saegmuller Solar Attachment which

was a great help to surveyors. After he became sole owner of Fauth and Company, he invented the telescopic boresight for the heavy naval guns. Before the Spanish-American War, with the assistance of Admiral Sampson, he developed a range-finder.

In the meantime, the newest conveniences were being added to Reserve Hill, such as running water piped from the spring in 1887. The county's first private phone line was run between Reserve Hill and Easter Spring Farm in 1894. A fine stone barn was erected in 1882, with the initial S carved on a soapstone plaque above the door; the date is on another plaque near the eaves. A chime-clock was installed in a high window of the barn. On top was a windmill for pumping cistern water to the stock.

The original house burned in 1892. As so often happens in panic, furniture and mirrors were thrown out of windows while mattresses were carried down the stairs. Mr. Saegmuller decided to rebuild on the same site a house reminiscent of his native Nürnberg. The new house, completed in 1904, was constructed of fine bluestone quarried on the estate. Tall white columns at the front show a Southern influence combined with that of a German castle. The house has twenty-two rooms plus baths. It was beautifully furnished with antiques and art treasures.

Just back of the house was built a stone watertower, which is an exact replica of a gatetower of the Nürnberg city wall. This was copied in minutest detail from a tankard replica of the tower which Mr. Saegmuller brought from Germany. It is now owned by his son, George Marshall Saegmuller. The family also has oil paintings of Nürnberg scenes by the noted artist Seibert, who was commissioned to go to Germany in 1907 to paint the set for Reserve Hill. Included is one of the Castle with the gate-tower from which the tankard was copied. [It was at Nürnberg Castle that Eppstein, the "robber knight", was imprisoned and condemned to be hanged. His last request was for a farewell ride on his stallion; it was granted; he jumped the wall and escaped!]

George Nicholas Saegmuller served his county as Chairman of the Board of Supervisors, and was influential in the choice of the Court House site, as related on page 132. He advanced money to meet county expenses during that period, and personally supervised construction of the new building. His interest in public education is told on page 170. It is my hope that when the current program of enlargement of James Madison School is completed, a suitable memorial plaque will be placed in the main hall honoring its early benefactor, George Nicholas Saegmuller.

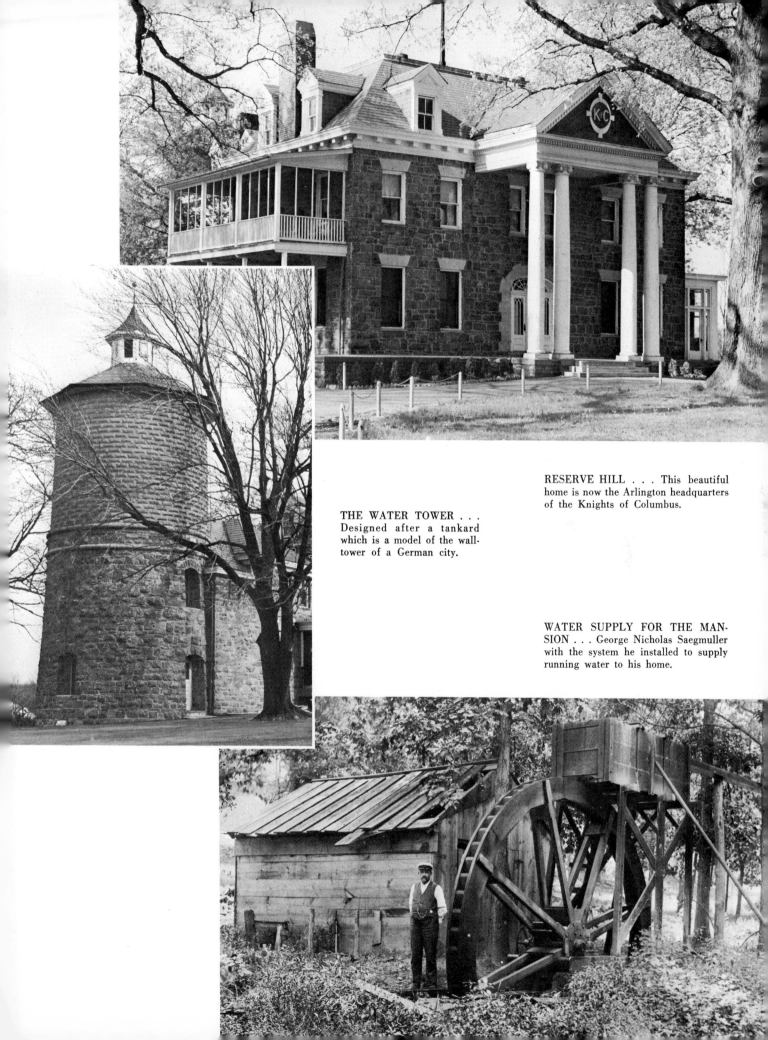

RESERVE HILL . . . This beautiful home is now the Arlington headquarters of the Knights of Columbus.

THE WATER TOWER . . . Designed after a tankard which is a model of the wall-tower of a German city.

WATER SUPPLY FOR THE MANSION . . . George Nicholas Saegmuller with the system he installed to supply running water to his home.

Vanderwerkens' "Falls Grove"

THIS attractive Virginia farm house is situated on a hilltop in a grove of fine oak trees at the northwest corner of Little Falls and Glebe Roads. It was built about 1852 by Gilbert Vanderwerken (1810-1894) who had married his cousin, Jane Vandenberg, whose brother built on the next hill to the west. The present residents are Mr. and Mrs. Arnim Hughes. Mrs. Hughes was Lillie Truett, granddaughter of the builder.

Gilbert Vanderwerken had an adventurous spirit. At seventeen he left his home in Albany, New York to be apprenticed to a coachmaker in Newark, New Jersey. This led to his operation of a coach line from Mexico City to Veracruz. While carrying a large consignment of silver for the Mexican government, he successfully escaped a band of desperados who had attempted to hold up the stage.

We next find him living in a house on the northwest corner of 30th and M Streets in Georgetown, and operating a coach line from the Aqueduct Bridge to the Navy Yard. This was the forerunner of the Capital Transit Company of Washington. The horses were kept in stables at the present site of the Georgetown carbarn at 3222 M Street.

In order to have a place to raise and pasture his horses, Vanderwerken bought a Virginia tract which included much of the extreme northern part of Arlington County. The house which he constructed was intended for the use of a tenant at times, and as a summer residence of the family. Besides the coach horses, he had some beautiful thoroughbreds. One was used by Clarke Mills, the famous sculptor who lived at the Glebe (see page 188) as the model for the equestrian statue of Andrew Jackson. A wooden replica of this horse was lost in the fire which destroyed the Georgetown barns.

Another enterprise of this family was the operation of stone quarries on the Potomac Palisades of Arlington. The excellent bluestone was loaded on barges and towed down the river to Washington, where it was used for many important buildings, including St. Patrick's Church, Georgetown University buildings, and the seawalls at Hains Point. The Italian quarry workers lived in shacks they built along Marcey Creek canyon of the palisades as related on page 142. They supplemented the local laborers from Chesterbrook and Halls Hill.

During the Civil War, the Vanderwerken family remained in Georgetown, having agreed to allow General Hancock to use Falls Grove as an Army hospital in return for a guarantee of protection of the buildings and fine grove of trees. The General used the two-story carpenter shop as his headquarters. President Lincoln came over to the farm to review the troops. Both Fort Marcy and Fort Ethan Allen were constructed on the property.

When the family returned after the war, they found initials of the hospitalized soldiers carved on the mantels and woodwork. These were filled in and painted over, with the exception of the word "Hospitol" [sic] carved on a door. As a memento of the war-occupancy, the door was moved inside to the dining-room with the carved work intact. Alas, the interior was recently redecorated, and an over-zealous painter filled in the word with plastic wood and painted over it! Among the treasured heirlooms in the homestead is a piano which was used for the concerts of Jenny Lind. Mrs. Hughes' grandfather had purchased it for her mother (neé Ella Vanderwerken) from P. T. Barnum, the business manager for the famous singer.

The Civil War map of 1864 shows Burnt Mill at the mouth of Pimmit Run below Chain Bridge. This was probably Hill's Paper Mill, which involves the tale of a duel between Hill and Vanderwerken about 1860. Vanderwerken's Georgetown house was on the northwest corner of 30th and M Streets, and Hill lived next door. Both these houses are preserved and have fine lines typical of early Federal architecture.

Charlotte Eleanor Vandenberg, who later married Henry Lockwood of Easter Spring Farm on Glebe Road, was spending the winter with the family of her aunt, Mrs. Vanderwerken, in order to attend school with her cousin Emma. Tension had been building up between Vanderwerken and his neighbor Hill, whose cellars connected. The latter collected odiferous rags for his paper mill and stored them in his basement. They overflowed into his neighbor's side. Repeated entreaty and warnings had been ignored.

One afternoon as the two girls returned from school, Charlotte took a short cut into the house by way of the side basement door. She was terrified to see her uncle and Hill with drawn pistols, each behind a stone pillar, and her cousin Charles on the staircase with a sword! Shots rang out, and Hill fell, seriously wounded. He eventually recovered and his threatened lawsuit was finally dropped. Sometime within the past century, a separating wall has been built between the two cellars.

FALLS GROVE . . . This home erected about
1852 by Gilbert Vanderwerken stands today in
the grove of handsome oak trees which sheltered
convalescing Federal soldiers.

AN ARLINGTON THOROUGHBRED . . . Gilbert Vandenberg's horse was used by Clarke
Mills as a model for the Jackson equestrian
statue in Lafayette Park.

Civil War at "Falls Grove"

THIS is the story of the old Vanderwerken homestead described on page 126. Nine years after it was built came the Civil War and the tranquility that had prevailed over the countryside was suddenly broken by vicious acts of civil strife. Of Northern background, the family's peaceful and neutral inclinations were at first misunderstood.

The first incident occurred immediately after the outbreak of hostilities, at a time when the family was living in Georgetown. Mr. Vanderwerken started out to the farm in his carriage, and enroute encountered his terrified coachman riding pell-mell toward him. He related that a neighborhood raiding party had seized the horses, wagons, and feed, and that lynchers were hiding in the house! Another group had ridden into the farm of his cousin, Gilbert Vandenberg, whom they had missed as he had already left for the city. Tired of awaiting his return, the bloodthirsty gang decided to go out to meet him. The intended victim was saved by his decision to use a much longer route he seldom traveled.

When the first flash of unreasonable feeling subsided, the Vanderwerkens came out to the farm for the summer before the Army took possession. They were in residence at the time of the Battle of Bull Run in July 1861. The defeated Federals fled toward Chain Bridge and Washington, along the Little Falls Road that passed within three hundred yards of the house. It was a hot July day, and a sudden heavy thunderstorm drenched the hordes of weary soldiers who made a dash for the protection of the house and porches. At sight of the wild mob racing across the lawn, the family fled upstairs and locked themselves in a bedroom. Within a few minutes the downstairs became packed with a sweltering, soaked mass of humanity!

There were amusing incidents to lighten the tension. Mr. Vanderwerken was often teased about the time he forgot the password necessary to enter the gate of his own property, and have to drive eight miles to Army headquarters in Alexandria.

Sentries had been assigned to guard the premises. One night a lad who had experienced his first skirmish that day and was still jittery, heard sticks crackling in the wood beside the road and assumed the enemy was sneaking up to capture him. His "Halt, who goes there?" received no reply, but a dark object broke from the woods and came straight toward him. The sentry fired and ran. The corporal of the guard arrived to find a dead calf!

The family remained in Georgetown during the period that the house was used as an Army hospital. Because so many soldiers had died in the house, it became the object of suspicion and dread among the superstitious people of the neighborhood. Some claimed to have heard music at night, or to have seen balls of fire dropping from the upper windows and rolling across the lawns. Those familiar with the story of the scared sentry would tell of seeing the calf with its bloody head hanging between its front legs cavorting along the road, crossing the lawn, and disappearing toward the house.

Another tale involves an old oak tree which leaned over the road near the gate and was cut down not too long ago. It was reputed to be haunted by the spirit of a spy who was hanged from it shortly after the war began. Years later another haunt was added: On an extremely cold moonlight night, a man on horseback had great difficulty getting his suddenly terrified mount to approach the tree. As they neared it, a man rose from the shadows and staggered down the road. Thinking it might be an inebriated neighbor in need of help, the rider called without response and was unable to overtake the figure at a gallop. When the man disappeared around a bend, the rider became terrified at the thought that he must have been chasing a ghost! Still upset by the harrowing experience of the night before, he rode back early next morning and found the frozen body of a man clutching a liquor bottle at the base of the tree!

After the war, the Vanderwerken family returned to the farm; but there was still another time of fear, the day following the assassination of President Lincoln. At the break of dawn, the family was awakened by banging on the doors. Ignorant of the tragedy that had occurred a few hours earlier, they were frightened to see their home surrounded by mounted Federal soldiers pointing their guns at the house. Without legal warrant or permission, they ransacked the place from cellar to garret, presumably hunting for the assassin.

The Union Army remained at the nearby forts for four years before demobilization. The Vanderwerken family were frequently serenaded during summer evenings by the officers and band from Fort Ethan Allen.

One evening four years after Appomattox, a large group of mounted officers formed their horses in a semicircle on the lawn facing the house. Following his custom of hospitality toward soldiers, Mr. Vanderwerken came out and passed around a box of cigars. Then, in the growing darkness, the officers sang their farewell, "I'm Smoking My Last Cigar," whirled their mounts and disappeared into the night. And so came peace to the house—a peace that has remained down through the years.

PIMMIT RUN BRIDGE . . . The stone abutment can still be seen today from the newer bridge some yards downstream.

"HANG TREE" . . . This handsome oak of Civil War legends was cut about 1940 for widening of Glebe Road.

Lockwoods' "Easter Spring Farm"

HENRY Alexander Lockwood came from New York in 1853 to accept a position in the Treasury Department. About five years later he built his home on a tract near Glebe Road and sent for his sister Jane to keep house for him. The address is now 3722 North Glebe Road. Mr. Lockwood married Charlotte Eleanor Vandenberg in 1868. Three of their daughters still live at the homestead: Margaret, Jane, and Sarah. His daughter Mary, wife of Bertram G. Foster was given a site for a home directly on Glebe Road, on land bought from Thomas Langton. Another daughter, Charlotte, married John R. Grunwell; we shall hear more about their home across Glebe Road in the next chapter. A son, William Lockwood, married Alice Prescott, and their daughter Carlotta is now Mrs. Bryce Weaver of 3841 Chesterbrook Road, Arlington.

The homestead received it name from the excellent spring down the hill to the west of the house. An old colored woman called Aunt Easter lived near the spring which had become identified by her name. The stone-lined spring is now in the garden of Mr. and Mrs. A. R. Gragg of 4607 41st Street North. Before the Graggs moved into their new home the spring had been mutilated, but they are attempting to restore its beauty.

Henry Lockwood, who built the house, was the son of Robert Lockwood, a surveyor of the Erie Canal; he had married Mary Catherine Alexander, who was the daughter of William Alexander, whose father, Robert Alexander, assembled the Hudson River boats that George Washington used at West Point during the Revolution. Henry Lockwood's half-sister, Jane Bowen Edwards established the first Methodist Sunday School at Walker Chapel. She was one of the original members of the Mount Vernon Ladies' Association.

In the Lockwood home are some of the finest heirlooms in this area, handed down through generations of their New York ancestors. The Frick Art Reference Library in New York City has had an expert catalog the family portraits. There is a silhouette of Gilbert Vandenberg in 1841 in his wedding suit, by the noted artist Edouard, whose work was all the rage among the elite. There is a grandfather clock which was a wedding gift to William Alexander, Henry Lockwood's grandfather. There is also a wall clock identical with one shown in Wallace Nutting's book on antique clocks, plate number 3405, identified as a "Curtis Girandole of 1810-18."

During the Civil War the troops at nearby Fort Ethan Allen used the attic window as a target, but fortunately most of the shot fell short.

In former times the Lockwood farm was noted for its excellent berries which were raised for the Washington market. Schools closed when the berries ripened so that the children and their parents could pick them.

Wages were at the rate of a cent and a half per quart for blackberries, two cents for strawberries, and three cents for raspberries. There were also fine fuits and vegetables; some of the old fruit trees remain around the house.

Henry Lockwood and his brother-in-law, George Saegmuller, built and maintained some of the early roads at their own expense. The first road to Chain Bridge crossed Pimmit Run by fording, which was dangerous when the water was high. On one such occasion the Lockwood wagon overturned and broke Henry's leg. He and George Saegmuller decided to build a bridge, which was used until fairly recent times when a heavily loaded truck broke through. It was called The Little Iron Bridge, and one can still see the masonry abutments upstream from the present bridge.

WALKER HOMESTEADS

Farther up Glebe Road are the homes of the Walker family. The Walkers have been identified with the area for generations. The first Walker of whom we find record was David, who was buried at the "Walker Grave Yard" which later became Walker Chapel Cemetery. His headstone reads, "David Walker, died Oct. 30, 1848; aged 54 years." The broken original stone is at the home of his granddaughter, Mrs. Harry Gutshall, having been replaced many years ago with a handsomer one at the cemetery.

A Civil War map of 1864 shows a Walker house at what is now 4446 North Glebe Road, the present Cornwell house. It has an old stone foundation and is constructed of logs, now covered with clapboard. It is assumed that this was built by David Walker some years before his death (1848), and where he and his wife, Nancy, raised their sons, Robert, James and George. Robert was born January 19, 1840, so if it was his birthplace, it dates to the 1830's or earlier. "Aunt Nancy's Spring" is on the White Pines estate on Military Road at what is now called Gulf Branch. The stream was known to the Walker family as Spring Branch, and is shown on the map of 1900 as Falls Branch. The derivation of its recent and less appropriate name remains a mystery.

Robert Walker was employed by Henry Lockwood to oversee his Easter Spring Farm. In 1871 he purchased land and built a log house (now stuccoed) for his bride, Margaret Mercer Havener, at what is now 4211 North Glebe Road. Their daughter, Maggie, married Harry E. A. Gutshall in 1903, and six years later moved into the home his father had built in 1880 within the earthworks of Fort Ethan Allen. When the county recently purchased the property for the Recreation Department, Mrs. Gutshall and her daughter returned to the Robert Walker home of 1871, to which they have added an attractive brick wing.

EASTER SPRING FARM . . . Now the home of the three daughters of Henry Lockwood, who built it in 1856.

RECENT DEVASTATION . . . A 1957 picture of the same spring (left) after devastation by an adjacent builder.

EASTER SPRING . . . Surrounded by ferns and wild flowers in a dogwood grove, this was a favorite picnic site for the Lockwood family, who named their farm for the spring.

Grunwells' "Bellevue"

THE attractive Virginia farmhouse at 3311 North Glebe Road, built soon after the Civil War, was the home of the Grunwell family until sold in 1946. Basil DeLashmutt bought it two years later and it was purchased in 1956 by William J. D. Hunter.

Into its construction went some of the timbers retrieved from Fort Ethan Allen which had been taken from the family property at the beginning of the war. There are a dozen spacious rooms with twelve-foot ceilings. The house has three fireplaces. A fourth one was originally in the kitchen, but has been eliminated to make room for modern equipment. One of the most unusual features of the house is a massive chimney which, as it passes through the attic, is corbeled in a spiral like a circular staircase. This was done so that the length of the rectangle would coincide with a balancing chimney at the other end of the house as the two chimneys emerge from the roof.

The house was appropriately named "Bellevue"; it has one of the finest locations in the area, on the crest of a ridge in an oak grove, facing west. To the northeast can be seen the taller buildings of Washington and the distant Maryland countryside across the Potomac.

The story of this house is the web of life that has woven into one fabric the lives of the families of the three hilltops which it faces: the Vandenbergs and Saegmullers of Reserve Hill, the Vanderwerkens of Falls Grove, and the Lockwoods of Easter Spring Farm. Just after the Civil War, Lieutenant Alfred Grunwell was stationed at a camp on Minor Hill to the west. One day he became lost in the woods of the Vanderwerken farm while attempting a short cut to Chain Bridge. He emerged from the forest to find himself on the lawn of a house. On the veranda a pretty young lady was reading. With cap in hand, he inquired the way, but added a few caustic remarks concerning the worthlessness of the country through which he had been floundering. It happened that the criticized area belonged to her father, and she promptly took exception to his uncomplimentary remarks. However, her mettle must have amused and interested the young officer, for he henceforth formed a habit of getting lost at every opportunity. By the time the troops were demobilized, he had acquired an advancement to captaincy and a bride. Their children were Charles Grunwell who married Margaret Vandenberg and John Grunwell, who married Charlotte Lockwood of Easter Spring Farm; these two brothers later developed Bellevue Forest. Another brother, Lieutenant Commander Alfred Gilbert Grunwell lived at 3405 Glebe Road. A sister, Susie, married and moved to the West.

Captain Grunwell took Jane, his bride, to Florida, where he was stationed during the difficult reconstruction period. His fairness and popularity in "alien territory" are proven by his subsequent election to public offices in Florida, first as county clerk and then as judge. They returned to Arlington at the time of the death of Mrs. Grunwell's brother Charles Vanderwerken, who had been manager of the family's quarry business. The elder Mr. Vanderwerken asked Judge Grunwell to take over the management, and as an additional inducement provided the home, Bellevue.

A little way up Glebe Road from Bellevue is the summer home of Judge Grunwell's daughter, Mrs. Louise Grunwell English. The house, whose street number is 3531, sets far back on a knoll in a grove of oak trees. It is named "Otley-on-the-Dee" for the English village from which the family came to America.

In 1896, Judge Grunwell became involved in another battle between the North and the South, again with a Northern victory. However, this dispute was purely local, between two parts of the county, as to which would become the site of the new court house. Formerly the town of Alexandria had been the county seat. Judge Grunwell was Chairman of the Board of Supervisors and was appointed to the Commission to choose the location of the new building. State Senator Frank Hume urged that it be at the south end of the county near Alexandria, the greatest concentration of population. Judge Grunwell pleaded to have it placed further north in what would be a more central location. George Nicholas Saegmuller, whose wife was Mrs. Grunwell's cousin, followed Judge Grunwell on the Board, and succeeded in having a referendum passed approving the more northernly Fort Myer Heights site.

The Grunwell estate extended to the palisades through a wilderness which has been developed by the Judge's sons into a beautiful residential area, (which the author of this book and her husband chose for the site of their home, built in 1950). Bellevue Forest subdivision is named in honor of the gracious home which was built nearly a century ago at the crest of the ridge to the west!

BELLEVUE . . . Appropriately named for its beautiful view from the crest of a ridge.

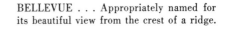

THE SPIRAL CHIMNEY . . . In order to achieve a harmonious relationship between the two chimneys as they emerged from the roof, one was "corbled" to turn in the attic so that the length of its rectangle would coincide with the other chimney.

Rixey Mansion and the Country Club

ONE of the most impressive homes in Arlington County is not actually old, but rose like a phoenix from the flames which destroyed a very early farmhouse. This is "Rixey Mansion", since 1948 the central building of Marymount Junior College (Parochial) at 2807 North Glebe Road. Civil War maps show that it was the home of Mary Hall, sister of Basil Hall of Hall's Hill. Her ancient spring was preserved until 1959 on the adjacent golf course opposite the 14th green.

Dr. Presley M. Rixey, a native of Culpeper, Virginia, became Assistant Surgeon General of the Navy and official White House physician under President McKinley. He advanced to Surgeon General with the rank of Rear Admiral on February 10, 1902. His town house was in Washington, but rural life appealed to him so much that he acquired two farms in nearby Virginia. One was in Falls Church. On it Camp Alger, named for the Secretary of War, was established during the Spanish-American War.

The other property was on North Glebe Road adjacent to the Grunwell estate, with a magnificent view of the Capital City. Here he spent his weekends, riding horseback along the country roads, often as host to President Theodore Roosevelt.

The Rixeys used the large old farmhouse until it burned. They lived in the tenant house while their mansion was being constructed in 1920.

The most lavish entertainment which ever took place in the mansion was the celebration on April 25, 1927 of the Rixey's golden wedding anniversary. Among the five hundred guests were the widows of two presidents, Mrs. Roosevelt and Mrs. Wilson. Admiral Rixey died the following year and his widow shortly thereafter.

Before his death Admiral Rixey helped organize the congregation of St. Mary's Episcopal Church and gave land for the building.

Few people realize that the Washington Golf and Country Club has changed both its name and location since it was organized in February 1894 by a group of members of the Metropolitan Club of Washington. The cover of the January 1897 issue of the magazine *Golfing* showed a photograph of the mustachioed members of the Washington Golf Club on the club-house porch. It was then listed among the seventeen clubs of the United States Golf Association. As the club was at that time three years old, it was probably one of the earliest clubs.

The original nine-hole course of 165 acres was at Arlington Heights above Rosslyn, on the present site of Colonial Village Apartments and Shopping Center. Fort Corcoran lay on the brink of the hill between Oak and Pierce Streets on the north side of Wilson Boulevard; its earthworks may have been included in the fairway hazards. The clubhouse was the pre-Civil War home of the Hoover family, at the rear of the grounds of the present Woodrow Wilson School. Jackson, the Hoover's old servant, "refreshed" the gentlemen before the large open fireplace after their matches.

Club members were required to wear the regulation outfit consisting of knickerbockers and scarlet coat with green collar. They termed a par score a "bogey". Their gutta-percha balls, called "gutties", had the resilience of a wadded-up sock and often had to be pressed back into shape between "swats". One hundred and fifty yards was considered a fine drive. Each hole had its own name, such as Arlington, Tarn, and Home.

The club had to seek a new site in 1907 when the lessor decided to subdivide and build on his property. A deal was consummated in March 1908 with Admiral Rixey for seventy-five acres of his estate on the east side of North Glebe Road. It was then that the name was changed to Washington Country Club because of a diversity of interests in addition to golf.

The eighteen-hole course was much shorter than at present and was truly a mountain-goat affair. The course was enlarged and revised in 1919, when 47 acres of the Grunwell tract were added. At that time a famous golf-architect said, "The Washington course, when completed, will be one of the most beautiful, enjoyable and sporting in the world."

The clubhouse, which was built in 1908 for fifteen hundred dollars, was demoted to Golf Shop the following year when a rustic type of clubhouse was built for eleven thousand dollars. It was gutted by fire in 1936 and was soon rebuilt. The clubhouse was replaced by a beautiful new structure opened officially on Thanksgiving Eve, 1958.

Soon after the purchase of the acreage from Admiral Rixey, it was discovered that the site of the present swimming pool was not included but was desired by the club. Therefore, a member of the Board of Directors, Dr. J. T. Johnson, challenged Dr. Rixey to a golf duel for the acreage. Dr. Johnson won the match and the land for the club!

At about that time the application of Percy Belmont, the New York socialite, was rejected because he had been divorced! By 1914, honorary members included Teddy Roosevelt and William Howard Taft. Woodrow Wilson was an active member.

Access to the club was best by way of Chain Bridge, although many used the Great Falls trolley. In 1915 the name of the club was changed to the present composite title, Washington Golf and Country Club.

Brick Wood, the caddy-master, is a link with the early days. He first appeared on the scene in 1917 as a pink-cheeked, red-headed caddy named William Wood. The other caddies experimented with the obvious nickname of Red, but a few bloody noses straightened that out. He has been Brick Wood to forty years of golfers.

RIXEY MANSION . . . Picture taken at the time it was purchased for Marymount School. It is now the center building of a vast educational group.

MARY HALL'S SPRING . . . Named for the owner of the original house on the site of the Rixey Mansion. The spring remained as a picturesque and historic site on the adjacent golf course until destroyed during the winter of 1958-59.

RIXEY MANSION DRAWING ROOM . . . Fine architectural details appear throughout the mansion.

Dawson-Bailey House, "Rio Vista"

I AM frequently asked how I discover the history of the early Arlington homes. There is no one place to seek it, nor one method of operation. Official documents have been scattered among the various counties of which Arlington was once a part, and many were destroyed during the Civil War. Besides, so many of the things which shaped the lives of our pioneer families are the unrecorded events which have been handed down as family traditions, known only to the old-timers.

Each case differs, but every one has the challenge of a mystery story, and requires a great deal of digging to find the clues which lead to the facts to weave into the history of the lives of our pioneers. It is a race against time to gather their fragments of history before it is too late.

Two years before my research started, Mrs. Bessie Bailey died on January 5, 1955, at the age of ninety-four. Her home is reputed to be the oldest in Arlington County. Her friends recall that she told them many interesting things about local history, but no one wrote them down! She had no children.

The "Bailey House" is above Rosslyn on the Dawson Terrace Playground on North Taft Street between 21st Street and the wooded palisades. It is a small two story structure of native stone. Architecturally, it could be the original patent house, but we have no proof. When the early land patents were granted, the patentee was required to build a house thereon within a year, or forfeit the right to the land. Stone was usually used as it offered good protection and was readily available.

On March 14, 1696, Thomas Owsley, Clerk of Stafford County Court and Captain of the Rangers, patented 640 acres extending up the Potomac to Spout Run. It is possible that he proved his patent by erecting this house. The Mason family acquired the land in 1717 with other patents within the Rosslyn area. Financial difficulties in the 1830's led to the holdings being taken over by the Bank of the United States. The bank had the land surveyed in 1836 and 1837 by Lewis Carberry. A house is shown on the Carberry map at the exact location of the existing one. It is also shown in a survey of 1785 made by Robert Brooks, to settle a lawsuit.

However, to contradict the rumor of great age; there is beneath the east window a large stone on which is deeply carved, "T. B. D. 1859". These are initials of Mrs. Bailey's father, Thomas Benonie Dawson, who we know owned the house during the Civil War. The carving indicated that the house was built by him at that date; yet the rumors of great age persisted, fortified by the architectural style.

The mystery was solved after more than a year of sleuthing, by a letter from "Tom" Dawson's granddaughter on Long Island! She said he had bought the house and eighty-five acres in 1859, and had en-larged the building on the east end, matching the original stone. It is possible the west portion dates back to 1696! The Dawsons named their home Rio Vista.

Thomas Benonie Dawson was born in Dawsonville, Maryland in 1816. On October 24, 1839 he married eighteen-year-old Elizabeth Jewell, daughter of Elizabeth and William Jewell of Georgetown. Besides their town-house on M Street, the Jewells bought a farm in Virginia just across Spout Run from the old stone house. Their house disappeared long ago and I can find no one who remembers it, yet I know that its color was red! Major General J. G. Barnard mentions it as "the red house" in a report of June 25, 1863 on progress of Fort Smith on Red Hill or Carberry Meadows. The fort's well and some of the earthworks are preserved on the Hendry estate at 2411 24th Street, North, across what was then the road from the Jewell home. The old spring house which can be seen from the Spout Run Parkway at its junction with Lorcom Lane may have been the Jewell spring.

The Dawson-Bailey spring is within the grounds of Dr. Jacobs' home at the end of North Randolph Street, beneath a giant poplar tree which shaded the soldiers during the Civil War. They had been given some sacks of walnuts which they cracked while resting at the spring; enough rolled away to start a walnut grove.

During the War, Fort Bennett was erected just east of Rio Vista, and the whole farm was taken over by Northern troops. None of the family could leave the yard without a pass. Two youthful officers of the 7th Regiment of New York were taken ill, and Mrs. Dawson was asked to take them into her home for better care. This led to a multiple set of romances; Mary Dawson married George Young; John Chumasow, the other officer, married Young's sister, Eva; and later, John's brother, Henry, married Anne Jewell Dawson!

The youngest Dawson daughter was Bessie Lola, born in the stone house in 1861; she lived there until her death in 1955. Bessie married a wealthy New Yorker, William Conway Bailey. His hobby was boating and boat-races upon the Potomac. When the Baileys wished to visit Georgetown they used their launch. They frequently visited the amusement park on Analostan Island.

Mrs. Bailey was a brilliant and charming little lady of elegant manners. Her home was furnished with heirlooms of excellent taste. She was pleased that the County purchased part of the farm for a playground, and expressed the hope that her home would eventually become a museum of early days. Following her death, it was bought by the County and added to the recreation center which is named for her father, Dawson Terrace Playground.

DAWSON-BAILEY HOUSE . . . The initials and date carved under the window at the right end of the house confused the dating of its erection. It may be the county's oldest.

FORT SMITH . . . Civil War fortification which was adjacent to the home owned by Mrs. Dawson's father across Spout Run.

The Doubleday Mansion Mystery

ONE of the handsomest homes in the county is situated at 2301 North Uhle Street, on the promontory of the Potomac Palisades between Spout Run and the River. It commands a magnificent view. Its white columns can be seen from Key Bridge.

For more than a year I delayed writing about it, hoping to fathom the mystery of its builders, Colonel Charles William Doubleday and his wife, Sarah Louise. They built in 1898 and departed eighteen years later. They were obviously wealthy and cultured and are said to have entertained notables of Washington and cavalry officers of Fort Myer. Their Virginia neighbors did not know them personally and are unable to tell me who they were, from whence they came, why they left such beauty, where they went, and whether or not they had heirs.

Their name is uncommon, and I wonder if there is a relationship to General Abner Doubleday who was recognized as the "father" of our national game, baseball. The couple is unknown to the Doubleday family of the well-known publishing company. The little we do know about Colonel and Mrs. Charles W. Doubleday comes from the land records at the Court House. These same records turned up some interesting facts about the site of the home and its various names.

This was part of the Thomas Going patent which, with the Owsley tract of the previous chapter, was later acquired by the Mason family of Gunston Hall and Analostan Island. John Mason's financial difficulties led to foreclosure in the 1830's by the Bank of the United States. It was sold in 1848 to William Jewell of Georgetown, as related in the previous chapter.

In 1877, the heirs of William Jewell deeded the land to The Ivanwold Syndicate for a sub-division. George Denning and Charles S. Bradley acquired Ivanwold and adjacent Woodmont. The Doubledays purchased approximately eighteen acres from them in the spring of 1898.

The Doubleday mansion shows evidence of having been built at different periods; beneath the white paint, the bricks of the wings are of a different color and bond. The older central section may have been built by Charles Bradley, a bachelor of Georgetown whose relatives had a liking for attractive country estates. His grandfather, Assistant Postmaster General Abraham Bradley had charge of bringing the official records by boat from Philadelphia to the new Federal City in 1800. Abraham had a townhouse in Washington and a country estate, "Chevy-Chase," which is the site of the Chevy Chase Country Club. In August 1814 when the British burned the Capitol, several Cabinet-members took refuge there, bringing important records. Another relative, William A. Bradley, purchased Analostan Island in 1855.

Included in the Doubleday tract is the site of Mason's Mill on the west bank of Spout Run, described on page 50.

The Doubledays extended the existing house on both sides, creating a beautiful pillared mansion, which they named The Cedars. On March 16, they sold to Harry Wardman, builder of Wardman Park Hotel (now the Sheraton-Park). Three years later it was purchased by the Richard Harlows. They named it Hockley for Mr. Harlow's ancestral estate in Maryland. Mr. Harlow was the builder of the Montana Railroad (nicknamed *The Jawbone*), and the owner of a large ranch in Montana. Their daughter, Catherine, married Theodore Wilkinson, and came to live at Hockley after the death of Mrs. Harlow in 1923.

During World War II, Vice Admiral Wilkinson commanded Halsey's Third Amphibious Force. Following Admiral Wilkinson's death at the end of the war, Mrs. Wilkinson moved to Washington. She later married Admiral Sir Henry Moore and now resides in England. Her daughter, Ann Wilkinson, inherited Hockley; she is now Mrs. Ralph W. Hunter of Hanover, New Hampshire.

Within a short period, Hockley had a variety of leasors. The sister of General Billy Mitchell lived there; then a group of Roosevelt's Brain Trust held Bachelor Hall, with no feminine invaders except for their famous Sunday brunches.

Then, in 1946, a lease of ten years with an option to buy was granted to Trans-World-Airlines through its president, the late Jack Frye. A token rent was to be supplemented by the lessee's investment of a specified amount in improvements. Mr. Frye remodeled the entire interior. Within two years, Howard Hughes, who owned the controlling interest in the corporation, and the lessor dissolved the lease by mutual consent.

It was then (1948) that the estate was purchased by G. Grant Mason, Jr., one of the founders of Pan-American Airways, an original member of the Civil Aeronautics Board and currently vice-chairman of the Board of Vision, Inc. The Masons were looking for a hotel-sized home with ample acreage for their six children and numerous dogs. It is good to see a mansion become a family home, its proper destiny. It is now named Peakleigh, which combines parts of the names of the mothers of both Mr. and Mrs. Mason.

DOUBLEDAY MANSION . . . Front portico which faces a magnificent view down the Potomac from the crest of the palisades.

REAR OF THE HOUSE . . . The roadway approaches the home from the rear which is almost as impressive as the front entrance.

Riverwood Was Phillips Estate

BEAUTIFUL Riverwood Estates, at the crest of the Potomac Palisades between Windy Run and Marcey Creek, was part of the Mason Tract. Assistant Secretary of State William Hunter of Georgetown was the next owner. The tract changed hands four times between 1850 and June 1853. John King of Washington acquired it and sold it to Ichabod and Achsah Thompson of Copenhagen, Lewis County, New York, who deeded it to John Brown of Alexandria. George Richardson Herrick of Geneseo County, New York, who had come to Washington in 1845 as a Federal employee, purchased the tract in 1853. Upon it he built a home.

The next owner was Robert Augustus Phillips, born in 1833 at Dryden, New York, of a prominent family. He was descended from the Reverend George Phillips, who came to Salem, Massachusetts, on the *Arbella* in 1630 with Governor Winthrop. Robert A. Phillips married Ann Elizabeth Boyer, whose ancestors were French Huguenots from the Eastern Shore of Maryland.

Phillips recognized the business opportunities across the Potomac from Washington, and during the Civil War bought up a number of tracts of timberland to supply lumber for Union fortifications. Attracted to the beauty of the area for a family home, he purchased the mile-square Herrick estate on July 5, 1865, and named it "North Arlington."

Upon discovering that sprouts from the large wild grapevine stumps on the cutover land made the astonishing annual growth of from ten to twenty feet, he decided to plant a vineyard, the area's first. In the spring of 1866 he planted three acres of Concord grapes, and the resulting crop exceeded expectations. So many interested visitors arrived one day to see the famous vineyard that Mr. Phillips suggested they form a Potomac Fruit Growers' Association, with monthly meetings to discuss horticulture. Fourteen assembled at the Phillips home on September 14, 1868, to organize. The report written in 1908 by Mr. Phillips, four years before his death, gave this account of the association: Their membership ranged from fifty to seventy-five, with monthly meetings except in summer, when they had an annual excursion down the Potomac by chartered steamer. Meanwhile, the membership evolved from fruit growers to fruit consumers who presented essays, songs, instrumental music, and other cultural achievements. Thus the Potomac Literary Club was born.

North Arlington house and its adjacent windmill stood until 1955, when they were demolished for the erection of the present residence at 2515 North Quebec Street. The old home was the birthplace of the Phillips children, two of whom performed important services to our country. Harry Phillips was the first superintendent and a heavy stockholder of the Washington, Arlington, and Falls Church Railway (electric trolley), which ran its first cars through the County in 1897.

In order to try to secure a franchise to operate to the Georgetown side of the Potomac, Harry Phillips attempted to secretly install the rail line across Aqueduct Bridge in the middle of the night and to run a car over it. However, the news leaked out and the plan was thwarted by Washington authorities, whose jurisdiction extended to the Virginia shore. (Phillips' chief electrician, who was at the controls the night of the bridge episode, was Howard Crocker, born in 1874. His grandfather, Brevet Brigadier General John S. Crocker of the New York 93rd Volunteers, had settled in Washington after the war. In June, 1869 he bought 4.28 acres from Robert Phillips for a summer home.)

The other Phillips son whose career included an important service to our country was Asa Emory Phillips, Sr., born at North Arlington in 1868. While Engineer of the Sewerage Division of the District of Columbia, he built for Washington what was then the largest pumping station in the world. He conceived and executed the plan to bring water from the District of Columbia to Arlington County by conduit suspended beneath Chain Bridge. In 1927-1928 he supervised construction of the one-and-a-half-million-gallon ground storage reservoir and the quarter-million-gallon tower on Old Dominion Drive at North 25th Street, the pumping station, and approximately thirty-six miles of service mains throughout the county, at less than estimated cost.

The next year he represented our Nation at the World Engineering Conference in Tokyo. He served on the Engineering Review Board of Chicago, assisted in solving the water problems of Boston and New York City, and was an engineer of the American Cemeteries and Monuments in France. He died in Washington January 1, 1936.

On the present north end of Quebec Street which remains undeveloped, Dr. Montgomery Hunter bought a tract in 1888. Although his office was in Georgetown, he administered to the needs of his country neighbors, day or night, at the rate of one dollar per house call. The late well-known Dr. Oscar B. Hunter, Sr., of Washington who died in 1952, was his son. Dr. Oscar B. Hunter, Jr., now operates the medical laboratory in Washington named in his father's memory.

In 1920, Mrs. Edith LeCompte purchased the Hunter tract and resided there until 1936, when she sold it to Miss Anna Hedrick, the present owner. The house was demolished a few years ago, but ivy-festooned trees mark the site.

Most of the Phillips estate has been developed within the past few years by John C. Wright as Riverwood Estates. Paul Stone is developing an adjacent acreage on which are Crystal Springs and the picturesque remnants of the Phillips stone springhouse in a lovely wooded glen. These springs help form Marcey Creek, which we hope the County may include in its proposed system of finger parks.

THE RIVER . . . Trees silhouette against the sparkle of sunlight dancing on the water.

RIVERWOOD SITE . . . Riverwood estates are just off the picture at the extreme left at the river bend. The homes overlook the parkway to views of Washington and Georgetown across the Potomac.

Little Italy Vanishes

ONE of our County's most unique and picturesque settlements was erased forever from the Marcey Creek ravine, with the beginning of the construction of the George Washington Memorial Parkway extension. Little Italy was the home of about twenty-four Italian and Sicilian quarrymen. A crew of about one hundred colored laborers (some came seasonally from Westmoreland County) supplemented their work.

The fine granite blue-stone was first quarried commercially by the Vanderwerken-Grunwell family who bought land along the palisades in 1851. Later the quarries were operated by the Potomac Stone Company, the Columbia Sand and Gravel Company, and finally by the Smoot Sand and Gravel Company from 1931 until they ceased operation in September 1938. Most of the workers drifted away, but those who had families or were too old to seek employment elsewhere sought to eke out their existence for the remaining years of their lives in the homes they had been permitted to build on company-owned land. The Smoot Company allowed them to remain, but as a control over the land, established a system of token leases at ten cents per month. However, no collections have been recorded since 1948.

When the National Park Service took title on March 8, 1956, the three remaining old men—Phil, Carl, and Josh—were advised that they must vacate before January 15, 1957. Phillip Matoli, born in Messina, Sicily, in 1876, came to America in 1904. After laboring in New Jersey for two years, ten hours daily for eighty cents per day, he heard of the local quarries and came down here as a dynamiter for the higher wages of $1.50 per day. Soon came Guiseppe (Josh) Conduci, born in Sicily in 1883, followed by his brother Carmelo (Carl) Conduci. They loaded the stone on barges to deliver at Georgetown and Washington.

In the days of quarrying, life in Little Italy was colorful, hard, and sometimes violent, resembling that of early western mining towns. Michele Dimeglio was an unofficial mayor who tried to keep things in line and looked after those in need. He had come from Naples in 1903 when he was a nineteen-year-old lad. While working in a quarry at Martinsburg, West Virginia, he met and married an Irish girl visiting there from Harrisonburg. They built a home in Little Italy and there reared their children. Michele's brother, Tom, and his family lived as neighbors. Another family was that of Ross Matoli, who ran the little store. The colony was isolated, with little policing and no fire protection. A quarryman named Patsy was burned alive when his shack caught fire late one night. The Dimeglio's home burned in 1936, and the family moved into the cottage of their son, Charles, who had taken the Anglicized name of Miller.

Boisterous fights were frequent, but were mostly settled among themselves. However, two acts of bloodshed, one fatal, brought in the authorities. In 1926 Mike Sunday, the colony's habitual trouble-maker, given to outbursts of mean violence, shot Michele Dimeglio, who spent two or three days in the hospital having buckshot dug out of his scalp but did not have Mike Sunday arrested. Three years later Mike tried to murder Carl Conduci, shooting him at close range and shattering both legs. While Mike was reloading the gun to kill, it was wrested from him by old colored Ed, saving Carl's life. While hundreds of spectators watched the rescue squad get the blood-drenched victim out of the canyon to the ambulance, Mike Sunday made his escape. Four years later, word came from New York that he had met a violent death. Carl recovered but was permanently crippled. His brother, Josh, is crippled from a lifetime of heavy labor and arthritis.

It was the violence of nature which maimed Phil and Ross Matoli; they were caught in a rockslide from the cliff. Ross' leg was sheared off by a sharp boulder, and Phil's heel was crushed. Two years in the hospital and skin grafts from his hip saved Phil's foot, but he still suffers with it a half-century later.

In 1936 Phil faced the choice of kill or be killed. Fourteen dollars, nearly a week's wages, had been stolen from his shack. He suspected Tex, a giant Negro quarryman. Tex heard of the accusation and threatened to kill Phil, whose friends warned him to be armed. The next day they saw each other approaching on the trail. Tex picked up a huge club and started toward Phil, who warned him to stop or be shot. As Tex came on, Phil shot him in the leg to try to stop him, but the enraged and bleeding Negro continued coming, swearing to kill. Phil's final warning was unheeded and he shot again, this time fatally. Tex lingered a few days. Phil was arrested but released upon the verdict of justifiable homicide.

In recent years, life has been peaceful for the three old quarrymen. Their needs were simple; their gardens and the river provided most of their food. With the pittance from their "pensh" (Social Security and County Welfare), they bought staples including their one luxury, pure olive oil for cooking. Sometimes there was enough for a bottle of wine to warm their blood and mellow their memories. The companionship of pet dogs and cats eased the loneliness.

The Conduci brothers raised thousands of beautiful flowers selling them to the residents of the fine new homes in nearby Riverwood Estates. Carl peddled them in a rickety wagon which the crippled brothers would load and draw up out of the canyon with ropes tied to trees.

It was a stunning blow to these men when the Park Service denied their appeal to be permitted to remain. They had planned to move their little shacks off the roadway site and spend their last days in the only way of life known to them. As they were being uprooted from the soil which had seemed theirs from years of patient toil, they dug up thousands of their cherished bulbs to give to people who had befriended them. Many went to the Shippens on Quincy Street, whose garden they had helped create.

Years ago it would have been Michele Dimeglio who would have helped these three with their bewildering problem, but he died in 1951. His son Charlie Miller (stone-masonry contractor) is now their benefactor. He arranged temporary quarters for the three. Phil has been given a home on the Prince William County farm of the McNutts, who live on North Quebec Street near the trail to Little Italy. Charlie Miller moved Phil and got him settled. He has undertaken the responsibility of the future welfare of Josh and Carl.

THE LAST THREE . . . Strong and weatherbeaten, the faces of the last three quarry workers resemble the Potomac cliffs where they worked and lived.

Roberts Lane to "Glenmore"

THE northern section of Bellevue Forest was developed between 1954 and 1958 along Roberts Lane which originally extended from the Potomac Palisades, along the crest of the hill between Gulf Branch and a tributary of Donaldson Run, to Military Road. In 1948, two blocks of Roberts Lane from Military Road to Pollard Street which now serves as its outlet were eliminated. From the air, Roberts Lane looks like a necklace laid upon green velvet, with pendant cul-de-sacs on each side.

This area was part of the vast Mason Estate. The portion nearest Military Road was acquired in 1851 by Gilbert Vanderwerken to pasture the herd of horses which he used to draw his fleet of omnibuses from Aqueduct Bridge to the Navy Yard. The acreage toward the River had been acquired by the Simmons family, the first known residents of the area. Their home was about one hundred feet northeast of the giant holly tree which is in front of the Rathbone residence at 3575 North Roberts Lane.

The daughter, Mary Ellen Simmons, married George W. Reid of Langley, Fairfax County. They built just across the lane on the other side of the forty-foot stone-lined well which still exists, although capped with concrete in recent years. George Reid purchased the farm from his wife's parents. After their death, he added to their pioneer cottage to make a barn and storage sheds for his berry crates. He developed a tremendous strawberry farm, during harvest season using as many as fifty pickers daily from daylight to dark. The berries were packed thirty-two quarts to the crate. One hundred twenty crates were taken daily in wagons to a Washington wholesaler for shipment.

By the time of the Civil War, George Reid had saved a neat sum of money. The rumor he had hidden the money in his house reached the men at nearby Fort Ethan Allen. Two drunken soldiers conceived a get-rich-quick idea. They broke into the back of the house, thinking it was empty, but were surprised by the owners. George Reid ran for his gun which was kept above the front door, but each thief seized an end of it to try to turn the weapon on their unexpected host. The terrified wife grabbed an axe and threw it at one of the attackers, wounding him severely. Reid was then able to wrest his gun from the other who fled but was shot dead before he got across the yard. That episode discouraged thieving on the Reid farm!

A daughter, Mary Frances Reid, now living on Military Road was born at the homestead in 1873, and married Samuel Phillip Morris, son of the John Morris who was living on the farm assisting Mr. Reid. Samuel and "Fanny" Morris' son, Charles, was born there August 5, 1895. Charles established the Morris Nursery at the intersection of Glebe and Military Roads, operated since his death in 1955 by his widow and son.

Another child of George and Mary Ellen Reid was Horatio, who, upon his marriage in the 1880's built a house on the crest of the gentle rise west of the homestead. We know that this was sometime before the birth in 1890 of their son, Howard, now living in Chesterbrook. It was constructed of sturdy dovetailed timbers on a "dry-wall" stone foundation two feet thick. The basic structure of the handsome residence built by the Rathbones in 1946 is the Horatio Reid house. The older Reid home burned down before 1900, and the site of the Simmons homestead is now marked only by the remnants of a lilac hedge.

In July of 1866, Oliver Cox, the preacher and pedagogue of Mount Olivet Church, made a survey of the Reid farm, apparently in view of a sale to the Gardiners of Washington of a ten-acre plot which included the mouth of Donaldson Run, and property up over the crest of the palisades. In 1876, the Gardiners mortgaged their plot to George W. Linville, also of Washington, who foreclosed in 1893.

About 1906, William Florian Roberts, a prominent printer of Washington, purchased the ten acre Linville tract and a few years later, the thirty-four-acre Reid farm. He erected a summer home designed especially for the rustic site by his friend, Appleton P. Clark, a noted architect. It was perched at the brink of the cliff, commanding a magnificent view from its large porch. Stone for the foundation and chimney were quarried from the palisades. The tremendous stone mantel was drawn up the cliff by a donkey-engine, and trees were cut on the site for the log walls. The estate was named Glenmore, the "more" a contraction of Mrs. Robert's maiden name. The family usually came by boat from Fletcher's Boat House across the Potomac. Young people rode horseback through the woodland trails. The Horatio Reid house was used by the son, Bertrand, as a vacation home for his family after his marriage.

Three generations of the Roberts family enjoyed the wilderness beauty throughout the summer months. During that time Glenmore was the site of many parties and oyster roasts. Prominent Washingtonians included members of the Gridiron Club, the Rotary Club, Temple-Noyes Masonic Lodge and the Analostan Boat Club. The latter paddled up the river in their long war-canoes from the clubhouse which was situated at the site of the Titantic statue.

Mr. W. F. Roberts died in 1929 and Mrs. Roberts in 1941. The house was bought in 1945 by Admiral Chester Ward. His cousin, Edward J. Calhoun, soon built nearby at 3450 Roberts Lane. Until recently, these were the only houses past the big holly. The George Washington Memorial Parkway now cuts across the brink of the promontory, so now all may share the magnificent view chosen a half-century ago by the Roberts family for their summer retreat.

GLENMORE UNDER CONSTRUCTION . . .
Built about 1906 by the Roberts family of
Washington which used it as a summer home
for three generations.

GIANT HOLLY OF ROBERTS LANE
. . . This holly tree which is over fifty
feet tall and measures 6½ feet in cir-
cumference at shoulder height may be
the oldest in Arlington County.

FARMHOUSE TO MODERN RESIDENCE
. . . The home built in 1946 by the Rathbone
family incorporates the Horatio Reid house
erected in the 1880's.

Minor Hill, the County's Highest

MINOR Hill, with an elevation of 460 feet, lies on the northwest side of Little Falls Road near the intersection of North Powhatan Street. Rockingham Street runs along its northern flank, crossing the Fairfax County line at Franklin Park. The advantageous location of Minor Hill naturally attracted early settlers. One block beyond the County line is the Minor homestead, brick veneer over logs. It may have been built by Simon Pearson or James Going when they patented the land in 1730. The following year when Simon Pearson and Gabriel Adams acquired adjacent land, Minor Hill is designated on the patent papers as Brandymore Castle.

George Minor, who was born in 1753 and married Ann Adams of Church Hill (see page 178) lived in this house. A back wing was added in the early 1770's, probably constructed under the supervision of their friend Colonel James Wren, the architect of The Falls Church. Its unusual construction of drymasonry walls covered with wood siding identified his style. That addition was removed a few years ago when a full second story was added to the original log house and the exterior brick added.

George Minor gave the ground (at Seven Corners) for Fairfax Chapel (Methodist). The site eventually became Oakwood Cemetery. The Minor Hill house is the home of Mr. and Mrs. William J. Hardy, Junior, who have furnished it with appropriate antiques. Mrs. Hardy told me of a tradition that a daughter of the Minor family who died during the Civil War was quietly buried beneath a lilac bush.

The first record we find of the Minor family is that of John Minor of Westmoreland County, whose son Nicholas was a justice as early as 1684. His son Nicholas II settled in Prince William County; Nicholas III pushed further into the wilderness. He purchased a plantation on the Alexandria-Key's Gap Road and erected an "ordinary" which became the nucleus of Leesburg. The grandfather of George Minor of Minor Hill, he was a captain of the Fairfax Militia and a member of the first County Court when Loudoun County was organized in 1757.

Minor Hill was a strategic spot during the Civil War. It was first occupied by Confederate snipers who exchanged shots with Federals en route to Bull Run. A Confederate casualty there may have been one of the first of the conflict. The ridge was soon taken by the Federal Army, a lookout tower was established on the crest, and troops were quartered along the flank for four years. This resulted in a claim after the war for eleven thousand dollars damages to local property.

Minor Hill was leased about 1867 to Eugene Crimmins of Ireland. He had come to America about 1863 and had served one year in the Union Army. His son, Francis X. Crimmins of 3577 North Powhatan Street was born in the Minor homestead. It is through the generosity of Mr. Crimmins that one of the original District of Columbia milestones, Northwest Number 1 (adjacent to 3611 Powhatan Street), is preserved.

Of the Minor family who lived in Arlington, John and his brother, Fairfax, both built homes on the northeast flank of Minor Hill. Neither house stands today. John's farmhouse site is now at 5600 35th Road North, a cul-de-sac. In the back yard of the new home at this location is an ancient walnut tree. A clear spring flowed down the slope to the north. John Minor and his two wives are buried on the south side of the tree. Their roughhewn gravestone was there until the recent real estate development turned the farmland into a residential area. The son, George, who married Annie Birch is buried in the Birch-Payne graveyard at North Sycamore and 28th Streets. The graves there have been vandalized.

Fairfax Minor's home was at the site of 3026 North John Marshall Drive. It was destroyed about 1920. The street divides around the four handsome oak trees that shaded the stone springhouse. The picturesque structure was demolished and the water diverted into a storm sewer. May the trees be preserved!

The east flank of Minor Hill came into the possession of the Vandenberg (later Saegmuller) family in the mid-1800's. George M. Saegmuller loaned me his abstract title, which revealed many interesting facts. The general area was known as "Elderfield" in 1816. A transaction of 1830 refers to the schoolhouse (see page 170) which furnished a clue as to the general location of the one mentioned in 1822 in the Birchland papers, the two properties being adjacent to each other.

By 1859, the east side of Minor Hill had changed from Elderfield to "Springfield", a most descriptive name for the area. Big Spring, whose site was on the north side of 3706 John Mason Drive was a popular spot with the Civil War soldiers living in the barracks nearby. Many returned after the war to get bottles of the fine water to take home. Rock Spring still exists in the block southwest of the intersection of Rock Spring Road and Old Dominion Drive. The source of water for the Saegmuller water-ram was Bennett Spring. Two Minor springs have already been mentioned, and Easter Spring (see page 130) was further down the same slope, to the north.

MINOR HILL'S COLONIAL KITCHEN . . . Generations of residents have sharpened knives on the fireplace bricks at the left.

CHERRY TREE ON MINOR HILL . . . A veteran of an ancient orchard soars above the homes on Williamsburg Boulevard on the west flank of Minor Hill.

SITE OF OLD SPRINGHOUSE . . . John Marshall Drive splits to save the pear trees and oaks which stood above the stone springhouse of Fairfax Minor, descended from the pioneer.

Birches: Pre-Revolutionary Pioneers

THE Birch family came from England to first settle in the "Northern Neck" of Virginia, where they owned land prior to 1690. Their home was near the headwaters of Tindall Creek, north of the York River. This was the birthplace in 1680 of John Birch, Sr., who died in Westmoreland County in 1729. His son, John Birch, Jr., moved to Stafford County, where he died in 1746. His will was probated there June 9, 1747.

Joseph Birch of the next generation lived at his town-house in Alexandria, but owned a large plantation in Fairfax County. He married Janet Bowmaker Robertson, daughter of James Robertson, who also owned extensive tracts on the north side of Four Mile Run, adjacent to Abingdon Plantation and extending through the present Lyon Park area. The Northern Neck Land Book shows that James Robertson received 800 acres in 1729 and 629 acres the following year.

James Robertson died in 1769, and his estate went to his son John Robertson and daughter Janet Robertson Birch. Interesting data on the family is given in a suit, Alexander versus Birch. Both families claimed title to acreage along present Shirley Highway, which was awarded to the Alexanders in 1790 by the Virginia Court of Appeals.

Joseph Birch and his wife, Janet, continued to add to their lands; in November, 1798 he acquired with John Ball part of the Breckin patent of 1716 adjacent to the Glebe lands. On July 15, 1799, he was appointed to the important position of Tobacco Inspector for the Town of Alexandria, which carried a bond of four thousand dollars.

Joseph and Janet Robertson Birch had eleven children. Samuel, born January 30, 1790, served as a colonel in the War of 1812. He established the Birch family in northwest Arlington with his purchase of a tract extending from present Lee Highway north to Little Falls Road, and from North Lexington to North Sycamore Streets. He built his large log home at the present site of 2450 North Powhatan Street. It stood about thirty feet northwest of the house at that address named "Allencrest", which was built about 1890 and is now owned by Howard Kleeb. The old log house was torn down about 1930, but the stone-lined well of the original pioneers remains as a picturesque feature of the front garden, beneath a wisteria vine.

Samuel Birch married Ann Richards of Alexandria, who bore him three children before her death. The home of their daughter, Carrie, was under the large maple trees at what is now the rear of the playground of Nottingham School.

His second wife was Ann Cleveland, whose family plantation was on the Leesburg Pike just west of present Wakefield School. There were ten children of this marriage. Two of their daughters, Margaret Amanda and Annie, married brothers, Asbury Rozzel Payne and Theodore Payne of Munson Hill. Margaret and Rozzel's home was between the giant maples in the present 6200 block of 30th Street, North; and their two living sons, John Edward and Harry Elmore, reside on part of the original farm. Annie and Theodore Payne's home site is at 2622 North Nottingham Street. Samuel Birch's other children settled in Falls Church, present Seven Corners, and Chantilly.

Rozzel Payne was the only member of the large family connection whose sympathies were with the North during the Civil War. He volunteered, and became a lieutenant in the First Maryland Cavalry. The ties of blood and marriage held strong, and his Southern in-laws helped him to reach home for occasional visits with his family during the period that the Confederates were encamped at nearby Minor Hill.

Rozzel was buried at Arlington Cemetery, but the rest of the Birch-Payne family were laid to rest in the cemetery at the southeast corner of North Sycamore and 28th Street, North. The graves include Colonel Samuel Birch (born 1790, died 1878), who fought in the War of 1812, his two wives, their children and grandchildren, and some husbands of both generations. There are also five or six of their colored servants buried in one corner of the graveyard. Samuel Birch's daughter, Sarah (1825-1881), inherited the portion of the land upon which the cemetery had been established. In her will, the one-acre burial ground was set aside and duly recorded in the County archives. It was attractively landscaped with fine fir trees, holly, and boxwood. The last burial was made in 1930, bringing a total of fifteen graves of the family plus the five or six servants. Since the development of Berkshire Gardens Subdivision in the area, the acre restricted for cemetery purposes seems to have shrunk to about one-third of an acre. Vandals have pushed over the headstones, and all but one have been taken for flagstones for gardens. The evergreen trees, holly and boxwoods, have been cut for Christmas decorations (what irony!), and the last time I examined the plot neighborhood children appeared to have been digging in search of bodies!

The most beautiful remaining landmark of the Birch-Payne families in northwest Arlington are two ancient oaks on the hill near the Shopping Center at Little Falls Road and North Sycamore Streets, shading the stone-lined well which was a favorite destination of Theodore Roosevelt when riding horseback with his friend, Admiral Rixey.

OAKS THAT SHADED BIRCHES . . . Beneath these trees adjacent to the shopping center at Little Falls Road and Sycamore Street is the capped stone-lined well of the Birch family. In the background is the water tower atop Minor Hill.

"Birchland" and Dittmar Road

I FIND Birch history all over the county, but that is not surprising, as Joseph Birch and his wife Janet bought, patented and inherited vast acreage in the mid-1700's (see page 148). Seven of their eleven children were sons who married and had families, most of whom lived on their inheritances. On North Glebe Road lived one of these sons, William Birch who named his plantation Birchland.

"Billy" Birch had five daughters, three of whom married and settled in the neighborhood. One was Elizabeth Ann who married Edward Karl Scarborough Deeble; former State Senator Frank Ball is a grandson. Two of their granddaughters reside at 3833 North Glebe Road in a home built by their father, Silas Wright Deeble about 1870. It sits back from the road in a grove of fine old trees.

Another daughter of Billy Birch was Martha Ann whose life was spent at the original Birch house, the site of which is now known as "The Weaver Place" at 3612 North Glebe Road. The Weavers come into the story later. The Birch home consisted of two double-storied log houses connected by a one story hallway. The kitchen was in a separate building, with a huge open fireplace, as was the custom in the better homes in early days.

Martha Ann Birch was a very interesting woman; she was a good cook, a spunky rebel, and twice a widow. Augusta McNeir Weaver, her first husband's sister was very fond of her. From Augusta's existing diary, we learn a great deal of what took place involving both of them and the family.

On February 4, 1843, Martha Ann Birch married the twenty-five-year-old Joseph Edward McNeir; on October 14 she became his widow! Their son, born January 13, 1844 was named for his father. She later married Samuel Titus, whom she also outlived. During the Civil War, Martha and her father remained at Birchland. Their hearts were with the Southerners, but they had to live for years with Fort Ethan Allen close by. At one time, General Hancock commandeered their home as temporary headquarters before moving to the adjacent Vanderwerken farm. Martha sold doughnuts and pies to the Union soldiers, while expressing herself freely as a Rebel.

An exciting incident befell her sister-in-law Augusta McNeir while visiting the Stalcup relatives at Langley. General George B. McClellan and his handsomely dressed staff of about twenty officers rode by enroute to take command of the Army of the Potomac from General Pope. That night all citizens in the neighborhood were ordered to leave their homes as a battle was anticipated. Augusta and the Stalcup family including four children rode by moonlight to Chain Bridge. They found that the Union soldiers had removed the floor boards from the bridge to prevent Confederate troops from crossing the river. They re-placed enough boards to allow the refugees to cross. The threatened battle did not eventuate.

Billy Birch died October 18, 1870 and his estate was divided among the daughters. He was probably laid to rest in the family burying ground which is now marked by three giant oak trees at the corner of 37th and North Abingdon Streets. Also buried there were his other daughter Mary and her husband Thomas Langton and their son Samuel Langton. Except for the trees, all traces of the cemetery have vanished since the site has become a residential area.

On January 29, 1863, Augusta McNeir married Charles Weaver of Whitehaven, an estate west of Georgetown. Martha Birch McNeir Titus died about 1890, and Augusta McNeir Weaver purchased her sister-in-law's home. About the turn of the century, her son Walter Thomas Weaver and his wife, Mary Britt Weaver, bought the property and erected the existing home in front of the log house and kitchen which were torn down. Theodore C. Hudson who had married their daughter, Mary, purchased the family home from the estate after Mrs. Weaver's death.

In 1889, Walter Weaver founded the hardware company in Georgetown now known as W. T. Weaver and Sons, Inc. He served as Supervisor on the County Board, and also as overseer of the roads for the northern part of Arlington. Senator Ball relates an episode which took place when he was about nineteen years old, acting as chainman for George Garrett, the County Surveyor. Walter Weaver met them on Dittmar Road which was very rough, and said, "Before you boys start I want to recite a little poem,

'This road is not passable
Not even jackassable
And those who would travel it
Should turn out and gravel it.' "

Forming a crescent along part of the east boundary of the original Birchland property is Dittmar Road which swings off Glebe Road in the 3500 block, and joins it again a mile north at Walker Chapel. This road follows in part, the lane which originally led to the farm house of Thomas Hitchcock which was built before the Civil War on land bought from Billy Birch. The Hitchcock house burned in 1952.

The road takes its name from Gustav Adolph Victor Hugo Dittmar who built a house on it about 1890. He had lost his first wife, and married a seventeen-year-old French actress, Blanche Juliette Marguerite LeComte who was a contemporary of his daughter Frida Alice Anna Dittmar. He died in 1909. His ashes were kept in an urn in the Victorian turret of the house at 4510 Dittmar Road until both Frida and Blanche died, in 1948 and 1949 respectively, and burials were made in Columbia Gardens. Just when I was planning to get a photograph of the house for my book, it caught fire shortly after midnight on April 30, 1959 and burned down!

BIRCHLAND . . . This home erected about 1900 adjacent to the then standing log home of pioneer William Birch.

Phillips Family of Minor Hill

ON the west flank of Minor Hill adjacent to Williamsburg Boulevard stand two well-kept farm houses which once belonged to the Phillips family. Nearby is the family burying-ground. James William Phillips, Senior, originally from Ohio, became a wealthy contractor in Washington around the mid-1800's. At that time, there was a stimulation of interest in Northern Virginia real estate, and Mr. Phillips was one of the many Washington businessmen who deemed it wise to invest in property here, and to establish a country home for the family to move to in the summers to escape the heat of the city.

Mr. Phillips bought a large acreage, mostly from William and Walter Tucker, who owned the south and west sides of Minor Hill. The Tucker log house stood near the present Somerset Street cul-de-sac, but was destroyed many years ago. When I first came to Arlington in 1935, I recall seeing the lilac and rose bushes on the hillside, where Little Falls Road curved around the homestead site.

Before the Civil War, there was a house on Mr. Phillip's estate, either another old Tucker home or one which Mr. Phillips had erected; it shows on the 1864 map with his name beside it. It was rumored to have been used by the Confederates as their headquarters at the beginning of the conflict. However, they soon withdrew and Minor Hill became a permanent Reserve Encampment for the Federals.

After the war, Mr. Phillips erected a handsome new home about fifty feet below the old house (which he tore down), using lumber from the nearby Civil War barracks. The new house originally faced uphill, so the two fine maple trees which framed the old one were in the front yard. However, the cutting of new streets in the area in recent years has put the closest outlet at the rear, so the entrance is now reversed. The present address is 3015 North Tacoma Street, the residence of Mr. and Mrs. John L. Harrison. They bought from the Beahns, who in 1912 and 1913 conducted an excellent private school there, Brempton Institute.

Just down the hill from the Phillips home was a fine stone-lined spring beneath huge oak trees. The water was of such excellence that people came from distances to fill jugs with it for home use. This spot of sylvan beauty is rumored to have been set aside in a previous sub-division plot for preservation for public use, but about 1950 it was destroyed in order to squeeze one more house into the block.

Mr. James W. Phillips, Senior, died in 1876, and his will reflects his keen business judgment besides his feeling of responsibility to his family's future welfare. Among other provisions, he refers to the fifty-eight-acre estate, Bloomingdale, which had been "improved by a large frame dwelling house containing 20 rooms . . . which shall be held as a homestead for my children where they can all gather as in my lifetime and have a home . . . the farm to be taken care of and worked by my sons, James W., Samuel D. and Stephen C. Phillips . . . they shall keep just and true accounts in book form . . . My desire is that my daughter, Lavina Annette shall have the privilege of taking boarders at the homestead during the four months of the year from June 1st to October 1st . . . the funds for her individual use." He further requested that the proceeds from the farm should be re-invested in improvements; that no part should be sold within ten years of his death, and then at a figure not less than he specified. This shows his awareness of the potential increase of land values a century ago, and of our County's desirability as a summer resort.

His sons eventually built their own homes on Minor Hill. The one that remains was erected in the 1870's by Charles Wesley Phillips, who probably also used timbers from the abandoned barracks. The land was given his bride, Rowena Kirby, by her father, Charles Kirby of nearby Kirbyville, and straddles the Fairfax County line. This house at 3111 North Rochester Street is a block up the hill from the father's home. It is now the residence of Judge and Mrs. Warren E. Burger, who purchased it in 1955. They have wisely made no attempt to glamorize it, but have enhanced its rural charm as a typical Virginia farm home, with such appropriate items as a cypress rail fence. Flanking the house are two giant oak trees estimated to be many hundreds of years old. It has a beautiful location near the crest of our county's highest hill, overlooking the rolling countryside and facing the sunset.

Down the hill from the two Phillips homes and slightly to the south is the lot set aside by the Tuckers and Phillips as a burial ground. It is between Little Falls Road and Williamsburg Boulevard on Tacoma Street. The temporary markers have disappeared from most of the graves, but depressions indicate the burials. One area is enclosed with an iron fence, and a large handsome stone reads: "In loving memory of our parents, James B. Phillips, died 1876 aged 71. Mary Conn Phillips, died 1894, aged 85 years. Monument erected by their daughter, L. Annette Phillips, died April 28, 1896, aged 55 years."

PHILLIPS-KIRBY HOME . . . Built in the 1870's by Charles Wesley Phillips for his bride Rowena Kirby on her dowery land. *3111 North Rochester Street.*

BLOOMINGDALE . . . Erected shortly after the Civil War by James William Phillips adjacent to an earlier home. *3015 North Tacoma Street.*

Marcey Memories

"MARCEYTOWN" was a familiar name around the turn of the century. It designated that area along Military Road between Donaldson Run and Marcey Creek. The Marcey family pioneered the area over a century ago, and many of their descendants are residing on inherited acreage to-day. The name is perpetuated by Marcey Road which leads off Military Road at Marcey Hill, towards the palisades. Also, by Marcey Creek, the site of the only well-documented Indian village between Analostan Island and Chain Bridge. The village is described in the recently published brochure *Indians of Arlington* by C. B. Rose, Jr.

Most of my information on the Marcey family came from an interview in July, 1957 with a very fine old gentleman, John Henry Marcey, who was born December 5, 1855. He died September 20, 1957, nearing his one hundred and second birthday. He lived with his daughter, Mrs. Ward at 2554 North Military Road, now a subdivision cul-de-sac.

From 1880 until 1929, John Marcey was head gardener of the grounds of Arlington House and the National Cemetery. During those forty-nine years, he and his family lived in one of the dependencies of the mansion. Some of his children were born and two were married there. His recollections have been of great value to the Arlington archives. He told of a stranger of courteous demeanor and genteel bearing who visited the garden one day when he was weeding, and asked if he might have a few pieces of the up-rooted pink clover. Mr. Marcey granted the humble request, and later learned that the visitor was a son of General Robert E. Lee, returned for a nostalgic glimpse of his mother's beloved garden.

The first pioneer members of the family were James Marcey, Sr., and his wife, who built before the birth in 1831 of James, Jr. (died 1922). Their house of which no trace remains was on the north side of 26th Street, about a block east of Military Road. Their picturesque rock-lined spring, across Military Road beneath two fine oak trees at the corner of 26th Road and Robert Walker Place, was needlessly destroyed by the County in 1954. Despite the entreaty of a Marcey descendant who lives across the street, Mrs. Fred Gamble, the County diverted the flow into a storm sewer and filled in the spring.

The pioneer couple, many of their descendants, and six unknown Civil War soldiers (see page 108) are buried beneath a giant holly tree at the crest of the hill beyond the spring site. The unmarked graves are in the north corner of the lot at 2641 North Richmond Street.

James Marcey, Jr., married Elizabeth Birch. They first lived at her parents' log home at 4572 North 26th Street, described on page 156, which is still standing. Before the Civil War, they built a home at 2632 North Military Road. The foundations of that house were recently found when excavations were made for the present house on that site.

The oldest standing Marcey home is a neat little cottage at 2657 Marcey Road, belonging to Mrs. Ernest Marcey. It is a log cabin, but the siding added many years ago hides its antiquity. Mrs. Marcey showed me the original 1843 documents of Lewis Marcey pertaining to the mortgaging of land to raise funds for the construction of the homestead and development of the farm.

Another old Marcey home is at 2666 North Military Road, recently sold to the Washington Presbytery for the site of a future church. It was the residence of Mrs. T. A. Barton, granddaughter of James Marcey, Jr.; the rear portion of the house was built by her father, Walter Marcey, in 1874. Red brick facing now covers the logs which were cut on the property. Walter Marcey was sent to the Philippines by the Government after the Spanish-American War, to take charge of shipment of bodies of our soldiers for burial at Arlington National Cemetery.

Mrs. Barton's mother, who died March 10, 1958, had told me of the family's Civil War recollections. Her father-in-law, James Marcey, Jr., who was then living just up the road at 2632, told of buried treasure. A frightened Union soldier begged him to keep, until cessation of hostilities, a large sum of money which he was carrying on his person. He feared that other soldiers would take it from him. Mr. Marcey refused the responsibility of either keeping it or of knowing of its exact hiding place, but loaned the man a pick to bury it nearby. He never returned to retrieve it. Where is this hidden treasure today?

In the early days of the County, in addition to taxes, every "tithable" was required to do a certain number of days of road maintenance. James Marcey's notices in 1871 from the County road overseer designated that his two days' work should "Commence at the big Poplar"; twenty years later it was still a landmark. Where was it, and why has it since been destroyed?

The Marcey family is outstanding for its longevity, the majority living into their nineties, with a number passing the century mark. Among the treasures of the late John Henry Marcey are birthday congratulations from Harry S. Truman and Dwight D. Eisenhower.

OAKS AT MARCEY SPRING . . . Between these trees was a picturesque stone-lined spring at the corner of North 26th Road and Robert Walker Place, destroyed in 1954.

MARCEY BURIAL GROUND . . . This ancient holly tree stands guard over the graves of the pioneer Marcey family and of Federal soldiers who died at homes used as military hospitals.

"Birchwood" — An Early Homestead

THE picturesque log house at 4572 26th Street, North, restored in 1939 by Mr. and Mrs. Walter Horn, was built about 1836 by Caleb Birch on land inherited from his grandfather James Robertson whose daughter, Janet, married Joseph Birch. (See page 148.) This was the second house, for during reconstruction, the Horns found the blackened foundations and a hearth of an earlier home which had apparently been burned. The first house was probably built at the time of Caleb Birch's marriage in September of 1800 to Mary Bowling. The second was a two-story log cabin, one room above another, measuring fourteen by sixteen feet. A larger unit was added a decade later, with a connecting roof over an open breezeway, then known as a dog-trot. Tradition is that the Birch boys used to race their horses through this opening.

Mr. John Marcey, the late centenarian, told me of his childhood recollections of living with his parents in this log house, after his grandfather Birch's death. Mr. Marcey's mother, Elizabeth Birch, had married James Marcey, Jr., who died when ninety-three; this couple are buried at Walker Chapel.

When Admiral Presley M. Rixey purchased the Mary Hall tract on Glebe Road in 1899 for his summer home, he also bought the Birch land including the homestead. The Hall house later burned and was replaced by the handsome "Rixey Mansion" in 1920, which is now part of Marymount School.

Admiral Rixey brought with him a colored valet named Richard Wallace, who also had duties as a footman at the White House. He daily drove Teddy Roosevelt's children to their classes at Friends School. President Roosevelt often visited Admiral Rixey, and the two friends rode horseback through the Virginia countryside. For these visits, it was Richard's duty to make the President's favorite ice cream.

Richard had made himself at home in the Birch cabin. He liked to tell of the day when Roosevelt came down to his cabin to ask him to prepare a freezer, and would demonstrate just where the President stood, resting his hand on the door jamb. The kindly darky had "taken a likin'" to the log cabin and spent much of his time there. He planted the apple trees which still grow beside the house.

When Admiral Rixey established the Washington Golf and Country Club golf course, he put Richard in charge of clearing the fairways. Green Number 10 was surveyed to be at the cabin site; Richard said nothing, but took it upon himself to engineer otherwise. The surprised Admiral approved the change, and realizing how fond his servant had become of the log house, deeded it to him with three acres which extended back to Donaldson Run.

The Horns, both school teachers, started looking for a homesite in the late 1930's. They wanted a small house mellow with age, a hillside, a stream, and old gnarled fruit trees. On April 1, 1939, they decided to explore a dirt road on the east side of Glebe Road past St. Mary's Church. Narrow, rough, and twisting, it led through thick woods over the brink of the hill; and at its end they found their Eldorado! The decrepit log cabin was basking in the spring sunshine, and by the door hung an old bread pan on which was crudely lettered a "For Sale" sign. They found Richard and consummated a purchase.

The Horns did most of the restoration themselves during summer vacation. They took the cabin apart and reassembled the fine old logs, and rebuilt the massive chimney. Three floors were found to have been laid, one upon another, and worn through. There were traces of the older foundation and hearth. Old coins in cracks between the logs dated from the late 1700's to 1880. Beneath the back porch were a Civil War bayonet, a sword-chain, a metal picket-stake, bullet mold, belt buckles, buttons, and minnie-balls. There was also a spur which appears to be of much earlier date. It may have belonged to Caleb Birch's brother Samuel who fought in the War of 1812.

Old Richard moved into Washington, but came out periodically until the time of his death a few years ago. He enjoyed seeing his home made beautiful. In season, he again ate fruit from trees he had planted. One of his philosophical sayings was, "Jes' don't you fret; the sun'll shine in youah kitchen doah!" It shines in Birchwood today because the Birches built with fine chestnut logs, old Richard's love of the place saved it, and Admiral Rixey's appreciation to a faithful servant preserved it until the Horns found it. Their vision of its potential charm and historical value have preserved what is one of the oldest standing houses in Arlington County. May others be so inspired to save our few remaining pioneer log structures! Since the Horn restoration, the area has been developed into a fine residential district.

Facing the sunrise from the hillside back of Marymount in a peaceful grove of ancient trees is the private cemetery of the Birch family, where Caleb and his wife are buried. There are some extremely old stones without inscriptions, some whose legends have weathered beyond reading; the earliest readable records a burial in 1841. I was deeply affected by one which read, "To live in the hearts we leave behind, is not to die." May I have the privilege of contributing in some small part to the immortality of Arlington's pioneer families by helping to bring their memories to live again in the hearts of present-day and future Arlingtonians?

BIRCHWOOD . . . Erected during the 1830's by Caleb Birch, it was beautifully restored as a private residence in 1939.

BENEATH GNARLED APPLE TREES . . . This restored homestead is now used part of the time as an exclusive nursery school and kindergarten.

The Donaldson Family

THE Donaldson family originated in Scotland, and first appeared on this area's census list in 1782. They have been closely associated with the history of this area since pioneer times. In 1808, The Glebe House was partially destroyed by fire, and the following year Andrew Donaldson was authorized to superintend the 516 acres of Glebe Lands. He was to prevent the stealing of timber by trespassers, to sell fallen timber, and to deliver every fourth load to the rector of Christ Church in Alexandria.

Donaldson homes are shown throughout the county on the 1864 Civil War maps. The only prewar Donaldson house still standing is at the end of Marcey Road. It is the present home of direct descendants, the Stewart family. Robert H. Donaldson was the first member of the family to own the tract, but the homes thereon were built by his sons: George, (1844-1926), who built the existing house; and Webster, (1851-1925), who built about halfway to the end of Marcey Road. Webster's home is long gone, but his log smokehouse remained intact until torn down early in 1959. They were adjacent to the home of his daughter, Mrs. Warren Horstman, at 2741 North Marcey Road.

The George Donaldson home is on the crest of a hill overlooking the Potomac, between Donaldson Run and Marcey Creek. I am told that when it was being built, Indian skeletal remains were unearthed during foundation excavation, and that nearby were other evidences of Indian burials. This was undoubtedly the cemetery of the Marcey Creek Indian village, which was situated where that stream flows into the Potomac. In the Smithsonian Institution are a number of artifacts which were excavated from the village site in the 1940's by Carl Manson. The evidence shows that it was a pre-17th century village, with traces of a culture which existed over two thousand years ago.

East of Marcey Road, between the Webster Donaldson house site and the George Donaldson home, is the half-acre family cemetery. A lovely spot, tranquil beneath the shade of an old pear tree, it contains about seventeen graves, dating back a century.

In early days, George Donaldson would take his farm produce by boat from the mouth of Donaldson Run to Georgetown for marketing. When the Civil War broke out, his boat was confiscated by the Federal troops. However, he was finally able to convince the authorities that his activities on the Potomac had no military significance, retrieved his boat, and secured a certificate allowing him to continue using it for marketing.

Before the waters were contaminated, the mouth of the run was a favorite swimming hole, and a boat-landing. Hence, it was called Swimming Landing Run. Thus it appears on all the old land records. The name was changed to Donaldson Run since the publication of the official county map of 1900.

That beautiful stream has witnessed both fun and tragedy. Mrs. George Donaldson became despondent, and committed suicide one wintry day about 1890. She first shoved two of her young children under the edge of the ice before drowning herself. A son escaped to report the triple tragedy. This was followed by another disaster in the family of the Hillerys who lived on 26th Street, North. Two young brothers were particularly devoted to each other; one died of pneumonia. The other, in loneliness and grief, drowned himself at the mouth of the run.

In a woodland vale of the Potomac Palisades between Marcey Road and Marcey Creek is the Donaldson Run Community Swimming Pool, one of the most attractively situated in Virginia. It was dedicated in August 1958 for the enjoyment of the members who are residents of the surrounding area. One could not find a lovelier sylvan setting at a mountain-top summer resort. The pool is approached from Marcey Road which follows the ridge-top. One looks down into the blue-green waters against a background of forest trees. The grassy slopes with shrubbery borders provide a natural amphitheatre from which aquatic sports can be viewed. The lighting effect at night is particularly beautiful.

The pool conforms to the natural topography of the gentle ravine, in the shape of an "L". One angle accommodates the twelve foot deep diving area, with racing lanes of the standard Olympic length along the deeper portions.

The County is at this time negotiating for the purchase of a fifteen acre tract on the other side of Marcey Road, to develop as a recreation area, and is considering the inclusion of Marcey Creek canyon in its proposed system of "finger-parks". The entire area along the brink of the palisades is now owned by the National Park Service as the setting of the George Washington Memorial Parkway. Therefore, we can be reasonably certain that this beautiful wilderness area will be preserved for the healthful pursuit of outdoor pleasure for present and future generations.

SMOKEHOUSE . . . Picture taken December 1958 a few months before this sturdy structure was torn down. It had been built about a century ago by Webster Donaldson.

DONALDSON CEMETERY . . . It lies between Marcey Road and the George Washington Memorial Parkway.

Train Tracks and Trolleys

IN the early 1800's most of Arlington's traffic was bound for destinations beyond its boundaries. The horsedrawn coaches operating between Richmond and Washington took thirty-eight hours for the trip until 1815 when the time was reduced to twenty-four hours with a night spent on a steamboat which ran from Aquia Creek to the Federal City. In 1834 a charter was granted to continue the rail line from Fredericksburg to Potomac Creek, supplemented by a steamer. The speed of ten miles per hour attained by the first train was considered amazing.

At times, the winter ice interfered with the steamboat operation on the Potomac, and it was necessary to resort to the old stagecoach to complete the trip. By 1842, the rail line was completed to Aquia Creek and an icebreaker boat kept the Potomac channel open.

The Alexandria and Washington Railroad began operations in 1858 in this county between the south end of Long Bridge and Alexandria. Later, the Alexandria and Fredericksburg line connected with the Alexandria and Washington line, providing through-transportation between Fredericksburg and Washington. A spur track was run to Rosslyn.

In 1904, it was agreed by all the railroad systems of the area that there was need for a freight classification yard on the south side of the Potomac in Arlington County. The Potomac Yard was put into operation in 1906 under one management which agreed to operate it until the year 2001 in the mutual interest of the five companies involved. In 1920 the Richmond Washington Company was organized by these companies which were issued equal shares of stock and together held a controlling interest. Other than railroad companies, the State of Virginia is the largest single stockholder.

Arlington County's rail line toward the west, the Washington and Old Dominion Railroad, is descended from two early systems. The first was the Alexandria, Loudoun and Hampshire Railroad organized in 1853. The line was in operation to Leesburg by 1859, although it never reached its original destination, the coal fields of Hampshire County.

During the Civil War, trestles and much of the track were destroyed by General Lee's retreating army. In 1870, the Washington and Ohio Company succeeded the bankrupt company. Although the company planned to extend their line to the Ohio River, it never got beyond Bluemont, a little resort at the crest of the mountain ridge west of Leesburg.

The other parent corporation of the present-day freight line westward from Rosslyn was the Great Falls and Old Dominion Electric Railway which operated a trolley through Cherrydale and McLean to the Falls. It was abandoned in 1935 after twenty-nine years of operation. The right-of-way from Cherrydale westward was taken over by Arlington and Fairfax Counties for highway purposes, and is the present Old Dominion Drive.

The railway line had in 1912 established a passenger-freight connection with the line running from Alexandria to Bluemont. Meanwhile that line had been taken over in 1894 by the Southern Railway System which leased the Bluemont Branch to the Washington and Old Dominion Railway until 1944 when the latter company purchased it. Passenger service was discontinued in 1951. Sixty-nine industries, fourteen of which are in Arlington County, have private sidings along the line.

The first trolley line in Arlington County operated from Rosslyn to Fort Myer. "Renny" Miller, who remained with the company until his death in 1944, was employed about 1896 to "drive" the car. He later became a motorman, but that first car had no motor; it was pulled up the hill by a horse which rode on the back platform when the car coasted back to Rosslyn.

The Washington, Arlington and Falls Church line evolved from the Fort Myer beginning. We learned on page 140 how Harry Phillips laid the line in 1897. There was quite a celebration in Ballston on July 4 when the first trolley came singing along the rails from Rosslyn, with Renny Miller at the controls!

It was not long before this line tied in with the Washington, Alexandria, Mount Vernon Electric Railway by constructing a link on what is present Washington Boulevard.

The Falls Church line suffered one major accident in 1906. Fortunately for Renny Miller, it was his day off. Will Nauck substituted as motorman on the city-bound passenger trolley, which met disaster after a confusion of signals at the Clarendon siding. A freight engine, with Bob Crack at the throttle, was pushing a flat car of steel rails up the grade from Rosslyn. It crashed into the trolley at the one blind curve (behind the present Sears Roebuck building). George Warren, a storekeeper of Ballston was killed. Will Nauck lost both of his legs.

The electric cars were replaced from 1936 to 1940 by "auto-railers" which could tuck their trolley wheels under their tummies and drive along the streets as buses. When these were later replaced by regular buses the County acquired the right-of-way for street purposes and appropriately named the street Fairfax Drive. Other trolley lines which operated from Rosslyn are mentioned on page 78.

On February 12, 1899, a Washington, Alexandria and Mount Vernon Electric Railway express with forty-five persons aboard was stranded overnight in a blizzard at Four Mile Run. Drifts up to fifteen feet high piled up around the tracks. An attempt by the Pennsylvania Railroad to rescue them with one car powered by four locomotives failed. They were dug out the next day, but had to walk two miles into Alexandria.

FALLS CHURCH STATION . . . Private vehicles
meet the trolley about 1900.

NORTHERN VIRGINIA TRAIN TRESTLE . . .
Civil War photo of Potomac Creek Bridge built by
Federal troops in nine days from standing timber;
called the "beanpole and cornstalk bridge."

Tapestry of Trees

"ON the twenty-first day of October in the sixth year of the reign of our Sovereign Lord George the third by the Grace of God of Great Britain France and Ireland King Defender of the faith . . .", the Justices of the County Court of Fairfax heard a plea from one Aminadab Seekright against Timothy Dreadnought. In the quaint style of the time, fictitious names were given to the plaintiff and the defendant who actually were John Carlyle and Charles Alexander. This was one more suit concerning the lands of the Alexanders, in 1767 still Arlington's largest landowners. In the course of the trial, depositions were taken from twenty-four witnesses whose testimony is very informative about the area and the people who lived there in the 1700's.

Much of the testimony concerns whether trees were old or young, or whether they had been marked as line or corner trees, and with what sort of instrument— a "howell", a large ax, or a small one—or, if any edged tool had been used. The dependence on marking trees to define property lines was not peculiar to early times, but the testimony shows the confusion which resulted from this practice.

Old John Summers who was born about 1697 and had lived since 1715 near where the "present Town of Alexandria is now", ended his testimony with a crotchety remark. He said he did not recall "whether the Chops on the north line were closed up with the Bark when Jinnings made his survey the Deponent not Expecting now to be asked such a Question nor half the other Questions that have this day been asked him."

Benjamin Talbert tells about looking for line and corner trees with Stephen Gray "who is dead" and that he went to Thomas Going the "day after Gray and he had been looking for the said bound Tree which . . . the Deponent Says Gray and he could not find and upon his describing the place where they had Looked . . . Going told him he had come Damnable near to it and . . . that if Gray would give him a Black Horse he possessed he would shew him the said bound Tree." Going is reported by Talbert to have said that he could find this tree "the Darkest Night that was." Talbert seems to have thought him something of a braggart as well as an extortionist. Considerable furor was raised by the claim that "one Samuel Vaughdry" had cut down a corner tree on Alexander's line.

* * *

We already know of the importance of George Washington's survey oak in Glencarlyn, described on page 64. Land records of the Cherrydale area refer to "A large, anciently marked poplar tree now [1860] in the middle of the road . . . at the corner of Jane Fall's lot on the Turnpike." This seems to have been the northwest corner of Lee Highway and Pollard Street, and the tree was probably destroyed when the Old Dominion trolley track was laid. It may have been the same poplar which was referred to in James Marcey's notices for road work, dating from 1871 to 1890. Just west of Glebe Road at Ballston was another giant tree which was described in records of 1760 as "a poplar tree . . . anciently marked as a corner". It was cut down in 1912 for construction of the track of the Washington and Old Dominion Railway.

Former Senator Frank Ball, said in describing Billy Birch's homestead on North Glebe Road, "Directly in front of the house was the largest hickory tree I have ever seen—very tall with a tremendous spread of limbs giving complete shade over the whole front yard. During the summer months, the family used the area under the shade of this tree more than they used the house." Perhaps the house site was chosen because of the tree. It was finally broken by a storm and cut down.

Throughout this book, I have referred to the existing landmark trees in the areas which were being discussed. To these, I would like to add the following:

One of the oldest oak trees of the Nation is in Country Club Hills next to 3215 North Abingdon Street. It was formerly in the meadow of Bellevue, the Grunwell estate (see page 132). A plot of land has been set aside for its perpetual protection.

There is a strip of evergreen forest extending from Little Falls Road along North Harrison Street and Little Pimmit Run to Old Dominion Drive. The trees were planted by George Nicholas Saegmuller (see page 124) who missed the evergreens of the Black Forest of his native Germany.

Although Arlington County has already lost a great deal of its forests through careless development of subdivisions, an awakened public concern over this priceless heritage will save a great deal of remaining beauty. Our stream valleys and palisades still possess true wilderness areas which must be preserved for posterity.

Our problem is not new; the city of Washington had it in the early 1800's. A friend of Thomas Jefferson wrote, in describing the site of the new Federal City, "Indeed the whole plain was diversified with groves . . . of forest trees which gave it the appearance of a fine park. Such as grew on the public grounds ought to have been preserved . . . the poorer inhabitants cut down these noble and beautiful trees for fuel. In one single night seventy tulip-poplars were girdled, by which process life is destroyed, and afterwards cut up at their leisure . . . Nothing affected Mr. Jefferson like this wanton destruction of the fine trees scattered over the city-grounds. I remember . . . his exclaiming 'I wish I was a despot that I might save the noble, the beautiful trees that are daily falling sacrifice to the cupidity of their owners, or the necessity of the poor.' 'And have you not authority to save those on the public grounds?' asked one of the company. 'No!' answered Mr. J., 'Only an armed guard could save them. The unnecessary felling of a tree, perhaps the growth of centuries, seems to me a crime little short of murder; it pains me to an unspeakable degree.' "

WOODLAND HOMESITES . . . Bellevue Forest residents, near the Potomac Palisades wilderness, have preserved native dogwood trees in their gardens.

COLONIAL VILLAGE GARDEN APARTMENTS . . . This was one of the nation's first garden apartments, 1,028 units erected on 44 acres 1935-40. Two streams bordered by forest trees were preserved by intelligent planning.

Luna Park and the Elephant Hunt

THE Washington, Alexandria, and Mt. Vernon Railway felt the loss of hundreds of daily passengers from Washington to St. Asaph Race Tracks near Alexandria which were closed in the clean-up campaign of 1904. Therefore, they immediately constructed Luna Park, an elaborate forty-acre family amusement park at the old Crane farm on the north bank of Four Mile Run just west of the Alexandria Canal, which ran adjacent to the road that preceded Jefferson Davis Highway. The trolley line ran parallel to the road and a spur branched off for the "Luna Park Special." Mr. Frank Travis, who was the motorman, is now employed at the George Washington Masonic Memorial, having spent his lifetime helping people enjoy their holidays. General Manager J. B. Holman lived in the Crane farmhouse. Mr. Travis relates that when he was a boy (born 1884) a hermit lived in a three-room cave in the hillside known as Wild Man's Cave.

A profusely illustrated sixteen-page booklet of 1906 elaborately describes Luna Park as "unquestionably the grandest and most complete amusement and recreative place between the great ocean resorts . . . architectural fashion plate, and the scenic beauty is unsurpassed in this country . . . magnificent buildings, ball rooms, restaurants, roller coasters, shoot-the-chutes, circus performances, exhilarating rides and exposition shows . . . It is an ideal outing place . . . the impressions will linger exquisitely in memory."

A concrete reservoir up the hill near Fort Scott supplied water for the eighty-foot lagoon. It remained intact until the recent installation of the radar towers at the site. The late Howard Birch Fields, who served this county as bailiff, constable, sheriff, and deputy U. S. Marshal, was at one time employed at Luna Park. Another employee was James Thornton Birch, who had charge of the flying horses. This kind elderly gentleman is now known locally as "Pop."

Various special features were brought in for short periods. These were rented from New York's Coney Island. One was a diving horse which leaped off a high platform into water. Another special event, much publicized in advance, was the importation of four trained elephants. A special stage had been erected for their performace, elevated enough to provide a shed beneath for their housing. Between acts they were to be chained to the heavy supporting columns.

The afternoon of their arrival by boxcar they gave a performance which delighted a large audience. The most popular act was that of the elephant barber who first lathered the face of his customer with a mop and a bucket of suds, then shaved him with a big wooden razor.

A violent storm came up during the night; the thunder and lightning frightened the animals. They stampeded, tore loose the columns which in turn collapsed the pavilion, adding to their terror, and disappeared into the blinding rain.

When the employees arrived at the park the next morning they were unable to find the beasts. Communication and transportation were still sketchy in those days, but finally a report came that the elephants had been seen eating hay in Mr. Whitehead's barn on Glebe Road near Columbia Pike. Five men from the park retrieved them and had driven them back almost to their destination when a white dog jumped barking at them from a hedge near the Army-Navy Country Club and panicked the nervous animals again. They bolted into a nearby swamp and escaped.

They were next located at the Lunt Farm up Four Mile Run, the present site of the Arlington County Property Yard. A second time a dog ruined the plans of the elephant hunters. He dashed barking into the barn and the elephants again stampeded and demolished the building in their frenzy to escape.

One elephant became separated from the others and came up Four Mile Run through Glencarlyn. The historian of that area, Miss Backus of 5514 5th Street South, has told me of her childhood experience. She was playing along the stream in the ravine back of their house one afternoon, but dashed home, terrified by the strange noises she had heard in the woods. The cause was not known until the following day. The next morning a path was found beaten around the home of their neighbor, Howard Young (now the Charles Stetson home at 605 North Carlin Spring Road). This lone elephant was lassoed in a cornfield that morning at Bailey's Crossroads and taken back to Luna Park.

The other three elephants remained at large for several weeks, roaming through farms in Lincolnia and west of the Virginia Theological Seminary. Mothers were frantic and kept their youngsters indoors. Farmers were furious about the destruction of fences, crops, and small buildings. However, the young blades of the community found the situation highly exciting—real elephants roaming through local woods!

They were eventually caught in Fairfax County, and loaded on a freight train at Burke Station on the Alexandria-Leesburg Railroad. Some farmers filed legal claims to hold the animals for damages. However, immediate reimbursement for claims was promised, much to the relief of all parties concerned. Had the elephants been held as collateral, these grey animals would have soon changed to "white elephants", in the opinion of the farmers saddled with their care! They were immediately shipped back to Coney Island, and Luna Park authorities were thereafter content with wooden animals.

A few years later, the park was badly damaged by fire and the project abandoned. The elaborate entrance gates and some of the buildings remained until a few years ago.

LUNA PARK . . . Entrance and the "Chutes."

Subdivisions and Streets

UNTIL around 1900, most of our County just grew like Topsey, without much plan or design. The first scattered farm houses and plantation homes were built conveniently near the river, and along the existing roads which led to the settlements in Fairfax and Loudoun Counties. Turnabout, sometimes the roads curved this way and that, to pass pre-existing homes. Some followed along ridges, swung around marked survey trees, detoured up or down a stream to a good fording place. Regardless of the reason, our early roads which later became streets meandered quite a bit.

However, by the turn of the century, subdivisions were laid out with streets. The location usually was determined by convenience to transportation. By that time, some of the roads were being improved, supplemented by railroad and trolley lines. Even though the latter have since been eliminated, the streets which replace them can be spotted easily by the late-Victorian houses which line them.

Let us refer to the 1900 map of the county for the names and locations of the early villages, beginning with the northwest corner. There was Falls Church, which was mostly in Fairfax County, but with East Falls Church on our side of the boundary.

Towards Alexandria on the west side of the railway was Falls Church Park; next on the east side was Fostoria, now Westover. Then came Bon Air, below present Wilson Boulevard. Just a skip further was Glencarlyn on the west side of the tracks, and another jump found Corbett at the crossing of Columbia Pike.

The next three villages down the track, Braddock Heights, Del Ray and St. Elmo have since been annexed by Alexandria, the first in 1915 and the other two in 1929. Later than this map, the town of Potomac was established in 1908 between Jefferson Davis Highway and Russell Road. It was acquired by Alexandria in 1929 and has since lost its identity.

On Arlington Ridge in 1900 was a subdivision called Addison Heights. The Addison home appears on both the 1864 and 1878 maps as on the southeast corner of what is now Ridge Road and 20th Street, South.

Before leaving the south end of the county, we swing back to the central section to find the colored village of Nauck on Glebe Road some blocks south of Columbia Pike, where it formerly made a sharp bend enroute to Alexandria. Up Glebe Road we find Fairview subdivision, on the east side bounded by present Walter Reed Drive and Columbia Pike.

Back toward the Potomac, was the remnant of Jackson City at the Virginia end of Long Bridge. As the railroad track swung toward Alexandria was Waterloo Station at Brick Haven Post Office. North and inland a bit was Queen City, another colored settlement at the intersection of Columbia Pike and Arlington Ridge Road. It was eliminated by the erection of the Pentagon and the Navy Annex.

Further north along the ridge was Arlington Heights northwest of the intersection of Columbia Pike and Court House Road. Fort Myer Heights was north of the military reservation. Rosslynn Farm was along the ridge above Rosslynn (then spelled with two n's). Above the palisades between Spout and Windy Runs was Ivanwold, an elaborate layout of streets on paper which never materialized. Much of this area is now in the Hendry estate which contains parts of Fort Smith. Up the Potomac at Marcey Creek were the scattered shacks of the Italian and Sicilian quarry workers called "Talleytown", a misnomer of Italy-town, later termed Little Italy. The area along Military Road at Marcey Road was known locally as Marceytown.

Clarendon had just been laid out on what is now Wilson Boulevard at its intersection with the new trolley line. Further out at the Glebe Road intersections was Ballston which had evolved from earlier Balls' Crossroads. Over on what is now Lee Highway was the settlement of Cherrydale. Just beyond the Glebe Road intersection was Hall's Hill, a colored settlement. It was shown on the north side of Lee Highway, with High View Park on the south side. Both are now known as Hall's Hill.

By the early 1930's, these villages had started to grow into one great residential area, with their variously named streets connecting with each other. New street patterns were being laid out across the intervening open areas. It became imperative to establish a system of street names which would carry across the entire county.

It was decided to divide the county in north and south areas, with Arlington Boulevard as the dividing line. Numbered streets would run chronologically east and west. Named streets running north and south would be arranged alphabetically in one, two and three syllable series starting at the river. Diagonal thoroughfares would become roads, drives and boulevards.

This helped a lot; newly named streets in some instances replaced seven or eight segments of various names. However, we have lost some historical and picturesque names which I wish could be applied to future streets. Among the former are: Analostan, Cathcart, Corbett, Mackey and Minor. Others lost were Cherry Valley, Indian Trail, Moccasin Trail, Orchardway, Laurel Lane, Forest Lane, Maplewood, Brookvale, Deepwood and Ferncrest; not important but pleasing.

One of the nice things about our county is that it is not a flat checkerboard. However, the hills and ridges interlaced with stream valleys cause many of our streets to curve, twist, jump and to do all manner of strange things. Especially in the palisades area, some streets skip along over seven or eight breaks. A real puzzler is where North Vernon Street intersects North Vernon Street at a right-angle, at the crossing of the headwaters of Donaldson Run. There are two intersections of Glebe and Dittmar Roads a mile apart. At North Taylor Street, 26th Street becomes 31st! These situations can cause a stranger on a rainy night to sprain his brain trying to find the home of his dinner host for the first time!

TOBACCO "ROLLING ROAD" . . . Hogsheads of tobacco being rolled to warehouses for shipment on sailing vessels. Their routes became known as "Rolling Roads." Sketch from Harper's Weekly 1869.

The Court House

NOW that our Court House is being enlarged and completely modernized, I have a belated appreciation for its Victorian turret as a symbol of an important and picturesque, if overly-ornate period. I shall quote from former Senator Frank Ball's article in the 1958 issue of the *Arlington Historical Magazine:*

"For fifty-two years after becoming a Virginia county, the County of Alexandria, now Arlington, had no building within its own limits to house any of its offices. The Court House was located at Columbus and Queen Streets in the City of Alexandria . . . The records were not voluminous and consisted mainly of those of the County Clerk . . . The Sheriff and Commonwealth's Attorney had no fixed offices and the official locus followed the person of the incumbent. This was also largely true of the Treasurer, who kept most of his official papers in his home . . . The Superintendent of Schools carried his office in his pocket.

"Both County and Circuit Courts were held in Alexandria City. County Court met every month. The Circuit Judge literally rode the circuit—holding court for two weeks at a time in each jurisdiction—Alexandria City, Fairfax and Prince William Counties.

"The demand for the removal of the County offices into the County itself reached its climax in 1896, . . . and the Board of Supervisors was authorized to set up a commission to make a selection . . . and to accept the lowest bid for the construction of the Court House, not to exceed twenty thousand dollars . . .

"The Commissioners unanimously decided to accept the offer of the Fort Myer Heights Land Company to contribute Block 8 of their subdivision . . . The deed specified . . . 'That no blacksmith, . . . livery stable, pig pen or bone boiling or similar establishment shall be erected or permitted on said lots, that no nuisance or offensive, noisy, or illegal trade, calling or transaction shall be . . . permitted thereon.' Whether the practice of the legal profession, especially in hotly contested cases, constitutes a noisy calling or transaction has never been decided . . ."

The Court House was built on the site of Civil War Fort Woodbury. In the downstairs hall is a tile mosaic which reads: "Erected by the Citizens of Alexandria Co., Va., A. D. 1898. Pursuant of an Act of the Legislature Passed February 1896. Board of Supervisors, Geo. N. Saegmuller, Chairman; Fred S. Corbett, W. Duncan. Arch., A. Goenner. Site Donated by Geo. P. Robinson, D. K. Trimmer."

"The writer [Senator Ball] has a very clear recollection of the dedication . . . There were five principal addresses by prominent men including J. Hoge Tyler, Governor of Virginia . . . There was a banquet, the part that I remember best was served at the southwest corner of Court House Square, where a whole steer was roasted over a charcoal fire and large pieces of beef were cut off and handed out with bread to all of us youngsters as well as to the grown ups . . . They had the steer turning on a spit for two days in order to get him cooked down to the point where the crowd could

go into raptures over the well-roasted beef . . . By nightfall, there was nothing left but a few bones . . .

"The other things most remembered . . . were the race for a greasy pig and the climbing of the greasy pole . . . at the top of which were a number of watches . . . and other items of some value. The climbing started early in the day, at which time a host of young boys could only get a few feet off the ground before they slipped back. There was a young chap by the name of Copperthite, who had come over from Georgetown who was a little too smart for all of us country boys. After making one or two attempts at the pole, he conceived the bright idea that with the aid of a little sand he could make it . . . he was able to reach the top, and take the choicest watch . . . By that time he was down, all the rest of the boys had their pockets full of sand and it was a battle royal as to who should have the next chance . . .

"The day was a beautiful one. Everybody in the County came early and stayed late. Everybody knew everybody else, and all the current gossip was hashed and rehashed and a glorious time was had by all . . . When Alexandria County laid down its sleepy head that night, it was complete for the first time in its history with its Courts and offices all housed within it borders."

* * *

Arlington County holds the national record for jurisdictional changes—eight. It is the third smallest county in America, with 25.5 square miles (New York County has 22 and Bristol County, Rhode Island, 24.91). It was the first to acquire by popular vote in 1932 a county-manager type of government. It maintained the national population growth record from 1930 to 1950, first doubling and then tripling its population. Since 1950 it has been outranked in growth by adjacent Fairfax County of which it was once a part. Although it is now the most densely populated area in Virginia, no towns or cities can be incorporated within its borders, and it still contains true wilderness areas along the Potomac Palisades. The George Washington Memorial Parkway runs the entire length of its river front.

The present name of our County has an ancient origin, tracing to an event in 1663 in the Court of King Charles II when he raised Henry Bennet, a successful adventurer, to peerage with the title of Baron, afterward Earl, of Arlington. He was the patron of John Custis II, who built a mansion before 1676 on Old Plantation Creek in Northampton County on the Eastern Shore of Virginia and named it for his friend. When George Washington Parke Custis built his home in 1802 in our County, he named it Mount Washington but his bride persuaded him to call it Arlington House in honor of his own ancestral home.

How suitable it is that our County should bear the name of Arlington. It is through the mansion of that name and the National Cemetery created upon the plantation, that the proud name of Arlington is known and respected throughout the world.

Arlington's Educational Evolution

EARLIEST education in this area was by the "fireside method". From the few books which they brought into the wilderness, including the Bible, families read aloud around the primitive hearths. This was often supplemented by the mother giving daily lessons to her own and sometimes neighbor's children. Finally, the more affluent families were able to employ tutors whom they shared. Others sent their children to board with relatives to attend tuition schools in Alexandria and Georgetown.

The first school documentation in our county records is in Deed Book U-M2 containing an agreement dated March 8, 1822 between William Birch (see page 150) and his neighbors, for the use of an acre of land for twenty years for a schoolhouse. The early records of Reserve Hill (see page 124) in 1830 refer to the schoolhouse, and again in 1859 to the "schoolhouse woods" near William Minor's land. Present Williamsburg Junior High School must be near the site of this early schoolhouse.

There is a report dated September 30, 1851, by the County superintendent of schools, of expenses for salaries and for coal. This could have been for the aforementioned school in the northern part of the County, or for Columbia School whose site was at the present southeast corner of Columbia Pike and Walter Reed Drive. No record has been found dating its erection, but it is the only school shown on the Civil War map of 1864.

Hume School, erected 1895 at 1801 South Arlington Ridge Road is the oldest standing school building in the county. It was named for Frank Hume who gave part of the land within its grounds. Last classes were held December 3, 1956.

In 1799, Thomas Jefferson proposed a plan for a State school system under local county administration, but interest was slight and nothing came of it. The General Assembly passed an act in 1846 providing for a primary system with funds to be supplemented by local taxation by county option. Among the few which adopted the plan were the City of Alexandria in 1848. Compulsory education was first authorized by the Constitution of 1869, subsequently by the Constitution of 1902, and finally enacted by Virginia in 1918.

Tuition schools had existed in Alexandria City since 1739, and the Episcopal High School since 1839. Our county had a tuition school in 1854 in Mount Olivet Church, conducted by Oliver Cox. Bennie Ball was another early schoolmaster, and may have held his classes in the room above Mortimer's Blacksmith Shop at Ball's Crossroads. Samuel Stalcup conducted private classes in a log cabin on the Febrey Farm on Wilson Boulevard during the Civil War.

Virginia set up a new school system in 1869 providing for the appointment of a superintendent in each area by the State Board of Education. Richard L. Carne was chosen for Alexandria City and County on September 17, 1870, but limited his activities to the County from 1872 through 1881 when he retired. Three public schools were operated in 1870: Columbia School, Walker School at Ball's Crossroads, and Arlington School for the colored at Freedman's Village on the Arlington Estate.

Carne School was built the following year on Glebe Road at 25th Street, North at the site of Saint Mark's Church, and named in honor of the superintendent. Samuel Stalcup, who had previously conducted his own tuition school, became Carne's first appointed teacher. Despite the fact that he had lost a leg, he was an excellent disciplinarian, with approximately ninety students of all ages. The one room was supplemented by a larger frame building in 1885, replaced in 1926 by the John Marshall School to the north.

There was need of another school in the northern part of the County. George Saegmuller advanced money for its construction in 1890. It was named for its benefactor and served until 1937 when it was replaced by James Madison School.

The first Fort Myer Heights School was held in the early 1900's in a Rosslyn building. It had formerly been a saloon in which a man had been killed. It was rented for twenty-five dollars per month and furnished with a wagon load of equipment retrieved by members of the School Board from an abandoned school near Soldier's Home in Washington. The first colored school at Hall's Hill was held in the Odd Fellows Hall, built in 1884.

In Glencarlyn, Mrs. William King held a small tuition school in her home. About 1895 her sister, Mrs. Maxwell, was employed by the County at twenty-five dollars per month to teach fourteen children in the east wing (since demolished) of the old Ball log cabin, which had been built about 1742. Two moves were made to private homes (still standing) before the erection of a schoolhouse about 1904 at the end of 4th Street at the woods above the glen. This location was an unsuccessful attempt to accommodate also the Barcroft area, but the parents there objected to their children traversing the long stretch of forest. Classes were finally moved to Carlin Hall, which is the oldest community house in the County and is still standing. The new school was built on Carlin Spring Road in 1955, the Kenmore Junior High School.

In 1912 there were only twelve public schools in the County, none giving instruction beyond the eighth grade. Mount Vernon School in Del Ray became our first high school in 1917 with thirty students and two teachers, but that area was annexed by Alexandria City in 1929. Washington-Lee School was built in 1925 as a junior-senior high, later changed to senior high only.

The tremendous population increase starting in the early 1930's resulted in a phenomenal educational evolution. Excellent modern schools are now scattered throughout the County, as related in the following chapter.

HUME SCHOOL . . . Named for Frank Hume who presented part of the land.

CARNE SCHOOL . . . Named for the county's first Superintendent of Schools.

SAEGMULLER SCHOOL . . . Named in appreciation of a benefactor.

School Names Reflect History

THE names of Arlington's forty-six existing public schools reflect an historical background. Many are named for famous Virginians or homes in which they lived. But some have been inadvertently left out —two are Presidents; William Henry Harrison, the 9th; and John Tyler, the 10th. Presidents from other States have been indirectly honored by having schools named for the streets on which they are located— Fillmore and McKinley. Some school names have no historical significance and for them or new schools, I suggest that we might honor the following famous Virginians:—

"Jack" Jouett, Revolutionary hero, the "Paul Revere of the South," who rode forty miles to warn Governor Jefferson and members of the Virginia Assembly of the British plan to capture them. (2) Andrew Lewis, founder of Staunton, hero of the French and Indian Wars. During the Revolution he drove the last royal governor, Lord Dunmore, from America. (3) Meriwether Lewis and William Clark, leaders of the 1804 expedition to open the Northwest Territory. (4) Thomas Nelson, signer of the Declaration of Independence. (5) General Winfield Scott, who served in the War of 1812, commanded our forces in the Mexican War, and was Commander of Northern forces in the Civil War.

Today, Arlington's public school system is made up of forty-six modern school buildings housing a student body of over twenty-three thousand pupils and a staff of over one thousand teachers. The curriculum, including grades one through twelve, offers a well-balanced six year elementary program of instruction and three years of junior high and three years of senior high school. Arlington is nationally known for its outstanding school program.

* * *

ABINGDON, 3035 South Abingdon Street, erected 1950. Named for Alexander-Custis estate.

ASHLAWN, 5950 Old Wilson Boulevard, erected 1956. Named for home of James Monroe, 5th President, near Charlottesville.

BARCROFT, 625 South Wakefield Street, erected 1924. Named for Dr. J. W. Barcroft, prominent citizen who developed the community which bore his name.

KATE WALLER BARRETT, 4401 North Henderson Road, erected 1939. Named to honor a woman physician of Alexandria, a leader in social service.

CHERRYDALE, 3710 Lee Highway, erected 1917. Named for the community which grew in Dorsey Donaldson's cherry orchard.

CLAREMONT, 4700 South Chesterfield Road, erected 1952. Named for estate on James River, patented 1649, house built later by Arthur Allen.

HENRY CLAY, 3011 North 7th Street, erected 1917. Named for "The Peacemaker," born in Virginia, 1777, moved to Kentucky, 1797, was a leading American statesman for nearly forty years and signed the peace treaty ending the War of 1812. He prevented war between the North and the South during his lifetime.

NELLIE CUSTIS, 712 South 23rd Street, erected about 1921. Named for the granddaughter of Martha Washington, raised at Mt. Vernon. (See page 14.)

DREW, 2410 South Lincoln Street, erected 1944. Named for Dr. Charles R. Drew of Arlington, a noted Negro surgeon whom Great Britain appointed as Medical Director of the Blood Plasma Research; killed in car accident, 1950. School originally called Kemper Annex, renamed, 1951 when large addition was built.

EDISON, 1800 North Edison Street, erected 1953. Named for Thomas Alva Edison (1847-1931), the great inventor.

FAIRLINGTON, 3308 South Stafford Street, erected 1944. Named for the apartment development in which it is located.

FILLMORE, 33 North Fillmore Street, erected 1953. Named for Millard Fillmore (1800-1874), 13th President of U. S.

GLENCARLYN, 737 South Carlyn Spring Road, erected 1955, the latest of a series of Glencarlyn schools dating from the past century. (See page 64.)

GUNSTON JUNIOR HIGH, 28th and South Lang Streets. Named for Gunston Hall, built 1758 by George Mason (1725-1792). (See page 68.)

PATRICK HENRY, 700 South Walter Reed Drive, erected 1925. Named for Patrick Henry (1736-1799), Revolutionary orator and Governor of Virginia.

HOFFMAN-BOSTON SENIOR HIGH, 1415 South Queen Street, erected 1916 and

HOFFMAN-BOSTON ELEMENTARY, 1520 South 14th Street, erected 1951. Named for Edward C. Hoffman, principal of the first school at the site, and Ella Boston, principal of the original Kemper School.

STONEWALL JACKSON, 855 Edison Street, erected 1926. Named for General Thomas Jonathan ("Stonewall") Jackson (1824-1863), famous Confederate officer.

JAMESTOWN, 3700 North Delaware Street, erected 1953. Named for Jamestown, first permanent English settlement in America.

THOMAS JEFFERSON, 816 South Walter Reed Drive, erected 1938. Named for Virginia's outstanding statesman (1743-1826) of more than 60 years of public service. He was 3rd President of the U. S., governor of Virginia, drafter of the Declaration of Independence and founder of the University of Virginia.

KEMPER, 2035 South Lincoln Street, erected 1924. Named for James Lawson Kemper, who led his brigade of Virginia troops in Pickett's charge at Gettysburg and was desperately wounded. As Governor of Virginia, 1874-1878, he took particular interest in Negro civil rights and education.

KENMORE, 200 South Carlyn Springs Road, erected 1956. Named for the Fredericksburg home of General Washington's sister, Betty, who married Fielding Lewis.

LANGSTON, 4854 Lee Highway, erected 1925. John Mercer Langston (1829-1897), Negro educator and diplomat, was Professor of Law and Dean of Howard

University. Appointed U. S. Minister to Haiti 1877, and in 1885 became President of Virginia Normal and Collegiate Institute. He was also a Congressman from Virginia.

ROBERT E. LEE, 5722 Lee Highway, erected 1926. Named for the famous Confederate commander and President of Washington College at Lexington, (now Washington and Lee University). He was a citizen of this county.

JAMES MADISON, 3829 North Stafford Street, erected 1937 on site of the former Saegmuller School, adjacent to Fort Ethan Allen. Named for James Madison (1751-1836), born in Port Conway, Virginia, who was our 4th President, 1809-1817.

JOHN MARSHALL, 4751 North 25th Street, erected 1926. John Marshall, born in Virginia 1755, was a Revolutionary Captain, then served thirty-four years (1801-1835) as the most famous Chief Justice of the U. S. Supreme Court.

MATTHEW MAURY, 3550 Wilson Boulevard, erected 1910, originally called "Clarendon Elementary." Named for the great geographer, Matthew Maury (1806-1873), called Pathfinder of the Seas. Born near Fredericksburg, Virginia, he was a Naval Officer and scientist and the author of standard textbooks on navigation.

McKINLEY, 1030 North McKinley Road, erected 1951. William McKinley (1843-1901) was 25th President of the U. S., from 1897 until assassinated in 1901.

JAMES MONROE, 2300 Key Boulevard, erected 1926. James Monroe (1758-1831) was the fourth Virginian to serve as President of the U. S. After fifty years of public service in almost every high office, he is immortalized as the author of the "Monroe Doctrine."

NOTTINGHAM, 5900 Little Falls Road, erected 1950. Named for the short street on which it corners.

OAKRIDGE, 1414 South 24th Street, erected 1950. Named for the area in which it is located.

THOMAS NELSON PAGE, 1501 North Lincoln Street, erected 1953. Named for the Virginia author of Southern plantation stories. Earlier Page Schools on Wilson Boulevard are now Hogate's Restaurant and the Northern Virginia Builders' Association Headquarters. The original Page School was the Ballston School at Ball's Crossroads (Wilson Boulevard and Glebe Road).

PEYTON RANDOLPH, 1320 South Quincy Street, erected 1947. Named for Peyton Randolph (1721-1775) of Williamsburg who was Chairman of the three Virginia Revolutionary Conventions, and President of the First Continental Congress, 1774.

WALTER REED, 1644 North McKinley Road, erected 1938. Named for Walter Reed (1851-1902), of Gloucester County, a medical officer in the U. S. Army, of yellow fever fame.

CHARLES STEWART, 2400 North Underwood Street, erected 1938. Named for a civic leader of Falls Church, near whose home the school was built.

STRATFORD JUNIOR HIGH, 4100 North Vacation Lane, erected 1950. Named for Stratford Hall in Westmoreland County, Virginia, built 1725-1730 by Thomas Lee whose sons, Richard Henry Lee and Francis Lightfoot Lee, were the only brothers to sign the Declaration of Independence, which was based on Resolutions introduced by Richard Henry Lee. Birthplace of Confederate General Robert E. Lee.

CLAUDE A. SWANSON, 5800 North Washington Boulevard, erected 1939. Named for Claude A. Swanson (1862-1929) a Governor of Virginia, U. S. Senator from Virginia, and Secretary of the Navy.

TAYLOR, 2600 North Stuart Street, erected 1953. Named for Zachary Taylor (1784-1850), 12th President. Born in Orange County, Virginia, son of Revolutionary officer, family moved to site of Louisville, Kentucky, 1785. Zachary Taylor was a national hero of Mexican War, died sixteen months after becoming President.

TUCKAHOE, 6550 North 26th Street, erected 1953. Tuckahoe was Indian name for Piedmont, Virginia, and name of plantation home of Jane Randolph, mother of Thomas Jefferson.

WAKEFIELD, 4901 South Chesterfield Road, erected 1953. Named for Westmoreland County plantation of the Washington family from 1665 and birthplace of George Washington, February 22, 1732.

WASHINGTON-LEE, 1300 North Quincy Street, erected 1925. Named for George Washington (1732-1799) and Robert E. Lee (1807-1870).

WILLIAMSBURG, 3600 North Harrison Street, erected 1954. Named for the early Colonial Capital of Virginia, which has been restored since 1927 by John D. Rockefeller, Jr.

WOODROW WILSON, 1601 Wilson Boulevard, erected 1910. First called "Fort Myer Heights School." Named for Woodrow Wilson (1856-1924), who was the 28th President of the U. S., born at Staunton, Virginia.

WOODLAWN, 4720 North 16th Street, erected 1940. Named for plantation given by George Washington to his wife's granddaughter, Nellie Custis. (See page 14).

WOODMONT, 2422 North Fillmore Street, erected 1926. Named for the area in which it is located.

YORKTOWN, 5201 North 28th Street, erected 1950. Named for Yorktown, Virginia, site of Cornwallis' surrender to George Washington, ending the Revolution.

"Not By Bread Alone . . ." Early Churches

THE pioneers and trail-blazers who laid the foundations of our permanent communities brought their faith with them, to light their paths into the unknown. Undoubtedly, the first religious services in Arlington County were family prayers before the hearths of pioneer cabins. To raise a family in the wilderness required courage, fortitude and a daily renewal of spiritual faith.

This is a record of only the earliest churches which served our community, including some across the later established county lines in Alexandria and Fairfax County. In recent years, Arlington has been one of the fastest growing communities in the Nation, and its churches of practically every denomination have kept pace. At this time, beautiful new edifices are in use throughout the county, with a number under construction and others contemplated. Our County will continue to flourish and stand high as a home community as long as our spiritual life keeps at this level.

This seems an appropriate time to record one of the strangest phenomenon which has occurred in this region within the memory of man. At precisely three o'clock on Good Friday afternoon, March 27, 1959, storm clouds became amazingly dark except for a weird sulphurous glow. This suddenly faded, leaving both earth and sky as dark as the deepest midnight. Street lamps which were automatically light-controlled came on, and cars drove with headlights burning. All of the Washington-Northern Virginia area was affected, but the most spectacular concentration of darkness was within the bounds of the original District of Columbia including Alexandria and Arlington County. The extreme darkness lasted for a quarter of an hour, followed by a torrential downpour.

The United States Weather Bureau explained that the situation was caused by haze at ground-level, a low ceiling of thick clouds, and a sudden pile-up of extremely dense, rain-laden storm clouds reaching to a height of thirty thousand feet, driven by strong winds. Despite the fact that the phenomenon was the result of an unusual combination of natural factors occurring but a few times in the history of the world, no explanation has been offered for the coincidence of time.

As worshippers came out of churches, they were awed by the identical situation which attended the crucifixion of Christ. The multitude witnessing the event was inclined to believe that it bore a religious significance. ". . . and there was darkness over the whole land . . . while the sun's light failed . . ." [Luke 23: 44-45].

EPISCOPAL

Arlington's early settlers were predominantly English, and therefore belonged chiefly to the Church of England. In 1765, a new Fairfax Parish, which took in the northern half of Truro Parish, was created to accommodate the up-river movement of settlers. George Washington was one of the twelve vestrymen and served on the Building Committee. The new parish included the original wooden "Falls" church of 1734 which was ordered rebuilt of brick, and a new edifice, Christ Church, in Alexandria. Colonel James Wren was commissioned as the architect for both.

The new Falls Church was completed in 1768. Christ Church, started in 1767 was not finished until 1773. In 1775, the Falls Church served as a Revolutionary recruiting station. During the Civil War, it was used by Union troops as a hospital and later as a stable.

To supply a "glebe" (rectory with farm for the minister's residence and maintenance) for the benefit of the clergyman who would serve the two churches, 516 acres were purchased from Daniel Jennings. In 1770, the construction of Glebe House was ordered, in accordance with detailed specifications which are still in the archives of Christ Church. This house was completed in 1775. Its present address is 4527 17th Street, North, a block east of Glebe Road.

Following the temporary ministry of Townsend Dade, David Griffith became the rector of Fairfax Parish. Griffith had served in New Jersey and Philadelphia before the Revolution, when he became a Chaplain. A friend of George Washington, he was unanimously elected to be Bishop of Virginia at the Convention of 1786, while living at the Fairfax Glebe. However, funds were not available to send him to England for ordination, and consequently he had not yet been ordained at the time of his death in 1787.

Griffith was succeeded at Fairfax Parish by the Reverend Colonel Bryan Fairfax who was ordained in 1789, and retired in 1792. The following year, he became the Eighth Lord Fairfax. In the meantime, Thomas Jefferson led in the adoption in 1779 of the Virginia Statute of Religious Freedom. A necessary consequence of this was the disestablishment of the Church of England. That was not formally accomplished, however, until 1785. The Episcopal churches in Virginia were not long allowed to keep their glebes. They were all confiscated by the Commonwealth pursuant to the statute enacted in 1802. The case of the local glebe was unique, in that Alexandria County had by that time ceased to be a part of Virginia. This was the defense offered by Edmund Jennings Lee in his arguments which saved the Fairfax Glebe (in Alexandria County, District of Columbia) from confiscation.

In the meantime, the Glebe House had burned in 1808. A rectory was needed in Alexandria, so the glebe lands were sold in 1815 to Walter Jones, a Washington attorney, and John Mason of Mason's Island (Analostan). The funds were used to purchase the Charles Lee home in Alexandria at the northeast corner of Washington and Princess Streets as a rectory, and for the erection of the Christ Church steeple and church-yard fence.

The Glebe House was rebuilt in 1820 by Walter Jones, and became the residence of a series of distinguished people, as related on page 188.

CHURCHYARD, CHRIST CHURCH, ALEXANDRIA . . . The fence erected with funds from the sale of the Glebe lands in what is now Arlington County.

CHRIST CHURCH INTERIOR . . . The land was given by John Alexander, and construction of the church was started in 1767, completed in 1773. James Wren was paid 8 pounds to write the Lord's Prayer, the Creed and the Ten Commandments on the panels on each side of the wine-glass pulpit. General Robert E. Lee attended services and was confirmed here.

CHRIST CHURCH STEEPLE . . .
Also erected from the Glebe funds.
118 North Washington Street.

Early Episcopalians

ARLINGTON CHAPEL

THE first house of worship in the County was the "Chapel of Ease of Arlington Plantation", built by G. W. P. Custis for the use of his "people", his neighbors and his own family who were communicants also of Christ Church. It was probably erected soon after the founding of the Virginia Theological Seminary in 1823, which provided student preachers. Indications are that it was at what is now the northwest corner of Columbia Pike and South Orme Street. A newer building at the site has served as a colored church and is now an Odd Fellows Hall. The earliest burials in the adjacent cemetery are of Custis servants. Furthermore, the Civil War map shows a road leading from Arlington House directly to this site.

One of the Seminary students assigned to Arlington Chapel from 1854 to 1857 was Henry Codman Potter, who later became Bishop of New York. He modestly ascribed his retaining the assignment to the fact that he kept a horse which enabled him to make the sixteen mile round trip from the Seminary. He once wrote, "Mr. Custis, who was an old man, often went to sleep when I spoke in Arlington Chapel and was fortunate in being able to do so, for very poor preaching it was, but his son-in-law, Colonel Robert E. Lee, afterwards the great Confederate General, was always singularly alert and reverent in his bearing. I shall never forget the constant kindness I received from the inmates of Arlington House."

Soon after the beginning of the Civil War, the Chapel was burned, and for nearly ten years, the southern part of the County was without an Episcopal Church. Following the war, Trinity Chapel was established by the former Arlington Chapel congregation, in a barracks left by the Federal troops on the south side of Columbia Pike, near the Army-Navy Club golf course. That building was likewise destroyed by fire. In 1877, a new chapel was built with neighborhood contributions. When Bishop Potter learned that the chapel in which he had conducted services had apparently been a casualty of the war, he was deeply distressed, and contributed a stained glass window for the new edifice.

In 1902, the entire building was moved intact to a new location at Columbia Pike and South Wayne Street. It was replaced in 1957 by a large modern church. The "Bishop Potter Window" did not blend with the architecture of the new building, and was therefore discarded. It was given to an employee of the construction company from Darcos, a village near Petersburg, West Virginia, and has been installed in the Darcos Baptist Church.

The threads of history are as gossamer as a spiderweb. Less than a year after the new edifice was completed, I had great difficulty in learning the fate of the "Bishop Potter Window" which had been one of the most cherished possessions of the congregation.

Bishop Potter and another local resident, Count Caleb Cushing (see page 188), were pallbearers of Dr. Elisha Kent Lane (1820-1857), America's great Arctic explorer, whose tragic love of Maggie Fox of the "Spirit rappings" of the 1850's is the basis for the historic novel by Jay and Audrey Walz *The Undiscovered Country*.

SAINT JOHN'S CHURCH

The story of Saint John's Church of Glencarlyn is told on page 64.

SAINT GEORGE'S CHURCH

Episcopalians of Clarendon and Ballston banded together in 1908 to establish a church. The question as to which of the two communities should be chosen for the building site was settled by erecting the church on the dividing line, Maryland Avenue which is now North Nelson Street, at 9th Street.

The first service was held in the new church on Christmas Eve of 1911. Five years later, the Parish Hall was financed by the Mothers' Club. The increased congregation by 1933 necessitated a larger hall. A member of the congregation made the auditorium lamps, and the antique walnut entrance doors were given by a couple who had found them stored in an old barn. The doors contained rare leaded glass panels which were removed and installed as windows on each side of the entrance, and walnut panels were substituted in the doors. The large stone in the vestibule floor was quarried for Pohick Church in 1769. The terrace before the Parish Hall is laid with bricks from about sixteen Colonial churches of Virginia and Southern Maryland, dating back to 1632, and from early Virginia plantations. In 1952 a new building was erected at the corner of Fairfax Drive and North Nelson Street. The original stone church is now used as a chapel.

SAINT MARY'S CHURCH

The first services of the St. Mary's congregation were held in 1925 in old Carne School. Admiral Presley M. Rixey presented the triangle of land for the erection of a church at the intersection of Glebe Road and Old Dominion Drive. Ground was broken on June 5, 1926 by Bishop Henry St. George Tucker. The cornerstone laid on August 5, 1926 by Bishop William Cabell Brown, with the trowel which George Washington used in laying the Capitol cornerstone in 1793. The first services were held in the church on April 1, 1927. An addition to the building was dedicated on October 19, 1952.

SAINT ANDREW'S CHURCH

St. Andrew's Episcopal Church at the southwest corner of Lorcom Lane and Military Road combines the congregations of two earlier missions; Epiphany which was organized in 1914, and Grace Chapel which was built about 1920. The two groups organized into one in 1950, and the new church was built. The first service within the edifice was held at Thanksgiving, 1951.

SAINT MICHAEL'S CHURCH

St. Michael's at 1132 North Ivanhoe Street is the newest Episcopal church of Arlington.

EPISCOPAL THEOLOGICAL SEMI-NARY OF ALEXANDRIA . . . Established 1823, it furnished student ministers to Arlington County's early chapels.

THE BISHOP POTTER WINDOW . . . Presented by Bishop Potter of New York to Trinity Church which was erected 1877 to replace "Arlington Chapel."

SAINT ANDREW'S CHURCH . . . The 1951 confirmation service was held under the great oak, before completion of the church.

Early Methodism and Adams Family

THE first Methodist services in this area were held just beyond the Arlington County line at Church Hill, a private home at 318 Leesburg Pike, now the residence of Mr. and Mrs. Donald Macleay. It was built in 1750 by Colonel William Adams (1723-1809) who owned 3,000 acres extending well into Arlington County. Colonel Adam's land was adjacent to the ninety acres patented by his father, Gabriel Adams in 1730 which George Washington subsequently acquired as part of his Four Mile Run tract. William Adams was sheriff of Fairfax County in 1767 and active in the affairs of the Falls Church. He operated a mill where Columbia Pike crosses Holmes Run. This was later Barcroft Mill, and the stone walls still stand. His son, Wesley Adams, inherited the house and plantation in 1809. The Honorable Simon Adams, born there, served in the Kentucky Territorial Legislature. The house came into the possession of the Payne family, through the marriage of Catherine Adams to William Payne, a carriage-maker of Georgetown. It acquired the name of the Adams-Payne House, and was later called the Dower House when granted as a widow's dower in an estate settlement.

The Adams home was a favorite stopping place of the first Methodist Bishop, Francis Asbury. Mrs. William Adams was the first of her family to become converted to the new sect and was considered a saint of pioneer Methodism.

Services were conducted at Church Hill until the erection of Fairfax Chapel about 1780 on the north side of what is now Seven Corners. The land was given by George Minor of Minor Hill, who had married Ann Adams. The first building was of wood, later it was rebuilt of brick. It was demolished in 1861 by the 121st New York Regiment, which was stationed nearby at Fort Buffalo. The churchyard is now Oakwood Cemetery.

Another Adams daughter, Sarah, married William Watters of Maryland, the first native American itinerant Methodist preacher. In May 1778, he attended the Sixth Conference of American Methodism (and the first in Virginia) in Leesburg, at what was probably the first Methodist Church in the Nation. The stone chapel erected in 1766 was abandoned after 1900 and torn down. Reverend Watters died in 1827 at his home, El Nido at Chesterbrook; a portion of his house re-remains standing. His grave and that of his wife are on private property behind St. John's Catholic Church, marked by a stone erected by the Virginia Conference of the Methodist Episcopal Church.

William Watters' autobiography vividly relates the death of his brother-in-law, Lewis Hipkins, from hydrophobia.

"On the 3rd or 4th of last June [1794] he was bit by a mad dog just as he stept out of the boat at Georgetown ferry . . . I felt much alarmed and went immediately to see him . . . He had been with a doctor and had sent to . . . Pennsylvania for medicine." A week later, Reverend Watters found that the patient had felt so well that he had failed to take the medicine. He continues, "I entreated him to do so, observing that in all such cases, though we hope for the best, we ought to prepare for the worst. He said he would take the greatest care of the medicine, and if he perceived the least approach of the complaint he would take it immediately."

On the 23rd of July he was taken with chills and fever, and two days later had his first convulsion. He suffered violent pains between his shoulders and in his chest, but his mind remained active. He realized he was doomed and by the 27th begged to be confined by ropes, lest he unintentionally bite someone during his increasingly violent seizures.

Finally, two strong men sat on each side of his bed to restrain him. After admonishing his wife, Sukey, to pray for their souls, he requested of her, ". . . and if you should ever have another husband, I pray God he may be a better one than ever I have been; and don't be in too great a hurry about it." His final minutes were peaceful. He stretched out his arms saying that he was dying in perfect love and peace with all men.

GRAVE OF WILLIAM WATTERS . . .
In Fairfax County near the Arlington line,
this first native American itinerant Methodist minister preached to pioneer Arlington families.

"CHURCH HILL" . . . *318 Leesburg Pike
at Munson Hill.* Just beyond the Arlington
County line, it was the first Methodist
preaching place in the area, visited often
by Bishop Francis Asbury.

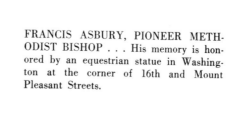

FRANCIS ASBURY, PIONEER METH-
ODIST BISHOP . . . His memory is honored by an equestrian statue in Washington at the corner of 16th and Mount
Pleasant Streets.

Early Methodist Churches

MOUNT OLIVET

MOUNT Olivet Methodist was the first church organized and erected through community effort in this County. By the mid-1800's, services were being held locally in private homes by itinerant preachers. In 1854, the local Methodists organized and chose a site for a church on the main thoroughfare between Alexandria and the upper Potomac communities (Glebe Road) at its intersection with Brown's Bend Road (16th Street, North). The chosen southwest corner was claimed by both William Marcey and John B. Brown, neither being able to prove full title to it. Therefore, a committee composed of the Ball brothers and William Minor was appointed to ask each contestant for the ground for the church, which resulted in an amicable settlement of their dispute.

The first contribution to the building fund was one hundred dollars from George C. Wunder who had recently established his farm at the present intersection of Glebe Road and Lee Highway, which was for many years called Wunder's Crossroads. Other men contributed funds and volunteered their own labor to erect the church. The women gave lawn parties and oyster suppers to raise funds.

The Reverend Oliver Cox was assigned to the new congregation. He also conducted a private day school in the church building. It was completed in 1860, and was a two story frame structure about thirty-six feet by fifty feet. The versatile Mr. Cox was also a surveyor as is shown by our County land records.

During the summer of 1861, the 22nd New York Regiment, retreating from the First Battle of Bull Run, encamped near Mount Olivet Church and commandeered it for their use. The church was used as a hospital for about three months, then as a commissary. Later, it became a guard post, and the lower floor a stable for the officers' horses. During the winter, the troops tore the building apart, using the lumber to floor their tents, to build bunks, and to burn for firewood. A claim of damages was settled in 1904 in the amount of $3,400 which was used to finance the parsonage.

During the tragic 1860's, services were again held in homes. In 1870, the Reverend W. C. Ames was appointed and the congregation made plans to rebuild. This time it was more difficult; homes and fields had been ravaged by war, stock and equipment destroyed. Self-sacrifice and cooperation prevailed and a long one-story church arose from the original stone foundations. This served the congregation until 1895 when the third building was constructed; with additions in 1920. The present handsome church was completed in 1948.

HUNTER'S CHAPEL

Hunter's Chapel is the only church other than Mount Olivet which shows on the 1864 Civil War map. It was on the northeast corner of Columbia Pike and Glebe Road, which was at that time called "County Road" and later "Telegraph Road". Funds were raised by the local residents and the chapel was built in 1857-1858. On May 24, 1859, Louisa A. Hunter, a widow gave the land; and a grateful congregation named the chapel in her honor. In the spring of 1861, the church was taken possession of by Federal troops for use as a picket post, then as a blockhouse, then as a commissary, and finally as a stable before it was torn apart to build barracks. Mrs. Hunter and her daughter had fled to Richmond, and their home was also destroyed.

After the war, the congregation held services in the one-room frame Columbia School House on Columbia Pike until Fred Bradbury donated ground for the new edifice in 1893. Again it was a woman who came to the financial aid of the little church, Sarah Elizabeth Bailey (neé Jenks, see page 88), mortgaged her farm to raise funds for its construction. Louisa Hunter who gave the land for the first chapel had bought her tract from Sarah Bailey's father, William Jenks.

The new church suffered a catastrophy when the steeple blew off in a violent storm September 29, 1896. All during those years, Sarah Bailey was working hard to get Congress to settle a claim for the destruction of the original building by Federal troops. The claim was finally paid March 19, 1900 with an award of three thousand dollars. A memorial window in honor of Sarah E. Bailey was placed in the church, which had become known as the Columbia Pike Methodist. The window was transferred and installed in the fine new Arlington Methodist Church, its successor, on the west side of Glebe Road at 8th Street, South.

WALKER'S CHAPEL

Walker's Chapel was the next church of our County, erected 1871 as a junior church of the Mount Olivet Circuit. Sunday School classes started by Mrs. Jane Bowen Edwards (see page 130) in 1869 in private homes were the forerunner of the Walker Chapel congregation. In 1871, fifty-eight men met at Mount Olivet Church to pledge their resources to build a chapel "at or near Walker's Grave Yard", the burial site of David Walker who had died in 1848. (See page 130.) His sons, Robert and James Walker gave the land for the new chapel, and those who offered to contribute their labor included the Reverend W. C. Ames of Mount Olivet. Some gave cash, and the ladies worked to raise funds by benefit suppers and strawberry festivals.

The first building was a small frame structure near the upper part of the cemetery. Past it on the west side went Little Falls Road, to connect with the McLean Road near Fort Marcy. In 1903, a new church was built at the other end of the cemetery by volunteer labor, with additions in 1952 and 1954. The original chapel of 1871 was used for Sunday School classes until 1930, when it was dismantled.

The focal point of the present church is a painting of Christ by Mrs. Cherry Ford White, presented in 1937. It is described as "a mural which is in itself a powerful sermon". A new church is under construction at the time of this writing.

WALKER CHAPEL . . . Erected 1903 to replace the original edifice of 1871. It is being replaced by a handsome brick church in 1959.

HOUSE ON WALKER HOMESTEAD FOUNDATIONS . . . *4446 North Glebe Road.* This house was built of logs, soon after the Civil War, by a Mr. Linther, who probably used the foundations of the pioneer Walker homestead. It was later covered by clapboard.

Presbyterians and Baptists

PRESBYTERIANS

THE First Presbyterian Church in Arlington County was founded February 22, 1872. It was organized by a Ladies' Mite Society at the home of Mrs. Alonzo G. Hayes. The first church services were held in June in the hall above Mortimer's Blacksmith Shop on the northeast corner of Ball's Crossroads. The Reverend Dr. David H. Riddle of Falls Church Presbyterian Church officiated, as the new congregation became a mission of his church.

In October of the same year, eleven acres were purchased for $1,200 on the northwest corner of Ball's Crossroads, for the church and a cemetery. A subsequent decision eliminated the cemetery, so nine acres were sold, two being retained for the church. Ground was broken April 18, 1873, and the sanctuary dedicated October 22, 1876.

The Church School was started in April, 1872, with twenty-two in attendance. The basement was made into a Sunday School room, and was first used for the Christmas Eve Festival on December 24, 1877.

On July 5, 1895, the congregation organized as a separate unit with their own pastor, under the name of the First Presbyterian Church of Ballston, later known as the First Presbyterian Church of Arlington.

The manse was erected in 1899. In 1912 electricity replaced the kerosene lamps. A pipe organ was installed and dedicated in 1931.

The congregation grew with the years, and by 1944 it was decided to sell the original site, which had increased greatly in commercial value, and to reinvest in a quieter residential area away from the main thoroughfares. On October 5, 1947, the trustees were authorized to purchase three and one-half acres of the Robert Veitch estate, about two hundred yards to the south of the original property, for $35,000. It was decided to first build the educational building and await church construction until the original property could be sold advantageously.

The Educational Building was dedicated on August 6, 1950. A month later a prominent real estate firm purchased the old property as a speculative investment for $200,800. The following January, construction of the new sanctuary and social hall was begun. After an appropriate farewell service at the old church on December 9, 1951, the congregation followed the Pastor and church officials, bearing the Cross and Pulpit Bible to the new church where worship was concluded on the steps.

The only furnishing of the old building to be moved into the new was the pipe organ. This was greatly enlarged and installed as a memorial to Arthur W. Cathcart, a gift from his family. (See page 84.) The old building was demolished, and all that now remains on the otherwise bare corner are a few fine old trees.

BAPTISTS

Early in 1909 a group of Clarendon residents of the Baptist faith began meeting together in the home of Thomas Garrison just west of Clarendon Circle at the present site of St. Charles Catholic School. The Reverend W. S. O. Thomas, an elderly minister of the Georgetown Baptist Church assisted in organizing a local congregation. Among the local leaders was George H. Rucker who had moved into the County two years before.

The congregation of twenty-three was formally organized at a meeting held on May 18, 1909, in the Clarendon Methodist Church.

During the first six years, services were held in a variety of buildings. From the Garrison home they moved to Mrs. Northrup's Undertaking Shop at 3173 Wilson Boulevard (now Mayer's Gift Shop), then to an uncompleted house on Wilson Boulevard loaned by a member. For a period in 1911, they paid ten dollars monthly rental for part-time use of the new Masonic Hall.

Toward the goal of a church site, they purchased three lots on Wilson Boulevard for the sum of $850. These lots were exchanged for the larger triangle formed by North Hartford and Highland Streets. Until funds could be raised for a building, a large tent was erected on this site for services.

In 1913, the Reverend H. L. Swain from Leesburg became the pastor, and the erection of a church was undertaken the following year. It appears that the whole congregation was not consulted as to the type of architecture chosen by the pastor, and some were disappointed that the edifice was neither Gothic nor Colonial.

Services were first held in the incomplete structure on February 19, 1915. Some of the finest food ever served in Clarendon resulted from the endeavor of the church ladies to amortize the building debt—ham dinners, oyster suppers, and strawberry festivals!

In 1935, a Sunday School Building was added. In 1947, a $300,000 new sanctuary was begun, with the first service held on December 31, 1950. During construction, services were held in the Ashton Theater, which was on the south side of Wilson Boulevard, a half-block below Clarendon Circle. The First Baptist Church of Clarendon is now housed in a beautiful colonial edifice which its congregation so well deserve, having worshiped in homes, a funeral parlor, an unfinished house, a Masonic Hall, a tent, and a movie theater!

Whereas the congregation of the Cherrydale Baptist Church did not organize until 1913, they immediately started their building program. The construction of their first building at North Quincy and 21st Streets took place at the same time as that of the First Baptist Church of Clarendon. A larger church was erected in 1925 and the original building became the Sunday School. A very beautiful new church was completed in 1959 at the southeast corner of Military Road and Lorcom Lane.

FIRST BAPTIST CHURCH
OF CLARENDON . . . Re-
placed by a fine brick edifice
1947-50.

FIRST PRESBYTERIAN
CHURCH . . . Erected on
the northwest corner of
"Balls Crossroads" in 1873-
76, it was replaced in 1951
by a new church at 601
North Vermont Street.

Catholic Progress

THE expansion of the Catholic Church in Arlington is but one phase of the growth of the Church in the Commonwealth of Virginia. The first time the Holy Sacrifice of Mass was celebrated within the bounds of our present State was in 1576 by a Dominican Priest at the future site of Jamestown, Virginia. Saint Mary's, the first Catholic Parish in Northern Virginia was founded in 1795 in Alexandria. The priests of Saint Mary's administered to the spiritual needs of the Catholic residents of our County.

The Catholic people and Church in Virginia were under the care of the Archbishop of Baltimore until 1820, when the Rt. Rev. Patrick Kelly was appointed the first Bishop of the newly created Diocese of Richmond, which comprised the present states of Virginia and West Virginia, with the Bishop residing in Norfolk. Difficulties beset the new Diocese, which two years later returned to the jurisdiction of the Archbishop of Baltimore. The Diocese of Richmond was re-established in 1841 under the Rt. Rev. Richard Vincent Whelan, D.D.

By 1880, there were enough Catholics in Falls Church to justify the establishment of Saint James, which also served the Catholic families in the upper section of our County. The Rev. Frederick P. Lackey who served Saint James in the early nineteen hundreds brought to the attention of the Bishop, the need of a parish in the Clarendon area. In 1909, the Rt. Rev. Augustine Van De Cyrr, 6th Bishop of Richmond ordered that a parish dedicated to Saint Charles Borromeo be founded, "to embrace the village of Clarendon and the surrounding country of Alexandria County for about forty square miles." The Reverend Father Lackey of Saint James became its founding pastor. He is presently the pastor of Saint Joseph's Church in Martinsburg, West Virginia.

Thus, Saint Charles Church at 3304 Washington Boulevard, one block west of Clarendon Circle, was the first established Catholic Parish in Arlington. The Church of Saint Agnes in Cherrydale, a former mission of Saint Charles was established as a separate parish in 1936. The Church of Saint Thomas More, 101 North Thomas Street was established in 1938. Parishes of more recent date are Our Lady Queen of Peace, 1945, at 19th and South Edgewood Streets; Our Lady of Lourdes, 1946 (from the parish of Saint Rita in Alexandria) at 23rd and South Hayes Streets; and Saint Ann's founded in 1947, at 10th and North Frederick Streets.

In recent years, the Church in Arlington has expanded to magnificent proportions. Besides its regular duties and services, it conducts a very fine school system which comprises five elementary schools, two high schools and one junior college. These provided educational facilities to over 3,600 elementary school children, 900 high school students and 220 college students in the 1958-59 term. The parishes which have their own elementary schools are Saint Charles, Saint Agnes, Saint Thomas More and Saint Ann's. Marymount School and Junior College for Girls, located at 2807 North Glebe Road, is beautifully situated at the crest of a ridge, with the Rixey Mansion as the nucleus of its numerous buildings. It was established in 1950 under the paternal guidance and care of the late Bishop Ireton, which gave Arlington County the distinction of having within its confines, the first Catholic College in the State. In 1957, the Bishop Denis J. O'Connell High School was opened, and served 775 students during the 1958-59 term. When operating fully it will accommodate fifteen hundred students. Two of Arlington's seventeen priests are engaged exclusively in work for the schools which are staffed by seventy-seven sisters; these figures as of the 1958-1959 term.

The other fifteen priests are engaged in regular parish work. There is also a staff working constantly at the Northern Virginia Branch of Catholic Charities which was established September, 1947 at 1225 North Lincoln Street. Since 1946, our County has been the home of the American Headquarters of the Immaculate Heart Mission Fathers, the ten priests and two brothers who reside at "Missionhurst" at 4651 North 25th Street. This beautiful residence was built in 1907 by Frank Lyon for his family, and called "Lyonhurst". The architecture suggests a Spanish castle, especially the water-tower, which commands a fine view of Washington. Lyonhurst was the first home in the County to use electricity, tapped from the adjacent trolley line (since abandoned, and now Old Dominion Drive). The Lyons sold the home in 1922 to Dr. and Mrs. Richard Sutton, and many people know of it as the Sutton Place.

A new field of Christian service is being opened in September, 1959 under the guidance of the Reverend Father Leonard J. Koster, the pastor of Saint Charles Parish. It is the establishment of a full-time school for retarded children. This is an outgrowth of the catechism classes which Father Koster established two years previously. During his forty years in the priesthood, his special field has been in counseling—asking questions and listening. He seeks to understand the problems of those who come to him in trouble, and to assist them in their solution. Therefore, he seems admirably fitted to help these most pathetic of human beings, retarded children.

SAINT CHARLES . . . The first Catholic Church of the County.

LYONHURST . . . Erected 1907 by Frank Lyon as a family home, it is now the American Headquarters of the Immaculate Heart Mission Fathers.

Potomac Disaster in 1844

THE *National Intelligencer* (newspaper) of February 29, 1844, carried the following headlines, "MOST AWFUL AND LAMENTABLE CATASTROPHE!". What had started out the preceeding day as a gala excursion on the Potomac participated in by President John Tyler, members of his Cabinet, military officers, statesmen, diplomats, prominent citizens and their ladies, including Dolly Madison, became a great national disaster. The happy group of two hundred gentlemen and one hundred and fifty ladies left the Federal City that morning on the steamboat *I Johnson* to glide past Arlington's shores, to Alexandria where they boarded the new Naval Steamer, *Princeton* for a run down to Mount Vernon, and to test the newly designed guns.

The *Princeton* was our Navy's first screw-propeller driven ship. It was designed by Captain R. F. Stockton. John Ericsson, later of *Monitor* fame had designed the engines. Captain Stockton described her thus: "She has an auxiliary power of steam and can make greater speed than any sea-going . . . vessel heretofore built. Her engines lie snug in the bottom . . . out of reach of enemy shot and do not at all interfere with the use of her sails . . . Making no noise, smoke or agitation of the water, and if she chooses, showing no sail, she can surprise the enemy."

The *Princeton* was armed with two long 225 pounder wrought iron guns and twelve forty-two pounder carronades. Wrought iron as a material for cannon had been attempted repeatedly without success except for very small calibers due to the difficulty in welding large parts together. Bronze was the metal most used, but was costly, and overheating with consequent distortion caused inaccuracy of fire. After final tests in January 1844, Captain Stockton reported, "As a gun, it is quite perfect, and I do not think that *any* charge of powder can injure it; and as a piece of forged work, it is certainly the greatest achievement up to this time." He had proceeded upon well-established facts and his decisions had been approved by men of science and practical experience.

The *Princeton* arrived at the Capital from Philadelphia where it had been constructed. President Tyler had accompanied Stockton on the ship's second trip down the Potomac to see the new guns fired. Members of Congress were on the next test-trip when the bow-gun named *The Peacemaker* had been fired thrice. A thorough examination of the gun after each firing, both inside and out, disclosed no defect. Public interest in the new guns and the ship prompted the excursion of February 28th which ended in tragedy. Aside from the 350 distinguished guests, there were 178 officers and members of the crew aboard.

In President Tyler's own words, "Never did the eye gaze on a brighter or more animated scene than that which the beautiful river exhibited during the forenoon on that fateful day. There floated the ship whereon had been concentrated so many hopes and anticipated joys . . . The decks were soon crowded with a host of happy visitors . . . A cloudless sky added to the brilliancy of the scene."

The ship left Alexandria at one o'clock and steamed down the river. With appropriate ceremony, Captain Stockton fired the gun. The crowd was thrilled with the thunderous report, the smoke and rumble, followed by the geyser of water thrown up by the accurately shot ball, thus fulfilling all their highest expectations. At 3:10, from near Mount Vernon, the ship started the return trip. Another shot was fired at 3:20 as the climax of the top-side events, followed by a sumptuous repast served below decks. Afterward, the guests remained below for singing. At 4 o'clock, word came down that some gentlemen had requested that one more shot be fired, which had been granted by the Captain with the approval of the Secretary of the Navy.

Miss Julia Gardiner, the twenty-three-year-old New York socialite who was engaged to the fifty-four-year-old widowed President, gives this account: "That moment someone called down to the President to come and see the last shot fired, but he said he . . . was better engaged. My father started with some gentlemen . . . When we heard the shot and the smoke began to come down the companionway . . . I heard someone say, 'The Secretary of State is dead' . . . 'Let me go to my father!', I cried, but they kept me back. Someone told me that there had been an accident, the gun had exploded . . . that drove me frantic . . . One lady, seeing my agony, said, 'My dear child, you can do no good. Your father is in heaven'. I fainted and did not revive until someone was carrying me off the boat . . . I learned afterwards that it was the President."

The gun had burst the breech, killing six men who were standing on the left side: Secretary of State Abel Upshur, Secretary of the Navy Thomas Walker Gilmer, Commodore Beverly Kennon (all three of Virginia), Virgil Maxcy, Charge d' Affairs of Belgium (a Marylander), and Colonel David Gardiner, New York State Senator, and two mortally wounded of the eleven seriously injured seamen.

The tragedy led to redesigning of cannon to bottle shape with increased strength at the breech, perfected by John A. Dahlgren for whom the Naval Ordnance Plant on the Potomac is named. Captain Stockton was exonerated from any blame and later won fame in California. Bereaved Julia Gardiner found happiness upon her marriage four months later to President Tyler. Following his term, they retired to his Charles City County plantation, Sherwood Forest, in Virginia.

U. S. STEAM FRIGATE, PRINCETON . . . Our Navy's first screw-propeller driven ship, it became the scene of a national disaster.

"MOST AWFUL AND LAMENTABLE CATASTROPHE!" . . . From a lithograph by N. Currier.

Glebe's Notable Residents

A SIDE from Arlington House, our County's most famous home is The Glebe at 4527 17th Street, North. Its erection and early ecclesiastical history are related on page 174. The wooden parts burned in 1808, and the property was sold in 1815 to Walter Jones and John Mason.

Walter Jones in 1820 built the Williamsburg-style brick house on the foundations and remaining masonry walls of the original Glebe House. He used it as a hunting retreat until 1826 when he suffered financial reverses. On October 9 it was sold at auction to General John Peter Van Ness.

This wealthy Congressman of New York in 1802 married the fascinating twenty-year-old Marcia Burns. Her father sold his farm, acquired in 1774, to the Federal Government for the site of the "President's Palace." General Van Ness was president of the Bank of the Metropolis and had erected a handsome home in Washington on the Burns homestead site now occupied by the Pan American Union. He purchased the Virginia estate as a shooting lodge, adding the John Mason acreage in 1836. He was the last owner of the entire glebe where Marcia Burns Van Ness probably spent many happy holidays.

Marcia's life exemplifies the type of immortality achieved by one whose kind deeds carry forward into the future. As a result of the War of 1812, many children were orphaned. Since there was no public provision for their care, a group of public-spirited women lead by Marcia Van Ness, Dolly Madison, and Eliza Lee met on October 10, 1815, in chambers of the House of Representatives to consider plans for them. This culminated in the establishment of an orphanage. Mrs. Van Ness gave a building lot. Each interested person contributed money and furnishings. Dolly Madison was appointed the first Directress and Marcia Van Ness the second. Each of these ladies visited the orphanage regularly to bring tenderness and affection into the lives of the children. An Orphan's Court was established and Richard Bland Lee was appointed first Judge. He served until his death in 1827.

Marcia Van Ness died in 1832 at the age of fifty, when her husband was mayor of Washington. The *National Intelligencer* of September 10 carried her obituary, containing the following tribute, "Of this lady may it be emphatically said that she was the guardian of the orphan and the benefactress of the poor." On her casket was placed a silver plaque inscribed with these words: "The citizens of Washington in testimony of their veneration for departed worth dedicate this plate to the memory of Marcia Burns Van Ness . . . and while we lament her loss, let us endeavor to emulate her virtues."

Her body was first placed in a mausoleum in the old Burns burying ground on H Street near St. John's Church in Washington as she had requested. About 1872 the mausoleum and caskets were moved to beautiful Oak Hill Cemetery in Georgetown, overlooking Rock Creek Park. The living memorial to Marcia is "A Children's Village", the present name of the former Washington City Orphan Asylum. A century and a half later it is still the refuge of the orphaned and the destitute children of our National Capital. On the grounds are memorial trees to Marcia Van Ness and Dolly Madison and bronze markers dedicated to their memory. Let us in Arlington sometimes think of Marcia Van Ness when we pass the home where she and her husband sought the quietude of our forests and fields.

Subdivision of the glebe lands began the year following the death of Van Ness in 1846. The next occupant of the house was Clarke Mills, the sculptor who designed the equestrian statue of Andrew Jackson. Cast from captured British cannon, it was erected in Lafayette Park in Washington in 1853. Clarke Mills completed a similar statue of George Washington in 1860. The unique octagon wing of the Glebe House may have been erected by Mills as a studio or by the next owner, Caleb Cushing of Newburyport, Massachusetts, who purchased the one hundred-acre house tract in 1870.

Caleb Cushing, our first Minister to China, negotiated with the Emperor a fine trade treaty in 1844. The Emperor had first refused him an audience because he was not of the nobility, whereupon President Polk conferred upon his emissary the title of "Count Caleb Cushing of the Commonwealth of the United States." Then the audience was granted and the terms of the treaty consummated. He served as attorney general from 1853 to 1857 and as Ambassador to Spain from 1874 to 1877. In appreciation of his services, the people of that country presented to him the hand-carved teakwood eagle which is still atop the octagon wing. Caleb Cushing used the octagon wing of The Glebe House as a studio in which to display his fine collection of art and curios. James Willett, Postmaster of Washington, was a later owner of this interesting house.

The Glebe House is now the home of former State Senator and Mrs. Frank L. Ball who purchased it in 1926. They are the longest residents.

The house is beautifully situated at the crest of a rise, and is surrounded by a two-acre garden containing some fine old trees which have their own histories. One of the most picturesque is a gnarled old catalpa, another is a huge ginkgo which Caleb Cushing may have had sent to him from China. The Balls have added to the history and beauty of both the home and garden. A presentation to honor garden-loving Marie Ball are the azaleas from the Government of the Netherlands in appreciation of her plea to our Congress to veto legislation forbidding the importation of Dutch bulbs when that courageous little country was striving to restore its economy following the Nazi devastation.

THE GLEBE HOUSE . . . This house grew from a Williamsburg-style cottage (extreme right) built 1820 on the walls and foundations of the burned "Glebe" (clergyman's house of Fairfax Parish) which was erected 1775. The octagonal wing was probably added before the Civil War.

Carrie M. Rohrer Memorial Library

IN June 1915, five members of the Ladies Guild of the Vanderwerken (now the Rock Spring) Congregational Church went on a picnic to Great Falls. The outing was not wholly for pleasure inasmuch as the group wished to choose a memorial to a fellow worker, Mrs. Charles W. Rohrer, a young mother who had died the previous winter. While their children played about under the trees that warm spring day, the idea of a children's library which would be open to the community took shape. They all knew the tedium of reading the same few stories over and over, yet books were expensive for people on government salaries and the nearest public library was at Seventh and K Streets in Washington, a long journey on the Old Dominion and Capital Traction trolleys. A circulating library at Neighborhood House, their combined church and community building, would be a boon to the community, a useful, living memorial to their friend.

To raise funds, the ladies decided to sell Christmas cards, for this would bring in "outside" money. That autumn they bought the first books, and preparing them for circulation, placed them in a large market basket. The collection had several homes over the years, for it outgrew the basket and occupied a bookcase donated by a Falls Church Sunday School. Its next home was a closet in which one of the husbands built shelves. In 1924, the men of the church were called into service to enclose the back porch of Neighborhood House at a cost of five hundred dollars for materials which the Ladies Guild agreed to pay. At long last, the library had a room, a table, chairs and even a gas heater for comfort whenever the building was unheated. When the brick church on the corner of Little Falls and Rock Spring Roads was erected in 1940, the library moved into a large room beneath the sanctuary. With the addition of another room when the building was completed in 1954, the memorial library found a pleasant and permanent home for the foreseeable future.

Money was a problem for a long time. For awhile, the Sunday School contributed the first collection of the month, so popular was the library, but this was an uncertain source of income and the sale of Christmas cards figured in all the early reports. Occasionally, funds raised for the library were used to pay the minister or even the coal bill, for the church was a small, struggling organization. Some members of the Guild and Library Committee also taught Sunday School and were from time to time members of the church's executive committee. No wonder their sympathies were divided and the money went where it was most acutely needed! One year a strong-willed chairman who decided she had had enough of this organized a lawn party for the library's benefit with the understanding not a cent would go for any other purpose. In 1924, the Ladies Guild began to set aside a monthly sum and has continued to do so, considering the library its major home community service. Nevertheless, until World War II, members of the committee not only bought, catalogued, mended and circulated the books, they also engaged in money-raising activities. The peak years were those preceding 1940 when they sold bags and rugs made by the North Carolina mountain folk. Profits went to purchase lighting fixtures, flooring and library furniture. To judge by the annual reports, one would think the ladies spent every spare moment on this project. Their comment was always, "It is so worth-while".

What began as a collection of children's books grew far beyond the first dream. The children matured and their interests changed. The committee kept pace as best it could and sometime during the twenties, decided to add adult books. Quality was the watchword. Chairmen were not afraid to buy expensive books if they were authoritative and assured of circulation. The early collection reflects the diverse interests and good taste of its readers, containing fine books on antiques, nature lore, religion, travel, history, and biography. Nor were those with a taste for light reading neglected. Novels of the best-selling variety as well as classics found their way onto the shelves.

Volunteer workers make up the library staff. The number has varied from half a dozen women to the present day thirty and more men and women. Never has a professional librarian been chairman of the committee although several have worked on it. From the beginning, leaders sought advice from professionals and one Washington librarian became so interested she came out many times to direct the change-over to the Dewey Decimal System when the simple method of numbering the books as acquired no longer sufficed.

At first, the library was open only after church and Sunday School and often committee members living nearby were called upon in emergency to leave dinner cooking and "tend library". Gradually, weekday hours were added until now, the library is open Monday through Friday from 3:30 to 5:00 and twice on Sundays. Circulation amounts to more than 6,700 books a year and use of the facilities for school work is increasing now that a subject catalogue is well under way. The five women who met at Great Falls forty-three years ago would be delighted with the development of their project, were they here to see it. The time and thought they lavished upon it laid the foundation of its present day usefulness. They established a memorial that has enriched the lives of many.

* * * *

The Arlington County Public Library, at present consists of seven branches, five of which were begun as volunteer projects. In 1937, these libraries were organized as a Department of the County Government. The libraries now have 125,795 books and their circulation was 767,789 in 1958-59. A new Central Library at 1015 North Quincy Street should be ready for service to the public in mid-1960.

ROCK SPRING CONGREGATIONAL CHURCH
. . . Corner of Rock Spring and Little Falls Road.

GREAT FALLS OF THE POTOMAC . . . Scene
of the birth of the idea which led to the establishment of the Carrie M. Rohrer Memorial Library.

NATIONAL AIRPORT . . . The geometric patterns of its runways and buildings occupy 750 acres.

TWENTIETH CENTURY ARLINGTON

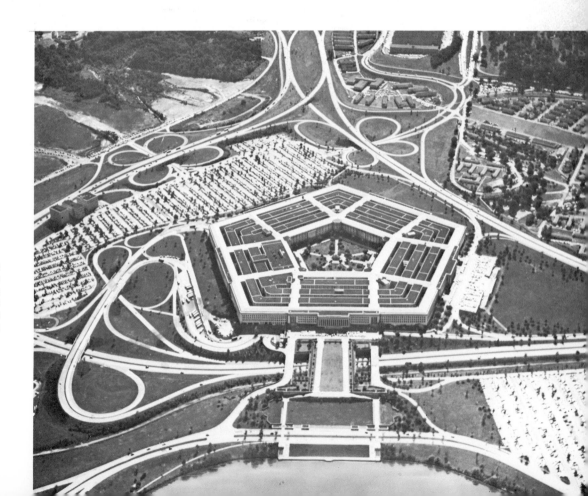

THE PENTAGON . . . This five-sided colossus, built in 1941-43, and having 17½ miles of corridors, is the largest office building in the world. Pentagon Lagoon is in the foreground.

THE POTOMAC PALISADES . . . Showers cannot dampen the enthusiasm of fishermen when the fish "run." *Scene taken from Chain Bridge by A. Aubrey Bodine especially for his book, "Chesapeake Bay and Tidewater."*

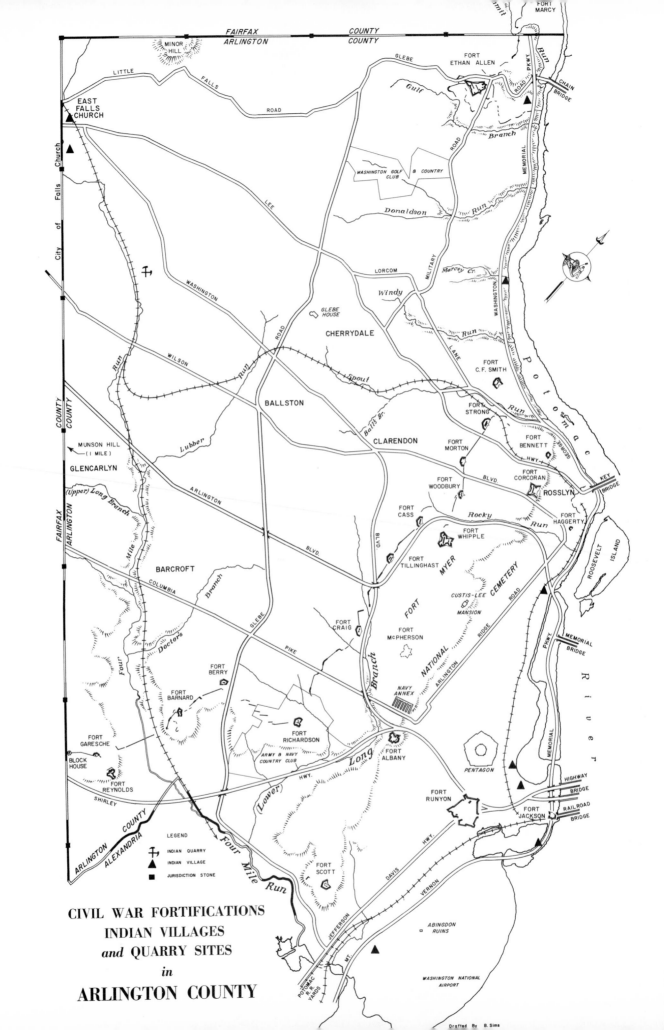

CIVIL WAR FORTIFICATIONS
INDIAN VILLAGES
and QUARRY SITES
in
ARLINGTON COUNTY

LEGEND

⚒ INDIAN QUARRY

▲ INDIAN VILLAGE

■ JURISDICTION STONE

Drafted By B. Sims

Acknowledgments

MY historical work would not have been possible without the whole-hearted cooperation of Arlingtonians and of members of pioneer families who are now living all over the Nation. They have shared with me their memories, family traditions, documents, and pictures. I have taken only the scattered threads of information to weave into a cohesive whole.

Space does not permit a list of all the hundreds of kind people who have assisted in this work. You each know of your own contribution, and of my gratitude. I hope that you will share my pride and pleasure in the result. This book is not MINE, but OURS!

I am indebted to the following for major contributions:

Miss Agnes M. Downey who prepared the eleven chapters on Arlington House, including some previously unpublished material drawn from the original research of Dr. Murray H. Nelligan, under whom she worked when first assigned to the Custis-Lee Mansion. Upon Dr. Nelligan's transfer to Philadelphia, Miss Downey became Park Historian at this home which she had learned to love so deeply. Her dedicated research, restoration, and interpretive programs have brought to this house an intimate warmth reminiscent of those who dwelt there. Assisted by the Staff and community volunteers, she inaugurated a series of programs on appropriate anniversaries which interpreted the interest of the Custis and Lee families in art, music, and gardening; and the celebration of patriotic anniversaries. She also supervised the creation of the Custis-Lee Mansion Museum before her transfer to other fields of historical research.

I have been greatly assisted in documentation of our Civil War forts by Stanley W. McClure, Assistant Chief Parks Historian, National Capital Parks. He is the author of *The Defenses of Washington 1861-1865.*

Cornelia B. Rose, Jr. contributed the chapters on Arlington Indians and Early Roads. Mollie Somerville, who furnished information on Analostan Island, is a free lance writer. Her special interest is the Washington metropolitan area, with particular emphasis on Alexandria and Northern Virginia. Mrs. Marion Thayer Suter is the author of the chapter on the Rohrer Memorial Library. Charles Grunwell gave me material on the Civil War episodes at Falls Grove.

Mr. Thomas Chapman, Secretary of the Fairfax Historical Society and Clerk of the Circuit Court, furnished material on our neighboring county. The Arlington Historical Society and its officers, past and present, have cooperated with me throughout and have granted me permission to quote from its publications.

Reverend Melvin Lee Steadman, Jr. of the Falls Church Historical Society has contributed the chapter on that charming city, and has assisted me greatly with his knowledge of early Methodism, and the genealogies of pioneer families.

The late Charles W. Stetson personally advised me in my early research before his death. His two books, *Four Mile Run Land Grants* and *Washington and His Neighbors* have been valuable sources of information on early patents. I wish to salute Dorothy Ellis Lee and Cecil Crittendon who each published a booklet in 1946 on Arlington County history, thereby blazing a trail which I have followed.

To my son, Robert Lee Templeman, my affectionate appreciation for the inspiration he gave me to create a permanent record of the history and beauty of an area we love, and in which we have shared many happy experiences.

The following busy people have taken the time and interest to read my manuscript before publication. Each is an authority in his own field such as history or journalism. Without their constructive criticism, I would not have been willing to publish this book!

Dr. Ludwell Lee Montague, former Historian of the Society of the Lees of Virginia. Author of *Richard Lee, The Emigrant,* published by the Virginia Magazine of History and Biography, January 1954.

Former Senator Frank L. Ball, the beloved patriarch of Arlington County. A fifth generation native, he has an unmatched knowledge of local history, and is currently the Chairman of the Civil War Centennial Committee.

Cornelia B. Rose Jr., Research Assistant to the County Manager of Arlington, Secretary of the Arlington Historical Society, and author of *The Indians of Arlington* and *A History of the Boundaries of Arlington County, Virginia.* She gave me daily guidance through the labyrinth of early County records and archives.

Emily W. Johnson, former editor on the staff of *Public Health Reports,* now publications writer, Staff of the Golden Anniversary White House Conference on Children and Youth.

Harrison Mann, Charter-President of the Arlington Historical Society, legislator and historian.

Arnold Sagalyn, Assistant-Publisher of the *Northern Virginia Sun,* and Una F. Carter, staff writer and historian.

Jane Nida, Arlington County Librarian, who, assisted by her husband, Dow, and the Library Staff, have proof-read my entire book, a colossal and deeply appreciated lift!

I am especially grateful to the present owners of the homes mentioned for their cooperation, and to the descendants of the builders and early residents, who have furnished valuable data. The following people have kindly allowed me to copy material from their own manuscripts or have made other contributions involving time and effort:

Arlington County Officials and Arlington School Administration Personnel, Arlington National Cemetery Staff, Misses Hadassah and Constance Backus, Willard Brown, John F. Burns, Bill Boley, Enoch Barnes, Mrs. Hugh Boyer, William Clarkson, Everett Coxen, Mrs. Mary Councell, Civil War Centennial Commission, Miss Helen Calvert, Mrs. M. E. Church, Columbia Historical Society, District of Columbia Library Staff, Mrs. Ivah Bailey DePue, C. J. S. Durham, R. Adm. E. M. Eller, Mrs. Opal Evans, Fort Myer Public Relations Staff, the late Lucien H. Greathouse, Miss Coralie Greenaway, Arlo G. Greer, Mrs. Elizabeth Goebel, Mrs. Frances Grillo, Frederick Griffiths, Paul A. Hill, J. Foster Hagan, D. C. Hastings, Meredith Johnson, T. Sutton Jett, Mrs. Ethel W. King, Mrs. Katherine McCook Knox, Mrs. Helen Payne Karlson, George Kennedy, Rev. Frank E. Mahler, Harry E. Payne, Mrs. N. Nelson Parker, Mrs. Dorothy Mills Parker, Rev. J. S. Payton, O. E. Penney, Mrs. Hendree P. Simpson, Mrs. Ruby Simpson, Julian R. Serles Jr., Judge Harry Thomas, Charles Thomas, U. S. Army and U. S. Navy History Divisions, Edward Wagstaff, James H. Webb Jr., Mrs. Emily Withers, Richard W. Westwood, Dr. T. R. Schellenberg, and the Washington Golf and Country Club.

* * * *

Photographs used in this book secured through the courtesy of the following: Book-jacket, (front) Ollie Atkins, (back) Harris & Ewing. Book Cover by Bill Little. Frontispiece by Arleen and Stanley Costa.

* * * *

Ollie Atkins, Alexandria Library, Robert N. Anderson, Judge Warren E. Burger, Charles Baptie, Joseph O. Bostrup, John D. Bostrup, Mrs. Charles Bittinger, Jr., Thomas R. Ball, A. Aubrey Bodine, Benton J. Boogher, Brady, the Costas, City of Alexandria, Mrs. Thomas Corbin, Mrs. Philip Campbell, Mrs. M. G. Chew III, Detroit Publishing Co., Frick Art Reference Library, P. I. Flournoy, Mrs. Charles Fenwick, Fairfax Chamber of Commerce, Federal Aviation Administration, O. B. Fanning, Mrs. Robert Goodale, Charles E. Gage, Maurice Grillo, George Mason Green Co., Glencarlyn Library, Frances B. Johnston, Bill Little, Library of Congress, C. G. Lee Jr., the Misses Lockwood, Hirst Milhollen (etching), Military District of Washington, Bob Milnes, James McDonald, J. D. Moore, Comdr. R. L. Mitten, Alpic, Miley, Argyle Mackey, National Capital Parks, National Archives, *Northern Virginia Sun,* Porter Studio, Erle Prior, Harry W. Parker, Abbie Rowe, Riggs National Bank, Bert Roberts, Randolph Rouett, Smithsonian Institution, B. Sims (maps), Courtland H. Smith III, George M. Saegmuller, Bob Templeman, Eleanor Lee Templeman, U. S. Army and U. S. Navy History Divisions, Virginia State Library, Mrs. Harry Wormald, Winslow Williams, George Worthington, Paul Walter, Mrs. Emily Withers, *Washington Evening Star, Washington Post and Times-Herald.*

* * * *

I have not knowingly or intentionally used any pictures or material in this book which would infringe upon any rights or wishes of others. I have published legal notices of my intention to use photographs and subjects of *Northern Virginia Heritage Calendar for Engagements 1958* which I compiled and edited, and the *Arlington Heritage* series of articles which were published weekly on the editorial page of the *Northern Virginia Sun,* which started in March of 1957. My notice stated that unless I received written and registered statement to the contrary before April 1, 1959, I would consider that there were no objections from photographers, home owners, persons, or families involved. I also repeatedly appealed to the public for corrections and additional historical facts. If errors are found in this book, I again ask for written corrections so that they may be included in future editions.

* * * *

INDEX